By Gardner W. Allen

A NAVAL HISTORY OF THE AMERICAN REVO-
LUTION. 2 vols. Illustrated.

OUR NAVAL WAR WITH FRANCE. Illustrated.

OUR NAVY AND THE BARBARY CORSAIRS.
Illustrated.

HOUGHTON MIFFLIN COMPANY
BOSTON AND NEW YORK

OUR NAVY AND
THE BARBARY CORSAIRS

OUR NAVY

AND

THE BARBARY CORSAIRS

BY

GARDNER W. ALLEN

BOSTON AND NEW YORK

HOUGHTON MIFFLIN COMPANY

The Riverside Press Cambridge

TO
THE MEMORY OF
MY FATHER
JOSEPH HENRY ALLEN

PREFACE

THE relations of the United States with the Barbary powers a century ago form an interesting and romantic episode in American history which has never before been presented as a complete story. While the picturesque exploits of Preble and Decatur are familiar, other adventures of American seamen and consuls among the pirates of the Mediterranean have escaped notice, or are barely mentioned in most histories. It has been necessary to explore original records for many of the details. The various events, scattered over a period of about forty years, are here brought together.

In the search for material many have given greatly appreciated assistance. The writer acknowledges especially his indebtedness to the officials of the Navy Department, the Library of Congress, the Boston Public Library, and the Massachusetts Historical Society. He is under particular obligations to Professor Albert Bushnell Hart of Harvard University, to Charles W. Stewart, Esq., Superintendent of Library and Naval War Records, Navy Department, and to Worthington C. Ford, Esq., Chief of Division of Manuscripts, Library of Congress.

GARDNER W. ALLEN.

BOSTON,
January, 1905.

CONTENTS

APPENDIX

ILLUSTRATIONS

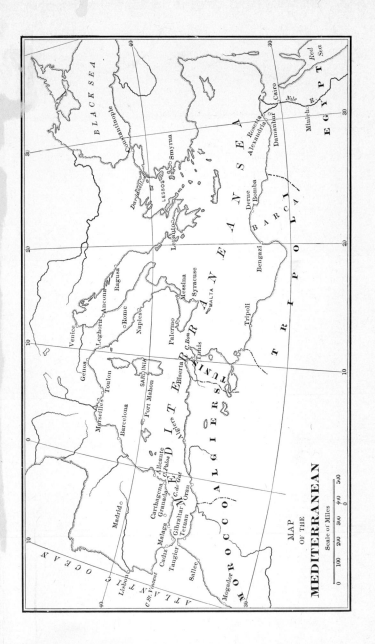

MAP
OF THE

MEDITERRANEAN

Scale of Miles

0   100   200   300   400   500

OUR NAVY AND THE BARBARY CORSAIRS

CHAPTER I

WHITE SLAVERY IN THE BARBARY STATES

ALONG the northern coast of Africa, between the Mediterranean and the Sahara, stretching from the Atlantic to Egypt, a distance of two thousand miles, lie the Barbary States. They are Morocco, Algeria, Tunis, and Tripoli, with the unimportant Barca on the east, generally included in Tripoli. Of these Algeria, formerly called by the name of its capital Algiers, and now a colony of France, was the most powerful and aggressive in the days of piracy.

Barbary is in the latitude of our Southern States, and is blessed with a mild climate and fertile soil. The coast is high and rocky from the Straits of Gibraltar to Cape Bon ; beyond that it is low, the water is shoal, and reefs extend far off shore. Most of the harbors are very open and exposed to the north. A strong current sets in from the Atlantic and sweeps along the African coast. From September to April frequent and severe gales blow, making naval operations difficult and dangerous, especially for sailing-vessels. Off the coast of Tunis and Tripoli and also about Malta and Sicily, the prevailing winds are northerly and northwesterly, and often have the force of hurricanes. In the spring violent easterly gales, called

levanters, are common. In the summer the weather
is generally mild, but even then gales are not infrequent.[1] These facts have a bearing on the history of
this region.

With its advantages of situation and climate, Barbary should have been a civilized and progressive
country. Its Mohammedan population, however, consisting of Moors, Arabs, Berbers, Kabyles, and Turks,
decided the character of the civilization. There were
also many Jews in Barbary. The cities were built with
extremely narrow streets, dark, and very dirty. The
houses were generally of one story, and the flat terraced
roofs approached so closely to each other that long distances could be traversed, passing from roof to roof.
A century ago the population of the city of Algiers
is believed to have been somewhere between fifty and
a hundred thousand; Tunis was larger and Tripoli
smaller.

There had been piracy in the Mediterranean from
the earliest times, and for centuries it was pursued
by Christians and Moslems alike. The captives were
reduced to slavery, and the condition of the Christian
slaves in Barbary excited sympathy throughout Europe. In 1199 was founded in Paris the " Order of
the Holy Trinity and Redemption of Captives." The
members, called Fathers of the Redemption or Mathurins, from the Church of St. Mathurin, devoted their
lives to the ransom of captives and the mitigation of
their plight. Missions were established and hospitals
maintained in Barbary.[2]

During the later Middle Ages the relations between
the Barbary powers and the Christian nations were

---

[1] Morris, pp. 5, 6. See Appendix I for authorities.
[2] Poole, pp. 251–255.

amicable. They traded together and made enlightened treaties. But with the dawn of the sixteenth century appears a change in the conditions, and hence-
forth a state of chronic warfare between Christians
and Moors. Then began the period of activity of the
Barbary corsairs which lasted about three hundred
years. This was chiefly the result of the conquest of
Granada in 1492, which was followed by the exodus
of thousands of Moriscos who passed over to Africa
and not only greatly swelled the numbers in Barbary,
but carried with them a hatred of the Spanish and
a thirst for vengeance which early found vent in
piratical raids along the Spanish coast.[1]

The first of the great corsairs were the brothers
Horuk and Khair-ed-Din Barbarossa, natives of Lesbos,
who had in youth joined a gang of pirates in the east
Mediterranean. Not finding free scope for his ambition so near the sultan's fleet, Horuk determined to
try his fortune on the Barbary coast. He first went to
Tunis in 1504, which he made his base. From Tunis
and later from other ports he cruised with brilliant
though not uninterrupted success, making many captures and collecting a strong fleet.[2]

In 1509 a Spanish expedition under Cardinal
Ximenes captured Oran, which was held by Spain for
two centuries. The Spaniards also took Algiers the
next year, but held only the small island, just off
shore, from which the city takes its name, and which
they fortified. This stronghold, called Peñon de Alger,
completely controlled the harbor and greatly interfered
with the movements of the corsairs. The island was
afterwards connected with the city by a causeway. In
1516 Horuk Barbarossa went to Algiers, having been

[1] Poole, pp. 7, 8.   [2] Ibid. ch. iii.

appealed to by Sheik Salim for assistance in driving
the Spanish from the Peñon. Instead, he murdered
the sheik, set himself up in his place, and soon had
control of nearly the whole country. In 1518, while
retreating from an overwhelming Spanish force, sent
against him from Oran, Horuk was overtaken and
killed, desperately fighting at bay.[1] The Spanish
might now have seized Algiers and put an end to its
piracy once for all, but the opportunity was stupidly
neglected.[2]

Khair-ed-Din Barbarossa succeeded his brother, and
began by putting Algiers under the protection of the
sultan at Constantinople, who made him governor-
general and sent him a guard of two thousand janizaries. In this way he greatly strengthened his power,
and finally, about 1530, was able to force the surrender of the Peñon de Alger. Soon after this, he was
given command of the Ottoman navy, and in 1534
captured Tunis, adding it to the sultan's dominions.
The next year, however, the Emperor Charles V led
an expedition for the conquest of Tunis in six hundred
ships commanded by Andrea Doria, the Genoese
admiral. The Goletta, or port of Tunis, was taken
and the city besieged. When Barbarossa came out
to meet the emperor, thousands of Christian slaves
escaped from the citadel and closed the gates of the
city behind him. In the encounter which followed,
he was defeated and put to flight. The city was then
taken and sacked by the Spanish. Thirty thousand
men, women, and children were massacred and ten
thousand carried away as slaves. Tunis was held by

[1] Poole, ch. iv; Prescott, Ferdinand and Isabella (Philadelphia,
1873), iii, pp. 314–322, 327.

[2] Poole, p. 53.

the Spaniards about five years. Khair-ed-Din departed from Barbary and did not return.[1]

In 1541 Charles V led another great armada across the sea, this time against Algiers. Hernando Cortes was one of his captains, and Andrea Doria commanded the fleet. Many non-combatants, including ladies, accompanied the expedition to witness the emperor's triumph. It was late in the season, and Doria, fearful of the gales that sweep the Barbary coast, counseled postponement, but was unheeded. Algiers was held by Hasan Aga with a small force. On the second day after landing, the army, without shelter, was drenched by a heavy rain and the next day a terrific hurricane wrecked the fleet at anchor. Over a hundred and fifty vessels were lost, and the sailors who succeeded in getting ashore were killed by the Arabs. Meanwhile the army was in the greatest distress, the stores not having been landed, and it was now necessary to undertake a three days' march to the bay where Doria had brought the remnant of the fleet. Many perished from starvation and exposure, and thousands were slain, or captured and enslaved. At last the emperor succeeded in reëmbarking the survivors and returned to Spain after one of the most disastrous defeats in history.[2]

The power of the Barbary States was now at its height. Khair-ed-Din was followed by a number of other famous corsairs, but with the decline of the naval supremacy of the Ottomans after their defeat at Lepanto in 1571, they degenerated into a race of

[1] Poole, ch. v, viii; Robertson, Charles V (Philadelphia, 1875), ii, pp. 237–242.

[2] Poole, ch. xi; Robertson, ii, pp. 347–352; Armstrong, Charles V (London, 1902), ii, ch. i.

petty pirates who continued to infest the Mediterranean until their extermination in the nineteenth century. Many of them were European renegades, and
they devoted themselves more exclusively to piratical
cruising, while the civil government fell into the hands
of the Turks. Until 1671 the rulers of Algiers were
appointed by the sultan or under his control, but
from that time a dey was elected by the janizaries
from their own number, and any common soldier was
eligible. The dey had despotic power, but was likely
at any time to be deposed and assassinated. Few deys
died a natural death; they followed each other in
rapid succession, and it was a long story of anarchy
and bloodshed. In Tunis after 1705 the ruler, called
bey, was elected by the soldiery. Tripoli became partially independent of the sultan in 1714 and was
ruled by a pasha. Morocco was, and still continues
to be, a sovereign power governed by a sherif or
emperor, now usually called sultan, who is an abso-
lute monarch. The Morocco pirates generally cruised
in the Atlantic, and Sallee was their chief port, but,
owing to its shallow harbor, their vessels were built
small and light, so that their operations were on a
smaller scale. They became unusually active toward
the end of the eighteenth century.[1]

In 1609 the final expulsion of the Moriscos from
Spain greatly recruited the strength of the Barbary
States. The corsairs not only scoured the sea, but
often raided the coasts of Italy, Spain, and the various
Mediterranean islands, sometimes advancing considerable distances inland, robbing houses and villages and
carrying off the inhabitants into slavery. As late as
1798 an expedition from Tunis landed on an island

[1] Poole, ch. xv; also pp. 22, 262, note.

off the coast of Sardinia and kidnapped nearly a thousand people, mostly women and children. Many of the pirates of the seventeenth century grew immensely and rapidly rich upon the plunder thus seized and the ransom of their captives.[1] With increasing boldness they extended their piracies into the ocean and along the European coast as far as the North Sea and even to Iceland. They ravaged the shores of England and Ireland, and seizing unsuspecting inhabitants bore them away into captivity.[2] Later, when better protection was afforded on the coast, that is after 1636, "those pirates still continued to take prizes in the ocean; and carrying their English captives to France, drove them in chains overland to Marseille, to ship them thence, with greater safety, for slaves to Algiers."[3]

England sent expeditions against Algiers in 1620 and against Sallee in 1637, which succeeded in liberating a number of slaves, and in 1655 Cromwell sent a fleet under Admiral Blake which chastised both Algiers and Tunis. The Algerines made several treaties with England, but quickly broke them. In 1661 the Dutch Admiral de Ruyter succeeded in releasing several hundred captives; and in 1682 and the following year the French under Duquesne bombarded Algiers, inflicting severe punishment.[4]

After this there were various demonstrations from time to time, but no serious attempt was made to subdue the pirates until 1775, when another great naval and military armament for the reduction of Algiers was fitted out in Spain under the command of Count

1 Poole, pp. 201–205; Eaton, p. 100.
2 Poole, p. 233; Sumner, p. 36.
3 Carte, History of England (London, 1747), iv, p. 231.
4 Sumner, pp. 36–46.

O'Reilly. This expedition is of interest to us from the
fact that Joshua Barney, later a gallant figure in our
naval annals, took part in it. At that time a boy of
sixteen, he was returning from the Mediterranean in
command of a ship bound for Baltimore. On putting
into Alicante he was impressed into the Spanish service with many other foreign shipmasters whose vessels
were required as transports for the thirty thousand
soldiers. The fleet of nearly four hundred vessels was
commanded by Admiral de Castijon. Owing to mismanagement, disagreement between O'Reilly and Castijon and lack of support on the part of the navy, the
expedition ended in defeat and disaster.[1]

Besides these warlike measures the redemption of
slaves was procured with money raised by missions,
contributions, and collections. Individuals and families sometimes impoverished themselves to ransom
friends and relatives. The slaves sometimes attempted
to escape, but generally without success, and when
discovered were cruelly punished. Many remarkable
escapes, however, are recorded. Among the captives
at different times were some famous men, such as
Cervantes, Vincent de Paul, and Arago the French
astronomer. Cervantes made repeated attempts to
escape and was finally ransomed.[2]

In the sixteenth century the vessels of the corsairs
were called galleys, galleots, or brigantines, according
to the size, the latter being the smallest, with twelve
or fourteen banks of oars, each oar handled by one
man. The typical galley was about one hundred and
fifty feet long with fifty-four benches or banks, twenty-
seven oars on a side, each pulled by from four to six

---

[1] Memoir of Commodore Joshua Barney (Boston, 1832), pp. 23–25.
[2] Sumner, pp. 16–18, 46–67.

men. The galleots were small galleys. The large galleys carried two hundred and seventy or more rowers, who with the officers, crew, and soldiers made a total of about four hundred. They were rigged with two masts and lateen sails which were spread when running before the wind. The galley slaves who manned the oars were chained to the benches day and night, perhaps for six months at a time. On the bridge between the two rows of benches stood two boatswains with long whips, with which they scourged the bare backs of the rowers. During a long chase these wretches would be compelled to pull ten, twelve, or even twenty hours at a stretch. When one fell from exhaustion he was directly pitched overboard. This slavery might last many years, or for life. This description applies to Christian galleys as well as to those of the corsairs of Barbary. The latter were manned by Christian slaves, the former by Moorish slaves or Christian convicts. Birth and rank gave no immunity; a Knight of Malta might be chained alongside any vile scoundrel in the galley of an Algerine admiral, who, if captured, would be forced to man the oar of the victor.[1]

With the seventeenth century sail-power came more into use. Larger and heavier square-rigged vessels were built, and longer voyages on the ocean were then undertaken. These vessels were called galleon, polacca, caravel, galleasse, etc., according to size and other characteristics; the last named was lateen rigged and a cross between the galley and the galleon.[2]

William Eaton, United States consul at Tunis, writing of the corsairs in 1799, says: " Their mode of attack is uniformly boarding. For this their ves-

<hr/>

[1] Poole, ch. xvi.   [2] Ibid. ch. xvii.

sels are peculiarly constructed. Their long lateen
yards drop on board the enemy and afford a safe and
easy conveyance for the men who man them for this
purpose; but being always crowded with men, they
throw them in from all points of the rigging and from
all quarters of the decks, having their sabres grasped
between their teeth and their loaded pistols in their
belts, that they may have the free use of their hands
in scaling the gunnels or netting of their enemy. In
this mode of attack they are very active and very desperate. . . . Proper defenses against them are high
nettings with chains sufficiently strong to prevent
their being cut away, buckshot plentifully adminis-
tered from muskets or blunderbusses, and lances.
But it is always best to keep them at a distance,
that advantage may be taken of their ignorance at
manœuvring." [1]

With the decline of the galley there was still occupation for the slaves; in fact by far the larger number had always been employed on shore. Their lot,
while not so wretched as that of the galley slaves, was
still bad enough. When captives were brought in,
some were reserved by the dey for his own or the
government service, while others were taken to the
slave market and sold at public auction. The treatment of the slaves depended chiefly upon the disposition of their master; sometimes they had an easy
time, but more commonly it was a hard, rough life.
They did every kind of household drudgery and farm
work. Next to the loss of freedom, the hardest thing
to bear, no doubt, for the proud and sensitive, was the
menial position, the contemptuous treatment by a barbarian master and punishment for trivial or uninten-

[1] Eaton, pp. 92, 93.

tional offense. The government slaves had the heaviest labor, especially quarrying stone and dragging it to the city on trucks. At night they were locked up in the bagnios, or prisons. They had some privileges, however, and a few were allowed to keep taverns frequented by renegades and soldiers, and by this means might save enough to purchase their freedom.[1] According to some accounts the treatment of slaves in Barbary was very commonly mild and humane.[2]

The attitude of Europe towards the Barbary States was cowardly and dishonorable from first to last. The action of the stronger powers was prompted largely by policy. In order to injure their enemies and to crush the commercial competition of their weak neighbors, they were willing to bribe and subsidize the corsairs, submitting to the indignity and dishonor of being tributary nations and encouraging a system of ruthless piracy and slavery. For two hundred and thirty years England sent consuls to Algiers who were forced to endure every insult and, if showing the least spirit, were recalled at the dictation of the dey and more obsequious substitutes sent with presents and friendly or apologetic letters. As late as the nineteenth century a Danish and a French consul were thrown into prison and made to labor with the slaves because of delay in paying tribute.[3]

There were English slaves in Algiers in 1816, when eighteen were liberated by Lord Exmouth;[4] although these had presumably been captured under the flags of other nations. Even after Exmouth's bombardment the insolence of the dey continued until the French

[1] Poole, ch. xviii.
[2] Sumner, pp. 119–129; Shaler, p. 77; Noah, p. 368.
[3] Poole, ch. xix.   [4] Ibid. p. 299.

conquest of 1830. In 1825 Sweden, Denmark, Portugal, and Naples were still paying annual tribute.[1] In 1817 Tunisian pirates cruised in the English Channel and North Sea and captured vessels from Hamburg and other Hanse towns.[2]

[1] Shaler, p. 39.
[2] Niles's Register, vol. xii, p. 334; vol. xiii, pp. 41, 95, 219.

CHAPTER II

AMERICAN CAPTIVES IN BARBARY

WE have records of American victims of the Barbary pirates during the colonial period. Two ships from Plymouth were seized in 1625 in the English Channel and taken into Sallee. Several cases from Boston and neighboring towns are mentioned, some of whom were ransomed and some died in slavery. Among them was Dr. Daniel Mason, a graduate of Harvard College, who sailed from Charlestown in 1678, was taken into Algiers, and never returned.[1]

But the real beginning of our troubles came after the peace of 1783, as soon as the pirates of the Mediterranean had learned to recognize the new flag as that of a young, weak power likely to fall an easy prey to their cruisers.

In October, 1784, the American brig Betsey, Captain James Erving, bound to Teneriffe, was captured by a corsair of Morocco and taken into Tangier. The crew were not enslaved, and after being held six months were released with the vessel. The emperor of Morocco expressed a wish for friendly relations with the United States, and gave orders that no other American vessels should be molested until there should be time to hear from Congress on the subject of negotiations for peace.[2]

July 25, 1785, the schooner Maria of Boston, Captain Isaac Stevens, bound to Cadiz, was captured

1 Sumner, pp. 67–70.   2 Blyth, pp. 41–43.

off Cape St. Vincent by an Algerine xebec of four-teen guns, and on the 30th of the same month the ship Dauphin of Philadelphia, Captain Richard O'Brien, was taken about fifty leagues west of Lisbon. Both vessels with their crews, numbering twenty-one in all, were carried into Algiers. James L. Cathcart, a seaman on the Maria, says: " I understood the Spanish language, which they all spoke, and was the only person on board who had any knowledge of the Barbary States. . . . We were welcomed on board [the xebec] by the Rais, or Captain, a venerable old Arab, who . . . informed me that they were a cruiser of Algiers, that they had come through the Straits in consequence of their having concluded a peace with Spain and of the arrival of a British consul, Charles Logie, who informed them that they might take all such vessels that had not passports of a particular cut." After much ill treatment and hardship they arrived at Algiers August 4. They were stripped, given filthy rags to wear, and marched through the streets. Later they were taken before the dey, Mo-hammed by name, and were put to work at various sorts of labor.[1]

The captives, soon after their arrival, addressed an appealing letter to the American consul at Cadiz set-ting forth their condition, stripped of their clothes and treated with barbarity; and they besought the consul's influence in obtaining for them an allowance for extra supplies and an early ransom. A second letter, written six months later by O'Brien to a com-mercial house of Lisbon, reports their being well pro-vided for by the French and Spanish consuls. This was in consequence of the intercession in their behalf

[1] Blyth, p. 47; Nav. Chron. p. 37; Cathcart, I, ch. i.

of the United States ministers, Jefferson and Carmichael, at the courts of Versailles and Madrid. The
captains had their own table and each had a small iron
ring on one leg as a badge of slavery. The men worked
at various trades and were allowed fifteen ounces of
bread daily.[1]

After making peace with Spain, Algiers went to
war with Portugal, and the latter power kept the Straits
of Gibraltar closed against Algerine cruisers, so that
American vessels in the Atlantic were safe from the
corsairs. Few Americans entered the Mediterranean,
and those that did were generally protected by the
Dutch, Portuguese, or Spanish cruisers. Sometimes
Americans had forged or purchased passes, so that
the Algerines could not distinguish them from English
vessels, with which they dared not interfere. These
passes were given to the vessels of nations having
treaties with Algiers. They were inscribed with Arabic
characters, and the corsairs tested their genuineness
by means of a stick with notches corresponding to
engraved figures on the margin of the pass.[2]

In 1793 a truce for one year between Portugal and
Algiers was suddenly concluded through the influence
of the English consul at Algiers, for the express purpose, as it is alleged, of allowing the Algerines to
cruise against Americans. In consequence of this,
four frigates, three xebecs, and a brig, comprising
nearly the whole cruising strength of the Algerine

[1] Blyth, pp. 48, 51, 52. Several other captures of Americans at about
the same time, some of whom escaped, are reported by Blyth (pp. 42,
44, 59, 62), but apparently on unreliable authority, as they are not
accounted for in the returns of captives finally liberated. See also
Boston Independent Chronicle, Oct. 20, 1785, April 27, 1786, Oct. 16,
1788; Amer. Museum, viii (Phila., 1790), appendix iv, pp. 4, 28.

[2] Carey, p. 34.

navy, passed through the Straits in search of prey.
Eleven American vessels with one hundred and nine
officers and men were captured in October and November, 1793, and taken into Algiers. After this the
courts of Lisbon and Madrid, for the protection of
their trade with the United States, granted convoys to
American vessels homeward bound to a certain latitude where they were beyond the reach of the pirates.[1]

October 8, 1793, the first of these later captures
of Americans were made, — the ships Thomas and
Hope and the schooner Despatch, and on the 11th
the brigs George, Olive Branch, and Jane were taken,
followed the next day by the schooner Jay. On the
18th the ship Minerva, Captain John McShane, of
Philadelphia, was captured off Gibraltar by a xebec
of twenty guns, and on the 23d the ship President,
Captain William Penrose, also of Philadelphia, was
taken off Cadiz. The last two victims were the brigs
Polly of Newburyport and Minerva of New York, the
latter being captured November 23.[2]

Letters from McShane and Penrose describe their
capture and captivity. The President, within a few
hours' sail of Cadiz, fell in with a xebec of sixteen
guns under Spanish colors and showed her American
flag. When within gunshot the xebec hauled down
her Spanish colors and hoisted the Algerine flag.
They lowered a boat, boarded the President, and at
once proceeded to loot the ship. They threw the crew
down and stripped them of all their clothes, fighting
savagely among themselves over the booty. The Americans were afterwards given a few dirty rags to put on.

[1] Nav. Chron. pp. 49–51; Carey, pp. 34, 35; Stephens, p. 68.
[2] Nav. Chron. p. 53; St. Pap. x, p. 338; Stephens, p. 69; Foss,
pp. 71–75.

They were tumbled and kicked into the boat, taken aboard the pirate, and brought before the commander, Rais Mahomet, an infirm old man described as "an emaciated, loathsome figure." Nearly one hundred and fifty Algerines were crowded into this small vessel, which was filthy in the extreme and swarming with vermin. They arrived at Algiers October 30 and were ordered to the Bagnio Baleck.[1]

The narrative of John Foss, seaman on the brig Polly of Newburyport, bound for Cadiz, is interesting. October 25, 1793, the Polly was overhauled by a brig flying the British flag. "When she came near enough to make us hear, she hailed us in English, asked from whence we came and were bound, which was immediately answered by Captain Bayley. The man who hailed us was dressed in the Christian habit and he was the only person we could yet see on her deck. By this time the Brig was under our stern; we then saw several men jump upon her poop to hall aft the main sheet and saw by their dress and their long beard that they were Moors or Algerines. Our feelings at this unwelcome sight are more easily imagined than described. She then hove too under our lee, when we heard a most terrible shouting, clapping of hands, huzzaing, &c., and saw a great number of men rise up with their heads above the gunnel, drest in the Turkish habit like them we saw on the poop. They immediately hoisted out a large launch and about one hundred of the Pirates jumped on board, all armed, some with Scimitres and Pistols, others with pikes, spears, lances, knives, &c. They manned about 20

---

[1] Carey, pp. 37, 39; Stephens, pp. 244–248. See also letters of Captains Newman and Smith of the Thomas and Polly in Mrs. E. V. Smith's History of Newburyport (1854), pp. 146, 147.

oars and rowed alongside. As soon as they came on board our vessel they made signs for us all to go forward, assuring us in several languages that if we did not obey their commands they would immediately massacre us all. They then went below into the cabin, steerage and every place where they could get below deck and broke open all the Trunks and Chests there were on board, and plundered all our bedding, cloathing, books, Charts, Quadrants and every moveable article that did not consist of the Cargo or furniture. They then came on deck and stripped the cloathes off our backs, all except a shirt and pair of drawers." The prisoners were then transferred to the corsair, where they found three of the crew of the ship Hope of New York, which had been captured several days before.[1]

They arrived at Algiers November 1, and were landed and " conducted to the Dey's palace by a guard, and as we passed through the streets our ears were stunned with the shouts, clapping of hands, and other acclamations of joy from the inhabitants, thanking God for their great success and victories over so many Christian dogs and unbelievers." The dey at this time was Hasan Pasha, his predecessor, Mohammed, having died in 1791. When brought before him he " told us he had sent several times to our Government, entreating them to negociate with him for a peace and had never received any satisfactory answer from them. And that he was determined never to make a peace with the United States, in his reign, as they had so often neglected his requests and treated him with disdain, adding, ' Now I have got you, you Christian dogs, you shall eat stones.' He then picked out four

[1] Foss, pp. 3-9.

boys to wait upon himself . . . and then ordered the rest of us to be conducted to the prison Bilic. When we arrived there we found several other Americans" and about six hundred Christian slaves of other nationalities "with wretched habits, dejected countenances and chains on their legs." After their names had been entered in the prison book, each man was given a blanket, a scanty supply of coarse clothing, and a small loaf of black, sour bread. They spent the night wrapped in their blankets on the stone floor.[1]

On the day after their arrival the captives were loaded with chains of twenty-five to forty pounds in weight fastened to a ring about the ankle, the other end being bound around the waist. They were then put at various sorts of labor. When there were no foreign vessels in port and there was no chance of escape, the slaves were relieved of their chains while at work, unless they were kept on as punishment for some misdemeanor. Many were employed in rigging and fitting out cruisers, discharging prizes, transporting the cargoes and other goods about the city, which, on account of the extreme narrowness of the streets, could be carried only by means of poles on their shoulders. Blocks of stone were carried from the mole to a new mosque the dey was building; these were suspended from wooden frames borne by four men, and for any but the strongest the load was excessive. Others were employed in blasting rocks in the mountains. Fragments weighing from twenty to forty tons were rolled down to the bottom of the mountain and placed upon heavy carts or sleds. These were drawn by teams of two hundred or more men to

[1] Foss, pp. 13–17.

a quay about two miles distant, whence they were transported on scows to the mole for the construction of a breakwater. This labor occupied the largest number of the slaves and was the severest that was imposed upon them; and they were cruelly beaten and driven by their overseers.[1]

There were about twelve hundred Christian slaves in Algiers at this time. Those in the government employ, as all the Americans seem to have been, wore an iron ring on the ankle, which was the badge of public service and protected the wearer from insult and abuse by the Turkish soldiers. Their daily ration was three small loaves of black bread with a little vinegar. The bagnio in which they were confined at night is thus described by Cathcart: "The Bagnio Belique is an oblong hollow square, 140 feet in length and 60 in breadth, is three stories high and may be about 50 feet high to the top of the terrace. . . . The lower story has no grating and is converted into taverns which are kept by the Christian slaves, who pay their rent and very high duties for permission to sell liquors and provisions in them. They are perfectly dark and in the day are illuminated with lamps, and when full of drunken Turks, Moors, Arabs, Christians and now and then a Jew or two . . . each singing or rather shouting in different languages, without the least connection, the place filled with the smoke of tobacco which renders objects nearly impervious to the view, some wrangling with the tavern keepers for more liquor and refusing to pay for it, . . . it must resemble the infernal regions more than any other place in the known world. . . . The second and third story of this dungeon is surrounded by a small corridor or gallery

[1] Stephens, pp. 71–77; Foss, pp. 19, 20, 28–30.

from whence are entrances into long, narrow rooms where the slaves sleep. They are hung in square frames one over another, four tier deep, and they repose as well as miserable wretches can be supposed to do who are swarming with myriads of vermin of all sorts, many nearly naked, and few with anything more than an old tattered blanket to cover them with in the depth of winter; for those who have the means of subsistence either live in the tavern or little boxes called rooms, built of boards, hanging round the galleries, for which they pay the Regency from twelve to fifty-four masoons per month. . . . The whole building is covered with a terrace. . . . It would be a great recreation to the slaves, especially in summer, were they permitted to walk or sleep there, but that is strictly prohibited." Cathcart kept a tavern for several years and was apparently able to lay by a considerable sum of money.[1]

For slight misdemeanors the punishment was the bastinado, which, as Cathcart relates, was inflicted as follows: "The culprit is thrown down on his face and by a pole six or eight feet long, with two loops of cord which are put about his ankles, his legs are held up by two men to present the soles of his feet; his head and hands, tied behind, are secured by one of the Guardians, who sits upon his shoulders, [and] the Guardian Bashaw and his Myrmidons are each furnished with hoop-poles an inch or more in diameter; two of them commence in very regular time to give him from one to five hundred blows, which are generally divided between the soles of his feet and the posterior. The culprit is then either put in chains, sent to labor, or to the hospital to be cured, according to circumstances."

[1] Foss, pp. 31–34; Stephens, p. 249; Cathcart, I, pp. 52–55, 136.

For serious transgressions the offender might be beheaded, impaled, or burned alive. A slave who murdered a Mohammedan was cast off the walls of the city upon iron hooks fastened into the wall, where he might hang suspended for days before he perished.[1]

The Americans were generally well behaved, yet were often severely punished for trivial offenses. All had their heads close-shaven and were not allowed a cap or other covering. When sick the slaves were sent to a hospital maintained by Spanish priests, where they were well treated, but could be removed at any time and sent back to work, which often happened before they were in a fit condition. The government authorities tolerated the hospital as it cost them nothing and saved the lives of many of their slaves. The plague raged in 1788, subsided the next year, broke out again in 1793, and continued as long as the American captives remained in Algiers. In an epidemic of smallpox in 1794 four Americans died.[2]

The captives addressed letters and petitions to the President, to Congress, to the ministers of all denominations, and to Colonel David Humphreys, United States minister to Portugal, who in a letter to the American people suggested a lottery as the means of raising the necessary funds for the ransom of their fellow countrymen. Humphreys, having deposited a sum of money with the American consul at Alicante in December, 1793, arranged to have it distributed to the captives through the Swedish consul, Mr. Skjöldebrand. The captains received eight dollars each per month, the mates six, and the men three dollars and

---

[1] Cathcart, I, p. 70; Foss, pp. 23-26.

[2] Foss, pp. 21, 22, 56; Stephens, p. 260; Carey, p. 44; Cathcart, I, pp. 112, 136, 137.

seventy-five cents. They were also provided with additional clothing. This was a great boon to the slaves and enabled them to procure extra food and a few other small comforts.[1]

The dey at first refused to consider the question of peace with the United States, but finally yielded, and in July, 1795, the captives were cheered by the news that Joseph Donaldson was on his way to Algiers for the purpose of negotiating with that potentate. Donaldson arrived September 3 ; on the 5th a treaty was concluded, and the American flag was given a salute of twenty-one guns. The overjoyed slaves now looked forward to speedy emancipation. In this, however, they were disappointed, for long delay in raising the money for their ransom kept them still in captivity. They were greatly disheartened, but somewhat encouraged in February, 1796, on receiving a sympathetic letter from Colonel Humphreys, and in March Joel Barlow arrived to assist in the negotiations. The dey became very impatient at the delay, and made dire threats of renewed hostilities and piracy. Finally Barlow succeeded in procuring the necessary funds from a Jew named Bacri, a merchant in Algiers.[2]

Meanwhile the plague had carried off many of the Americans, and the numbers were reduced to eighty-five. The custom was that for all slaves dying after the conclusion of a treaty ransoms were paid just the same, and the dey exacted the stipulated amount for all the Americans who died after the 5th of September, 1795.[3]

At last, on the 13th of July, 1796, the ransomed

---

[1] Blyth, pp. 69-71; Sumner, pp. 78-82; Stephens, p. 260 ; Foss, pp. 54, 55 ; Nav. Chron. pp. 51, 52.

[2] Foss, pp. 52, 53, 58-65.　　　　[3] Stephens, pp. 87, 249.

slaves set sail for Leghorn, in the ship Fortune, a vessel owned by Bacri. On account of a fresh outbreak of the plague on board the ship, they put into Marseilles, where they were quarantined for eighty days. From this point the survivors found their way home.[1]

[1] Foss, pp. 66, 67.

CHAPTER III

FIRST NEGOTIATIONS

TROUBLE with Barbary, as a result of the loss of British protection, was early foreseen. In the plan of a treaty with France which Congress agreed upon September 17, 1776, one article provided that the king should protect the inhabitants of the United States against all attacks on the part of the Barbary cruisers.[1] The American commissioners to France were unable, however, to get this inserted in the Treaty of Amity and Commerce of February 6, 1778, but in accordance with Article VIII of that treaty the king " will employ his good offices and interposition with " the Barbary States " for the benefit, conveniency and safety of the said United States . . . against all violence, insult, attacks, or depredations." [2]

A few months later the commissioners, Benjamin Franklin, Arthur Lee, and John Adams, requested the king's good offices in behalf of certain American vessels then in Italy and in fear of Barbary pirates. This led to a correspondence with the Comte de Vergennes, minister of foreign affairs, and M. de Sartine, minister of marine, as to the best policy to be pursued by the United States towards the Barbary powers. The result was that by the advice of the ministers the commissioners applied to Congress for authority to treat with the Barbary powers and for funds to be expended

[1] Secr. Jour. ii, pp. 10, 28 ; Davis, p. 30.
[2] See Appendix II.

in presents. No further steps were taken at that time.[1]

The emperor of Morocco showed a friendly disposition, and claimed to have been the first sovereign to recognize the independence of the United States. He opened his ports to American vessels, and expressed a wish for a treaty of peace with the new republic. His overtures were made through M. Caille, a resident of Sallee, who corresponded with Franklin and Jay on the subject. In 1783 Franklin received letters from M. Crocco, another agent of the emperor, to the same effect.[2] The lack of response on the part of Congress to these advances may have been in some degree answerable for the seizure of the brig Betsey in 1784.

British jealousy of the rising commerce of the United States was not unnatural, and was shown in the defeat in parliament of a bill introduced by Pitt in 1783, which provided for free trade between the two countries. Lord Sheffield published a pamphlet on American commerce, aimed at this bill, which is a strong protectionist argument, as will appear from the following : " It is not probable the American States will have a very free trade in the Mediterranean ; it will not be the interest of any of the great maritime powers to protect them there from the Barbary States. If they know their interests, they will not encourage the Americans to be carriers — that the Barbary States are advantageous to the maritime powers is obvious. If they were suppressed, the little States of Italy, &c. would have much more of the carrying trade. The

---

[1] Stevens's Facsimile MSS. (London, 1895), xxiii, nos. 1953, 1972, 1978 ; Dipl. Corr. Rev. i, pp. 431, 453, 462, 465, 484, 491 ; iii, p. 92.

[2] Dipl. Corr. Rev. iii, p. 92 ; iv, pp. 135, 176, 179 ; vii, pp. 389–398.

French never shewed themselves worse politicians than in encouraging the late armed neutrality. . . . The armed neutrality would be as hurtful to the great maritime powers as the Barbary States are useful. The Americans cannot protect themselves from the latter; they cannot pretend to a navy." [1]

Franklin, while minister to France, received a letter from a certain M. Salva dated Algiers, April 1, 1783, which related the narrow escape of two American vessels which had recently sailed from Marseilles, adding: " Some secret enemies, whom I know, having given information to this Regency of their departure, nine armed ships immediately sailed to wait for them at Cape Palos. It is to be presumed that the Americans had passed the Straits." Franklin wrote to R. R. Livingston, Secretary of Foreign Affairs, on the subject, July 25, 1783, as follows : " You will see by the enclosed copy of a letter I received from Algiers, the danger two of our ships escaped last winter. I think it not improbable that those rovers may be privately encouraged by the English to fall upon us and to prevent our interfering in the carrying trade ; for I have in London heard it is a maxim among the merchants, that if *there were no Algiers, it would be worth England's while to build one.* I wonder, however, that the rest of Europe do not combine to destroy those nests and secure commerce from their future piracies." [2]

Concerning the importance of peace with the Barbary States, John Adams, at that time peace commissioner in Paris, wrote to the President of Congress September 10, 1783 : " There are other Powers with

[1] Commerce of the American States (2d ed. London, 1783), p. 115, note.

[2] Dipl. Corr. Rev. iv, pp. 95, 149.

whom it is more necessary to have Treaties than it
ought to be; I mean Morocco, Algiers, Tunis, and
Tripoli. . . . If Congress can find funds to treat with
the Barbary Powers, the Ministers here are the best
situated. . . . Ministers here may carry on this negotiation by letters, or may be empowered to send an
agent if necessary." [1] Congress accordingly issued a
joint commission, May 12, 1784, to Adams, Franklin,
and Jefferson, with David Humphreys, secretary,
granting them or a majority of them, plenary power
to negotiate treaties with various powers, including
Morocco, Algiers, Tunis, and Tripoli, and a year later
authorized them to appoint agents for the purpose. [2]

The first employment of the commissioners appears
to have been in behalf of the Betsey, captured by
a cruiser of Morocco, when they addressed a letter,
March 28, 1785, to Vergennes asking his advice and
the interposition of the king with Morocco, in accordance with the treaty of 1778. They were advised to
request the emperor to refrain from further interfer-
ence with American commerce until Congress should
have time to send him a consul. [3] Not long after this
the Betsey and her crew were released through the
friendly interposition of Spain. [4] Franklin soon returned to America, leaving Paris July 12, 1785,
and was reported to have been captured by Algerine
pirates on the way. [5] After his departure Adams and
Jefferson, who was now minister to France, appointed
Thomas Barclay, consul-general of the United States

[1] Dipl. Corr. Rev. vii, p. 161; Davis, p. 31.
[2] Dipl. Corr. U. S. i, p. 501; Secr. Jour. iii, p. 536.
[3] Dipl. Corr. U. S. i, pp. 566–573.
[4] Jefferson, i, pp. 385, 392.
[5] Jefferson, i, p. 449.

at Paris, to negotiate peace with Morocco, and he was commissioned October 5, 1785. His mission was entirely successful and satisfactory. He arrived in Morocco June 19, 1786, and within a month concluded a treaty [1] which contained very liberal principles, especially as to neutral rights and the exchange of prisoners. This treaty required ratification by the new emperor in 1795, and there were slight difficulties in 1802, 1803, and 1804; with these exceptions there was no further trouble with Morocco. The expense, moreover, was small, being less than ten thousand dollars in presents at the outset and twenty thousand for the ratification in 1795; no tribute was paid. [2] Congress passed resolutions of thanks to the king of Spain for his interposition with Morocco in our behalf, and to Barclay for his services in procuring the treaty. [3]

The situation in Algiers was complicated by the capture of the Maria and Dauphin, and involved the question of ransom of the captives as well as of peace. These vessels were taken as a result of a peace concluded between Algiers and Spain, which allowed the Algerines to pass the Straits. July 19, 1785, only a few days before the first capture, William Carmichael, our chargé d'affaires in Spain, wrote to Jefferson: " I am alarmed on account of the Algerines. Their peace with Spain has opened a large field to their piracies." [4]

The man appointed to the difficult task of negotiat-

[1] Appendix II.

[2] Dipl. Corr. U. S. i, pp. 656, 657, 805, 814; ii, pp. 693, 694 *et seq.*; St. Pap. x, p. 42; Lyman, Diplomacy of U. S. (Boston, 1828), ii, pp. 345–351.

[3] Secr. Jour. iv, pp. 367, 368.

[4] Dipl. Corr. U. S. i, p. 633. For other letters of Carmichael see iii, p. 299 *et seq.*

ing with Algiers was John Lamb, who knew the
country, having been engaged in the Barbary trade,
and who had been recommended by Congress. He
could speak only English, however, and appears not
to have been well qualified for the work. Adams and
Jefferson apparently had no great confidence in his
ability, and sent with him a clerk named Randall, in
whom they could trust. Lamb arrived in Algiers
March 25, 1786, and had three interviews with the
dey, Mohammed, who expressed admiration for Washington and a desire for his portrait. His estimate of
Washington's fellow countrymen in his power seems
also to have been a high one, for when the question
of ransom came up he declined to part with them for
less than six thousand dollars apiece for three captains,
one of whom had been a passenger on the Dauphin,
four thousand each for two mates and two passengers,
and fourteen hundred for each of the fourteen seamen,
which with eleven per cent. added, according to custom, made a total of nearly sixty thousand dollars, or
an average of about twenty-eight hundred dollars a
captive, while Lamb had authority to offer only two
hundred. Under the circumstances, therefore, the
best of agents must necessarily have failed. Lamb
retired to Spain to wait for a better opportunity, which
he thought might occur. He was urged by Adams
and Jefferson to return to America in order to explain
the situation to Congress; but pleading ill health he
declined to do this, or to report in person to them.
He then resigned his office.[1]

[1] Dipl. Corr. U. S. i, pp. 652, 656, 657, 661, 737, 773, 800, — pages 728
to 756 relate chiefly to this subject; see also iii, pp. 22–26; Nav. Chron.
pp. 37, 38, 41; Jefferson, i, pp. 438, 569, 581; Schuyler, American
Diplomacy (N. Y. 1901), pp. 205–207.

It was commonly believed that the European powers and their representatives at Algiers were not only indifferent to the success of our negotiations, but that most of them actively intrigued against it. Captain O'Brien, one of the captives, writing to Carmichael, June 24, 1790, says, on the authority of the vekil hadji, or secretary of foreign affairs: "That after the Americans had freed themselves from the British, that the British nation had demanded as a favor of this Regency, not to make a peace with the Americans, and that some time before the American ambassador [Lamb] came, the French [consul?] and Conde d'Espilly [Spanish ambassador] tried all their influence against the Americans' obtaining a peace." The vekil hadji expressed a warm desire for peace with the United States, stating that in that event he should expect as a present, for his private use, a twelve-gun schooner. Lamb found d'Espilly indifferent and the French and English consuls polite. D'Espilly told Carmichael of intrigues on the part of the British consuls at Barcelona and Algiers, regarding which, in his letter to Jefferson of July 15, 1786, relating the circumstances, Carmichael says that it "must arise from the court, for their private characters are good and they are men of liberal and humane principles." [1]

Concerning the attitude of France, Vergennes wrote, August 25, 1786, to M. Otto, the French chargé d'affaires in the United States: "You can assure the Congress that the King will seize with eagerness all occasions to facilitate their good intelligence with the Barbary Powers. This assembly without doubt have been informed of the support that his Majesty affords

[1] For. Rel. i, p. 118; Dipl. Corr. U. S. i, pp. 773, 801.

to the American Commissioners who negotiate at
Algiers and at Morocco; the treaty which has been
recently signed with this last Power, and which will
probably be published in America, will be the best
refutation of the suspicions which many public papers
are willing to inspire against our system of policy." [1]
The friendly disposition of France was indicated a
year earlier, when a letter from M. Soulanges, dated
Toulon, July 14, 1785, just before the captures of
Americans, was addressed to the consular authorities
in French ports informing them that the Algerines
were about to cruise against Americans, and saying:
"I give you immediate advice of this circumstance,
gentlemen, as well on account of the interest your
place may have in the cruise of these vessels, as to
enable you to give notice of it to American captains." [2]

Early in 1786 Adams, then minister to England,
had an interview with Abdurrahman, the Tripolitan
ambassador in London, which he describes in a letter
to John Jay, secretary of foreign affairs, dated February 17, 1786, in the course of which he says: "It
is sufficient to say that his Excellency made many
inquiries concerning America, the climate, soil, heat,
cold, etc., and observed, 'It is a very great country,
but *Tripoli is at war with it.*' In return it was asked
how there could be war between two nations when
there had been no hostility, injury, insult, or provocation on either side. His Excellency replied 'that
Turkey, Tripoli, Tunis, Algiers and Morocco were the
sovereigns of the Mediterranean; and that no nation

---

[1] Dipl. Corr. U. S. i, p. 242.
[2] Sherburne, Life of John Paul Jones (New York, 1851), pp. 254,
255, 270, 271.

could navigate that sea without a treaty of peace with them.'" In another letter to Jay, five days later, after discussing the probable cost of buying peace with the Barbary States, Adams says: " If it is not done, this war will cost us more millions of sterling money in a short time, besides the miserable depression of the reputation of the United States, the cruel embarrassment of all our commerce, and the intolerable burthen of insurance, added to the cries of our countrymen in captivity. . . . If a perpetual peace were made with these states, the character of the United States would instantly rise all over the world. Our commerce, navigation, and fisheries would extend into the Mediterranean. . . . The additional profits would richly repay the interest, and our credit would be adequate to all our wants." [1]

At Adams's request Jefferson visited London, in order that they might confer together on the subject, and they had an interview with Abdurrahman. The result they reported to Jay, March 28, 1786, which was to the effect that, according to the Tripolitan, a perpetual peace, which would be best, because inviolable by future pashas and cheapest in the long run, would cost thirty-three thousand guineas, of which three thousand would be his own share. A treaty with Tunis would cost about the same, and for Algiers and Morocco he could not answer, but each of them would probably demand about twice that sum. This would make a total of about a million dollars, whereas Congress had appropriated only eighty thousand. Jay reported to Congress on the subject, May 29, 1786, that " it would be expedient to leave terms of treaty " to Adams and

[1] Dipl. Corr. U. S. ii, pp. 565–573; Adams, viii, pp. 372, 373, 379.

Jefferson, but they might not be able to borrow money in Europe; therefore it would be better to inform the states of the amount needed and "that, until such time as they furnish Congress with their respective proportions of that sum, the depredations of those barbarians will, in all probability, continue and increase."[1]

This report illustrates the weakness of Congress under the Confederation and the poverty of the government, which is again emphasized by Jay in a letter to Jefferson of December 14, 1786: "If Congress had money to purchase peace of Algiers, or redeem the captives there, it certainly would, according to their present ideas, be well to lose no time in doing both. Neither pains nor expense, if within any tolerable limits, should be spared to ransom our fellow citizens; but the truth is, that no money is to be expected at present from hence, nor do I think it would be right to make new loans until we have at least some prospect of paying the interest due on former ones."[2]

About this time there was talk of its being necessary to send an ambassador to Constantinople to make a treaty with the sultan as a preliminary to peace with the Barbary States, or at least to facilitate that object. Jefferson therefore obtained the opinion of Vergennes on the subject, which he communicated to Jay May 23, 1786, and which was to the effect that a treaty with the porte would be very expensive and "would not procure us a peace at Algiers one penny the cheaper."[3]

[1] Dipl. Corr. U. S., i, pp. 604–608.
[2] Ibid. p. 811.
[3] Jefferson, i, p. 575.

Adams and Jefferson held radically different views as to the attitude that should be assumed toward the Barbary States. The former favored a policy of peace with the payment of tribute, while Jefferson preferred war. Adams wrote to Jay, December 15, 1784: " Some are of opinion that our trade in the Mediterranean is not worth the expense of the presents we must make the piratical states to obtain treaties with them. Others think it humiliating to treat with such enemies of the human race, and that it would be more manly to fight them. The first, I think, have not calculated the value of our Mediterranean trade. . . . The last have more spirit than prudence. As long as France, England, Holland, the Emperor, etc., will submit to be tributaries to these robbers, and even encourage them, to what purpose should we make war upon them ? The resolution might be heroic, but would not be wise. The contest would be unequal. They can injure us very sensibly, but we cannot hurt them in the smallest degree. . . . Unless it were possible, then, to persuade the great maritime powers of Europe to unite in the suppression of these piracies, it would be very imprudent for us to entertain any thoughts of contending with them, and will only lay a foundation, by irritating their passions and increasing their insolence and their demands, for long and severe repentance." [1]

Jefferson wrote to John Page, August 20, 1785: " You will probably find the tribute to all these powers make such a proportion of the federal taxes as that every man will feel them sensibly when he pays those taxes. The question is, whether their peace or war will be cheapest? But it is a question which should be

[1] Adams, viii, p. 218.

addressed to our honor as well as our avarice. Nor does it respect us as to these pirates only, but as to the nations of Europe. If we wish our commerce to be free and uninsulted, we must let these nations see that we have an energy which at present they disbelieve. The low opinion they entertain of our powers cannot fail to involve us soon in a naval war." [1]

In the summer of 1786 Adams and Jefferson carried on an interesting correspondence. Adams wrote to Jefferson, July 3, as follows : " I lay down a few simple propositions. 1. We may at this time have peace with them, in spite of all the intrigues of the English or others to prevent it, for a sum of money. 2. We shall never have peace, though France, Spain, England, and Holland should use all their influence in our favor, without a sum of money. 3. That neither the benevolence of France, or the malevolence of England, will be ever able materially to diminish or increase the sum. 4. The longer the negotiation is delayed, the larger will be the demand. From these premises, I conclude it to be wisest for us to negotiate and pay the necessary sum without loss of time. . . . Give me your opinion of these four propositions. . . Perhaps you will say, fight them, though it should cost us a great sum to carry on the war. . . . If this is your sentiment, and you can persuade the southern States into it, I dare answer for it that all from Pennsylvania, inclusively northward, would not object. It would be a good occasion to begin a navy. . . . The policy of Christendom has made cowards of all their sailors before the standard of Mahomet. It would be heroical and glorious in us to restore courage to ours. I doubt not we could accomplish it, if we should set

[1] Jefferson, i, p. 401.

about it in earnest ; but the difficulty of bringing our people to agree upon it, has ever discouraged me."[1]

To this Jefferson replied July 11 : "Our instructions . . . having required us to proceed by way of negotiation to obtain their peace, it became our duty to do this. . . . I acknowledge, I very early thought it would be best to effect a peace through the medium of war. . . . Of the four positions laid down in your letter of the 3d instant, I agree to the three first. . . . As to the fourth . . . this will depend on the intermediate captures; if they are many and rich, the price may be raised ; if few and poor, it will be lessened. However, if it is decided that we shall buy a peace, I know no reason for delaying the operation, . . . but I should prefer the obtaining it by war. 1. Justice is in favor of this opinion. 2. Honor favors it. 3. It will procure us respect in Europe ; and respect is a safeguard to interest. 4. It will arm the federal head with the safest of all the instruments of coercion over its delinquent members. 5. I think it least expensive. 6. Equally effectual. I ask a fleet of 150 guns. . . . So far, I have gone on the supposition that the whole weight of this war would rest on us. But, 1. Naples will join us. . . . 2. Every principle of reason assures us that Portugal will join us. . . . I suppose then, that a convention might be formed between Portugal, Naples, and the United States, by which the burthen of the war might be quotaed on them, according to their respective wealth ; and the term of it should be, when Algiers should subscribe to a peace with all three, on equal terms." [2]

In reply to this Adams writes, July 31 : "Your favor of the 11th instant I have received. There are

[1] Adams, viii, pp. 406, 407   [2] Jefferson i pp. 591-593.

great and weighty considerations urged in it in favor of arming against the Algerines, and, I confess, if our states could be brought to agree in the measure, I should be very willing to resolve upon external war with vigor, and protect our trade and people. The resolution to fight them would raise the spirits and courage of our countrymen immediately, and we might obtain the glory of finally breaking up these nests of banditti. But Congress will never, or at least not for years, take any such resolutions, and in the mean time our trade and honor suffers beyond calculation. We ought not to fight them at all, unless we determine to fight them forever. This thought, I fear, is too rugged for our people to bear. To fight them at the expense of millions, and make peace, after all, by giving more money and larger presents than would now procure perpetual peace, seems not to be economical. I agree in opinion of the wisdom and necessity of a navy for other uses, but am apprehensive it will make bad worse with the Algerines. I will go all lengths with you in promoting a navy, whether to be applied to the Algerines or not. But I think at the same time we should treat. Your letter, however, has made me easier upon this point. Nevertheless, to humble the Algerines, I think you have undercalculated the force necessary." [1]

In his hopes of a perpetual peace Adams's confidence in the good faith of the Barbary States was not justified by their record in diplomatic history from the earliest times, and their subsequent relations with our

[1] Adams, viii, pp. 410, 411. In a footnote the editor, C. F. Adams, says: "The argument of Mr. Adams is one of expediency, drawn solely from the condition of the country at the moment." Subsequently Adams was a strong supporter of the navy, as is well known.

government showed that their idea of a treaty was
a compact by which they were to abide just as long as
it pleased them. This confidence was not shared by
Jefferson, who in a letter to Monroe, May 10, 1786,
in speaking of his interview with the Tripolitan
ambassador, and the proposition to purchase peace of
all the Barbary States, says: " The continuance of this
peace will depend on their idea of our power to enforce
it, and on the life of the particular dey, or other
head of the government with whom it is contracted.
Congress will, no doubt, weigh these circumstances
against the expense and probable success of compelling a peace by arms." [1] Adams seems to have had the
better appreciation of what was practicable in view
of the empty treasury and the weakness of the government, and Jefferson of what alone would be effectual in view of the sort of people with whom they had
to deal.

Jefferson's plan for using force was by means of
a perpetual blockade by an international fleet. He
had obtained the opinion of D'Estaing on the subject,
who wrote to him May 17, 1786: " I am convinced
that, by blocking up Algiers by cross-anchoring and
with a long tow, that is to say, with several cables
spliced to each other, and with iron chains, one might,
if necessary, always remain there, and there is no
barbarian power, thus confined, which would not soon
sue for peace. . . . Bombardments are but transi-
tory. It is, if I may so express myself, like breaking
glass windows with guineas. None have produced
the desired effect against the barbarians. Even an
imperfect blockade, were one to have the patience
and courage to persist therein, would occasion a per-

[1] Jefferson, i, p. 565.

petual evil; it would be insupportable in the long
run." [1]

In his autobiography Jefferson says: " I was very
unwilling that we should acquiesce in the European
humiliation of paying tribute to those lawless pirates,
and endeavored to form an association of the powers
subject to habitual depredations from them. I accordingly prepared and proposed to their ministers at Paris,
for consultation with their governments, articles of a
special confederation. . . . Portugal, Naples, the Two
Sicilies, Venice, Malta, Denmark, and Sweden were
favorably disposed to such an association, . . . and
nothing was now wanting to bring it into direct and
formal consideration but the assent of our Government
and their authority to make a formal proposition. . . .
But they were in no condition to make any such engagement. Their recommendatory powers for obtaining contributions were so openly neglected by the
several states, that they declined an engagement which
they were conscious they could not fulfill with punctu-
ality; and so it fell through." [2] Jefferson also describes
his plan in a letter to Monroe, August 11, 1786, and
goes on to say: " Were the honor and advantage of
establishing such a confederacy out of the question,
yet the necessity that the United States should have
some marine force, and the happiness of this, as the
ostensible cause of beginning it, would decide on its
propriety. It will be said there is no money in the
treasury. There never will be money in the treasury,
till the confederacy shows its teeth. . . . Every ra-
tional citizen must wish to see an effective instrument

---

[1] Dipl. Corr. U. S. i, p. 753; St. Pap. x, p. 54.

[2] Jefferson, i, pp. 65, 67, where the plan is given in detail; also iii,
p. 164, and ix, pp. 307, 424.

of coercion, and should fear to see it on any other element than the water. A naval force can never endanger our liberties, nor occasion bloodshed ; a land force would do both." [1]

Early in 1787 Jefferson had an interview with the general of the religious order of Mathurins on the subject of the redemption of the American captives. He entered into the project with zeal, and proposed to employ for the purpose his agents already on the spot. The consent of Congress was obtained and negotiations with the Mathurins began in September, 1787. It was considered necessary to keep the matter a profound secret, for if the concern of the United States in the transaction should become known, the Algerines would not only demand exorbitant ransoms, but future redemptions by the order would be rendered more difficult and expensive. "These ideas, suggested to him by the danger of raising his market, were approved by the minister plenipotentiary [Jefferson] ; because, this being the first instance of a redemption by the United States, it would form a precedent, because a high price given by us might induce these pirates to abandon all other nations in pursuit of Americans ; whereas the contrary would take place, could our price of redemption be fixed at the lowest point." With the same object in view, an assumption of indifference and neglect on the part of the government was considered expedient and the allowance which had been given the captives was withdrawn. As it was not thought safe to let them into the secret, they naturally complained bitterly of their abandonment. After Jefferson's departure from Paris in 1789, correspondence with the Mathurins was continued by William Short,

[1] Jefferson, i, p. 606. See also Ford's Jefferson, iv, pp. 10, 11, 89.

chargé d'affaires. Nothing ever came of the plan, however, for the dey persisted in demanding excessive ransoms ; and finally, after three years or more of vain effort and weary delay, the Revolution in France put an end to the negotiations by the abolition of the Mathurins with other religious orders.[1]

The adoption of the Constitution and the inauguration of a stronger government in 1789 gave hope of more vigorous measures for the solution of this vexed problem, but even then Congress was slow to take decisive action.

[1] Dipl. Corr. U. S. ii, pp. 25, 86, 148, 182, 324 ; St. Pap. x, pp. 56–67; Nav. Chron. pp. 37–43.

CHAPTER IV

PEACE WITH ALGIERS

OWING to hopes of success attending the efforts of the Mathurins, and the secrecy necessary to be observed, it was not until the end of 1790 that the matter was made public, nor, in the mean time, were other measures taken. On December 28 of that year, Jefferson, then secretary of state, made two reports: one to the President, on the situation at Algiers, called forth by a petition addressed to Congress by the captives; the other to the House of Representatives, on Mediterranean trade. The first of these was transmitted to Congress two days later with a message from President Washington.[1]

These documents cover the events already related in the preceding chapter. In the Mediterranean report Jefferson continues to advocate force, and repeats his recommendation of coöperation with other powers for the blockade of Algiers. This latter proposition, apparently, was never seriously considered, and on account of the convulsions in Europe, just beginning, would probably then have been impracticable. A vigorous policy, however, was beginning to win favor. On the 6th of January, 1791, the Senate committee on Mediterranean trade reported "that the trade of the United States to the Mediterranean cannot be

[1] These reports, with accompanying documents, will be found in St. Pap. x, pp. 41, 56, and in For. Rel. i, pp. 100, 104, and the first also in Nav. Chron. p. 37.

protected but by a naval force; and that it will be proper to resort to the same as soon as the state of the public finances will admit." [1]

In March, 1791, the emperor of Morocco having died, Congress appropriated twenty thousand dollars for the purpose of obtaining from the new emperor recognition of the treaty made with his father. With this object, Thomas Barclay was appointed consul to Morocco, but on the way to his post he learned that there was a civil war in progress in Morocco, the throne being in dispute between several sons of the late emperor. He therefore remained in Lisbon, awaiting a favorable opportunity. The war, however, proved a long one. At this time, all that could be done for the captives at Algiers was to renew their allowance, which was done through Colonel David Humphreys, the United States minister to Portugal. [2]

In July, 1791, Jefferson, still in the hope of being able to send a naval force against Algiers, wrote to Paul Jones, with the approval of the President, suggesting that he attempt to enlist the coöperation of Holland, and intimating that he would be chosen to command the American squadron, should one be sent. Jones met with little encouragement in Holland, and thought that it would be far better for the United States to act alone in the matter. He believed that Algiers could be brought to terms by a force of two frigates and two or three sloops-of-war. He had been deeply interested in the fate of the captives from the first, and in 1787 had suggested to John Jay that a fund be raised for their redemption by deducting

---

[1] For. Rel. i, p. 108; Rep. Sen. Com. iv, p. 5.

[2] St. Pap. x, pp. 254–260; For. Rel. i, p. 288; Rep. Sen. Com. iv, pp. 5, 6; Nav. Chron. pp. 44–46.

a shilling per month from seamen's wages throughout the country.[1]

February 22, 1792, the Senate favored paying one hundred thousand dollars annually for peace with Algiers, Tripoli, and Tunis, and forty thousand dollars ransom for the captives. May 8, in response to a message from the President of the same date, the Senate passed resolutions stating its readiness to ratify treaties with Algiers providing for peace at a cost of forty thousand dollars at the outset and annual tribute of twenty-five thousand; and also for ransom of the captives, then thirteen in number, for forty thousand. Congress at once appropriated fifty thousand dollars for the expenses of the mission, and on June 1 Paul Jones was appointed envoy to treat for peace and ransom, and also consul at Algiers. Secrecy was considered of such importance that Jones's long and minute instructions were made out by Jefferson in his own handwriting. The following extracts will serve to bring out the attitude of the administration towards the question : " We have also understood that peace might be bought cheaper with naval stores than with money, but we will not furnish them with naval stores, because we think it is not right to furnish them the means which we know they will employ to do wrong and because there might be no economy in it as to ourselves in the end, as it would increase the expense of that coercion which we may in future be obliged to practice towards them. . . . It has been a fixed principle with Congress to establish the rate of ransom of the American captives with the Barbary States at as low a point as possible, that it may not be the interest

[1] Buell, Paul Jones (New York, 1900), ii, pp. 285–287; Sherburne's Jones, p. 270.

of these States to go in quest of our citizens in preference to those of other countries. Had it not been for the danger it would have brought on the residue of our seamen, by exciting the cupidity of these rovers against them, our citizens now in Algiers would have been long ago redeemed, without regard to price. The mere money for this particular redemption neither has been, nor is, an object with anybody here. It is from the same regard to the safety of our seamen at large, that they have now restrained us from any ransom unaccompanied with peace; this being secured, we are led to consent to terms of ransom to which, otherwise, our government would never have consented." [1]

The papers were intrusted to Thomas Pinckney, who was about to set out for Europe as minister to Great Britain, and who had authority to turn the business over to Barclay in case anything should prevent Jones's serving. On Pinckney's arrival in England he heard of Jones's untimely death in Paris on July 18, 1792. Much time was lost in finding a trustworthy messenger to convey the papers to Barclay and in accomplishing the journey for that purpose. Finally Barclay received his instructions and had made preparations for his mission to Algiers when he was suddenly taken sick in Lisbon and died January 19, 1793. As soon as this became known to the administration, Humphreys was appointed; but owing to further delays, due chiefly to the difficulty of the messenger in getting transportation to Lisbon, it was not until September, 1793, that he received his commission and instructions. He proceeded to Gibraltar, and while waiting for a passage to Algiers came the

[1] St. Pap. x, pp. 260-268; For. Rel. vol. i, pp. 133, 136, 290; Rep. Sen. Com. viii, p. 6.

news of the truce with Portugal that resulted in the numerous captures of 1793. After this the dey positively refused to receive our minister. Humphreys, foreseeing the danger to American commerce, at once dispatched a vessel to the United States to give warning to merchants.[1]

It was the opinion of Colonel Humphreys, and of Edward Church, United States consul at Lisbon, that this truce was made through the influence of the British consul at Algiers and without the authority of the Portuguese government, which, although desirous of peace, had intended first, according to the Portuguese secretary for foreign affairs, to give " timely notice to all their friends, that they might avoid the dangers to which they might otherwise be unavoidably exposed. . . . But the British Court, zealous overmuch for the happiness of the two nations, Portugal and Algiers, in order to precipitate this important business, very officiously authorized Charles Logie, the British consul-general and agent at Algiers, not only to treat, but to conclude, for and in behalf of this Court, not only without authority, but even without consulting it." Church says : " The conduct of the British in this business leaves no room to doubt or mistake their object, which was evidently aimed at us." Humphreys, however, was of the opinion that Logie had acted on his own responsibility. Pinckney was assured by Lord Grenville that England " had not the least intention or a thought of injuring us thereby ; that they had been applied to by their friend and ally the Court of Portugal to procure a peace for them with the Algerines, and that Mr. Logie had been instructed to use

[1] St. Pap. x, pp. 268–276; For. Rel. i, pp. 292–294; Nav. Chron. pp. 47, 48.

his endeavors to effect this purpose; that he, finding the arrangements for a peace could not immediately take place, had concluded the truce; that in this they conceived they had done no more than their friendship for a good ally required of them." [1]

Church took measures to warn American shipmasters in neighboring waters of their danger. He also obtained from the Portuguese government convoy for several vessels, but this, of course, could only be depended upon as an occasional arrangement, and, as Humphreys wrote to Jefferson, December 25, 1793: "It appears absurd to trust to the fleets of Portugal, or any other nation, to protect or convoy our trade. If we mean to have a commerce, we must have a naval force, to a certain extent, to defend it." Captain O'Brien also wrote from Algiers, to the President, November 5 and to Humphreys December 6, strongly urging force as the only effectual means of securing immunity from the pirates.[2]

At last, informed of the added dangers to commerce, the House of Representatives, January 2, 1794, resolved by a majority of two "that a naval force, adequate to the protection of the commerce of the United States against the Algerine corsairs, ought to be provided." A bill was reported January 20 by the Committee of Ways and Means providing for the construction of six vessels at a cost of six hundred thousand dollars. The opponents argued that the finances of the country did not justify the expense, and that the public debt must first be discharged;

[1] St. Pap. x, pp. 278–284, 305; For. Rel. i, pp. 295, 296; Nav. Chron. pp. 49, 50; Barlow, pp. 120, 121.

[2] St. Pap. x, pp. 284–291; for correspondence relating to the captures, see pp. 309–342; For. Rel. i, pp. 414–422; Nav. Chron. pp. 51–53.

that we should follow the example of Europe by buying peace, or should hire a European navy to protect
our trade; that a navy is a menace to liberty. The
advocates of a navy predicted an improvement in the
national finances resulting from the protection to commerce and saving of insurance, and contended that
the friendship of Algiers could not be relied upon,
and that to subsidize a European navy was not consistent with national dignity. Madison opposed the
bill partly on the ground that a navy would lead to
international complications, particularly with England, and this opinion was shared by others. The bill
passed the House by a vote of fifty to thirty-nine.
Its passage, however, was only made possible by the
insertion of a provision that in case of peace with
Algiers all work on the frigates should stop. Having
passed the Senate, it was approved March 27, 1794.
The law authorized the President " to provide, by
purchase or otherwise, equip and employ, four ships
to carry forty-four guns and two ships to carry thirty-
six guns each; or . . . in lieu of the six frigates, a
naval force not exceeding, in the whole, that by this
act directed, so that no ship thus provided should carry
less than thirty-two guns; or he may provide any
proportion thereof, which in his discretion he may
think proper." The full complement for each ship
was prescribed, also the pay and ration. A subsequent
act appropriated $688,888.82 to defray the expenses
of the naval armament.[1]

This legislation is of special interest and import-

[1] Nav. Chron. pp. 53–56; Benton, Debates of Congress (New York,
1857), i, pp. 473–482. The opposition to the navy was mostly from the
South; the representatives from Massachusetts, Rhode Island, and
Connecticut were unanimously in favor of the bill.

ance because it marks the beginning of the present navy, the Revolutionary navy having been allowed to lapse completely. The work was well begun, and the selection of Joshua Humphreys, a shipbuilder of Pennsylvania, to design the ships, was a most fortunate one. He was a man of exceptional ability, and his views as to the type of ships most suitable at that time showed great wisdom. He had previously written a letter to Robert Morris, then in the Senate, on the subject, in which he proposed to build " such frigates as in blowing weather would be an over-match for double-decked ships, or in light winds may evade coming to action by out-sailing them; " and added : " If we build our ships of the same size as the Europeans, they having so great a number of them, we shall always be behind them. I would build them of a larger size than theirs, and take the lead of them, which is the only safe method of commencing a navy." In his report of December 23, 1794, Humphreys says : " As soon as Congress had agreed to build frigates, it was contemplated to make them the most powerful, and, at the same time, the most useful ships. . . . From the construction of those ships, it is expected the commanders of them will have it in their power to engage, or not, any ship, as they may think proper ; and no ship, under sixty-four, now afloat, but what must submit to them." The secretary of war, General Henry Knox, in whose department the work was done, the navy department not yet having been established, reported December 27, 1794 : " That the passing of the said act created an anxious solicitude that this second commencement of a navy for the United States should be worthy of their national character. That the vessels should combine such

qualities of strength, durability, swiftness of sailing,
and force, as to render them equal, if not superior, to
any frigate belonging to any of the European Powers."
This policy of building the best ships of their class was
thus begun and was followed until the period of the
Civil War, and has been since, to a great extent. The
line-of-battle ships, which composed the fighting
strength of the navies of that day, were slow and
unwieldy, and a fast frigate could keep out of their
way. The resources of the United States at that time
were not equal to the construction of the heavier and
more expensive ships.[1]

Meanwhile efforts at making peace with Algiers
were not abandoned. The number of captives had
now been increased to a hundred and nineteen, and
their redemption had become correspondingly difficult
and expensive. The Swedish consul, Matthias Skjöldebrand, and his brother were much interested in the
fate of the Americans. The consul, on account of his
official position, felt obliged to keep himself in the
background, but his brother, Pierre E. Skjöldebrand,
thenceforth took an active part in the negotiations
between the United States and Algiers. November
13, 1793, the brothers wrote letters of sympathy and
advice to Colonel Humphreys. One piece of advice
was to break relations with a Jew merchant in Algiers,
named Bassara, who had been employed by the Americans as an agent and who was out of favor with the
dey, and transfer the business to Bacri, another Jew.
This was done and helped to facilitate matters. But
the dey was indisposed to peace. He said: "If I were
to make peace with everybody, what should I do with
my corsairs? What should I do with my soldiers?

[1] Narr. and Crit. Hist. vii, p. 360; Nav. Aff. i, pp. 6, 8.

They would take off my head for want of other prizes, not being able to live upon their miserable allowance." [1]

Humphreys came back to America in 1794, and returned in April, the next year, to Lisbon with Joseph Donaldson, Jr., who had been appointed consul to Tunis and Tripoli and was to assist in the negotiations with Algiers. For peace and ransom Humphreys had been authorized, July 19, 1794, to spend eight hundred thousand dollars, and was later given minute instructions. Humphreys did not go to Algiers, but exercised a general supervision of affairs. He went to Paris in June, 1795, where he conferred with Monroe, the United States minister, received assurances of coöperation on the part of the French republic, and secured the services of Joel Barlow to assist in the negotiations. The dey persistently refused to receive any American minister or to treat for peace or ransom, but finally relented and Donaldson was sent over. [2]

Cathcart, one of the captives of 1785, was at this time secretary to the dey, Hasan Pasha, and appears to have had a good deal of influence with him. According to his own account it was only through his persuasion that the dey consented to receive Donaldson. As soon as he yielded, Skjöldebrand chartered a Ragusan brig which sailed at once for Alicante, where Donaldson was waiting, and brought him over. He arrived at Algiers September 3, 1795. Cathcart gives an interesting account of the negotiations, in which he acted as a medium of communication between the dey and Donaldson, who had as advisers Skjöldebrand, O'Brien, and Bacri. The dey began with an

---

[1] St. Pap. x, pp. 313–318; For. Rel. i, pp. 414, 415.
[2] St. Pap. ii, pp. 144, 229, 425–427; x, pp. 448, 449; For. Rel. i, pp. 528, 529, 553; Nav. Chron. pp. 62, 63; Davis, p. 33.

exorbitant demand and Donaldson with a rather modest offer, and both were obstinate. Donaldson was with great difficulty persuaded to increase his offer to a figure which the dey was finally induced to accept, as he said, to spite the English. The treaty was signed and the American flag saluted September 5. Then followed much discussion as to presents and other details, and at last O'Brien sailed September 11 with the treaty to be delivered to Humphreys, and bearing a letter from Skjöldebrand, in which he says: "The Jew Bacri . . . has been the person who, in concert with Mr. Cathcart, have executed in public with the dey, the plans and directions on which Mr. Donaldson, in concert with me and Captain O'Brien, privately agreed; and all have had their share of merit in removing all the difficulties invented by your enemies here, who have used all their endeavors, even with lies, to create in the dey an ill disposition towards the United States." The French consul was apparently one of these unfriendly persons.[1]

Humphreys was informed of the treaty while still in France, and did not get back to Lisbon until November 17, where he found O'Brien with the document awaiting him. There was now great delay in procuring the funds necessary to carry out the stipulations. O'Brien was sent to London in the American brig Sophia for the money, and Barlow, who had already purchased a number of presents, went to Alicante to be ready to cross directly over to Algiers as soon as O'Brien returned. But owing to the disturbed condition of European politics it was impossible to obtain coin in England, and O'Brien was obliged to return empty-handed. Both gold and silver could have been

[1] Cathcart, I, ch. x, xi, xii; For. Rel. i, p. 530.

procured in Lisbon a little earlier, but Humphreys
was then in Paris, and the opportunity was lost.[1]

Meanwhile the dey became very impatient and
threatened to abandon the treaty and again to send
out his cruisers against Americans. The captives also,
who had expected prompt release, were becoming disheartened. Barlow then waited no longer, but proceeded to Algiers, arriving March 5, 1796, with the
hope of being able to soothe the dey. He, however,
became more and more angry, and in April gave Barlow and Donaldson eight days' notice to leave Algiers,
declaring that he would send out his cruisers at the
end of thirty days, if the money had not then been
paid. Affairs seemed now to be in a very critical state,
and the American envoys assumed the responsibility of
offering the dey the additional present of a thirty-six
gun frigate as the only chance of saving the treaty.
This had the desired effect. The dey was mollified
and granted further time. Donaldson then went to
Leghorn to endeavor to raise a loan there. Cathcart
was sent to America with letters from Barlow and the
dey. At last Barlow succeeded in borrowing from
Bacri a sum of money sufficient for the ransom. This
money in reality belonged to the public treasury of
Algiers; it had been borrowed by the French consul,
and deposited with Bacri, and was now taken with the
knowledge of the dey. The captives were then hastily
shipped off before the dey should have time to change
his mind. Barlow says of these unfortunates, in a
letter to the secretary of state: "Our people have
conducted themselves in general with a degree of
patience and decorum which would become a better
condition than that of slaves." They were taken in the

[1] St. Pap. x, pp. 449, 459; Pickering, xxxvi, p. 46.

ship Fortune, belonging to Bacri, but under American colors, to Marseilles, where they were cared for by the United States consul, Stephen Cathalan, Jr. The Fortune, still under the American flag, was afterwards captured and condemned by the British. Thereupon Bacri, holding the flag responsible, demanded forty thousand dollars, for which Barlow was forced to give bonds. Cathalan sent most of the liberated captives home in the Swedish ship Jupiter, which arrived in the United States in February, 1797.[1]

Humphreys, not wishing to assume the responsibility of the frigate to be presented to the dey, sent O'Brien to America in the Sophia to refer the matter to the government. Upon receiving the report, Timothy Pickering, secretary of state, wrote to Humphreys June 11, 1796 : " There appears no eligible alternative but to confirm the engagement of Messrs. Barlow and Donaldson." O'Brien returned to Lisbon in July. In the mean time Humphreys had succeeded in negotiating bills on London in Lisbon for two hundred and twenty-five thousand dollars. This was embarked on the Sophia, and O'Brien set sail for Algiers August 4. On the way he was captured by a Tripolitan corsair and taken into Tripoli. Another American vessel was taken about the same time. The pasha of Tripoli was loath to give up such a rich prize, but he dared not disregard O'Brien's Algerine passport ; so after holding him three weeks, he released him, and the Sophia arrived safely at Algiers in October. The treaty stipulations were now fulfilled, and the dey was so pleased that he offered to lend Barlow ninety thousand piastres

[1] St. Pap. x, pp. 450-453 ; For. Rel. i, pp. 553-555 ; Nav. Chron. pp. 63, 64 ; Barlow, pp. 117, 120, 125, 129-136 ; Cathcart, I, pp. 265-267 ; Pickering, x, pp. 117, 155 ; xxxvii, pp. 57, 150.

(Spanish dollars) for the treaties with Tunis and Tripoli. Barlow remained in Algiers during the negotiation of these treaties, and finally took his departure the following summer.[1]

In the mean time the war in Morocco was brought to an end in 1795 by the victory of one of the aspirants to the throne, Muley Soliman, over his brothers. James Simpson, United States consul at Gibraltar, was at once sent over to obtain from the new emperor recognition of the treaty made with his father. In this he was successful, and in December, 1795, the President received from the emperor an effusive letter to this effect.[2]

The treaty of peace and amity [3] with Algiers, of September 5, 1795, which was ratified by the Senate March 2, 1796, cost up to January, 1797, nearly a million dollars, including $525,500 for ransom of the captives, various presents, and miscellaneous expenses; this was exclusive of the annuity in naval stores, valued at something over twenty-one thousand dollars, according to the estimate, which afterwards proved to be far too low. Naval stores comprised ship-timber, spars, cordage, and many other articles for the use of ships. Presents were an important feature in dealing with these barbarians; they were called usance, and were of three kinds, — a present of twenty thousand dollars with each new consul, biennial presents to government officers of about seventeen thousand, and

[1] St. Pap. x, p. 450; for details of the financial difficulties which hampered and delayed the negotiations, see Report of the Secretary of the Treasury, Jan. 4, 1797, and accompanying documents, St. Pap. x, pp. 453–463; Barlow, pp. 139–141, 148; Pickering, xxxvi, p. 108.

[2] St. Pap. x, pp. 403–408; Nav. Chron. p. 58.

[3] Appendix II.

incidental presents, which could not be estimated.[1]
The treaty was not so liberal as that with Morocco
and was the only one with the Barbary States which
stipulated the payment of tribute. This tribute, consisting of naval stores, and the frigate afterwards
given, furnished the Algerines with means of waging
war upon us and upon other Christian nations, but
it was found impracticable to avoid this, and the position taken in the instructions to Paul Jones, already
quoted,[2] could not be held.

The page of our history recording these dealings
with Algiers is not one to take pride in, and it is greatly
to be regretted that the weight of opinion at that time
was not in favor of the early and energetic employment of force. It is now easy to see how such a course
would have saved time and money and won respect.
But to judge the question fairly it is necessary to look
at it from the point of view of that time. Most of
those who favored following the precedent of Europe
by paying tribute to barbarians, and who opposed a
navy, did what they thought was best for the country,
and many of them were among the foremost public
men of the day.

On the ratification of the treaty, the provision of
the act of March 27, 1794, that work on the ships
should cease, took effect. President Washington,
therefore, in a message to Congress, March 15, 1796,
called attention to the loss and disadvantage that
would result from abandoning the work already well

[1] St. Pap. x, pp. 453–463 ; Nav. Chron. p. 65; Davis, p. 34 ; Rep.
Sen. Com. viii, p. 7 ; For. Rel. i, pp. 549, 555 ; iii, p. 33. For details
of expenses of intercourse with the Barbary powers at a later period,
see Amer. State Papers, Misc., ii, pp. 20–45.

[2] See above, p. 45.

advanced. Two days later a committee of the Senate reported that " it will be expedient to authorize the President of the United States to cause to be completed, with all convenient expedition, two of the said frigates of forty-four, and one of thirty-six guns," and this recommendation was adopted by an act of Congress of April 20.[1] These three ships, launched the following year, were the United States, Constitution, and Constellation. They were the first of a long and honorable list containing many famous men-of-war, and the two last are still on the Navy Register.

In his annual message in December, 1796, Washington said : " To an active external commerce, the protection of a naval force is indispensable. . . . The most sincere neutrality is not a sufficient guard against the depredations of nations at war. To secure respect to a neutral flag requires a naval force, organized and ready to vindicate it from insult or aggression. This may even prevent the necessity of going to war, by discouraging belligerent powers from committing such violations of the rights of the neutral party, as may, first or last, leave no other option. From the best information I have been able to obtain, it would seem as if our trade to the Mediterranean, without a protecting force, will always be insecure, and our citizens exposed to the calamities from which numbers of them have but just been relieved. These considerations invite the United States to look to the means, and to set about the gradual creation of a Navy." [2]

[1] Nav. Aff. i, p. 25 ; Nav. Chron. pp. 59-61; Rep. Sen. Com. iv, p. 6.

[2] Nav. Chron. p. 62.

CHAPTER V

PEACE WITH TRIPOLI AND TUNIS

As before mentioned, Mr. Barlow remained at Algiers during negotiations with Tunis and Tripoli. He secured the services at Tunis of a Frenchman named Joseph Famin, who had been recommended to him by the French consul. Famin concluded, without expense, a truce for six months between the United States and Tunis, beginning June 15, 1796.[1] In a letter dated September 1, Barlow mentions the capture of two American ships by the Tripolitans, one of which turned out to be the Sophia with O'Brien and the money for the Algerine treaty; the other ship, he says, was broken up and the cargo confiscated. These vessels were taken by the Tripolitan corsair Peter Lisle, a renegade Scotchman known as Murad Reis. October 9 Barlow speaks of the capture of a vessel by the Tunisians, apparently in violation of the truce. October 12 he writes: "Another large ship, richly ladened, the Betsy of Boston, Captain Sampson, has been taken at Tripoli. The crew are in slavery; they will soon be free." No further details of these captures are given. Upon the conclusion of peace with Tripoli, which soon followed, the Betsy was retained by the pasha, but her crew were released.[2]

Taking advantage of the dey's good humor on receiving his money, Barlow asked his influence, which was supposed to be powerful, in treating with Tunis

---

[1] St. Pap. x, p. 451; For. Rel. i, p. 554.
[2] Barlow, pp. 137–140, 142; Stephens, pp. 82–84.

and Tripoli. The dey not only promised this, but advanced the necessary funds — fifty thousand piastres for Tunis and forty thousand for Tripoli. O'Brien at once set sail for those cities with the money, letters, and presents. On his arrival at Tunis, the bey, Hamuda, demanded three times his original price, and this caused delay.[1] With Tripoli things went more smoothly. A treaty[2] was concluded without much difficulty, November 4, 1796, at a cost of nearly fifty-six thousand dollars. After being signed by the pasha, Yusuf Karamanli, it was brought by O'Brien to Algiers, where it was signed by Barlow and the dey, January 3, 1797. It was ratified by the Senate June 10. The treaty[3] with Tunis was at last concluded by Famin in August, 1797, at an estimated expense of one hundred and seven thousand dollars. It was sent to Colonel Humphreys, who approved it, November 14, and transmitted it to the State Department.[4] The expense of these treaties was subsequently much increased by yielding, at least partially, to the repeated demands of the Barbary rulers.

In June, 1797, the dey of Algiers having requested that two cruisers should be built and equipped for him in the United States, at his expense, President Adams, considering the United States "to be under peculiar obligations" to the dey, on account of his aid in our dealings with Tunis and Tripoli, recommended that this request be complied with. "The expense of navigating them to Algiers may perhaps be compensated by the freight of the stores with which they may be loaded, on account of our stipulations by treaty with

[1] Barlow, pp. 140–144. [2] Appendix II.
[3] Appendix II.
[4] For. Rel. ii, pp. 18, 123, 125, 126 ; Rep. Sen. Com. viii, pp. 9, 10.

the dey." [1] The frigate which had been promised to
the dey by Barlow as a condition of preserving the
treaty was built at Portsmouth, N. H., was called the
Crescent, and is borne on the United States Navy list.
She sailed for Algiers in January, 1798, loaded with
naval stores, and taking as passenger Captain Richard
O'Brien, who had been appointed consul to Algiers
and consul-general to all the Barbary States. The
consulship had been offered to Pierre Skjöldebrand,
but he declined it. [2]

The treaty with Tunis was laid before the Senate
February 21, 1798, and upon its consideration objection was made to three articles. One of these, the
fourteenth, related to the tariff and provided that American goods in American vessels should pay three per
cent. in Tunis, that American goods in foreign vessels
or foreign goods in American vessels should pay ten
per cent., while Tunisian goods, under any flag whatever, in United States ports should pay but three per
cent. It was suspected that Famin had the obnoxious
clauses of this article inserted for his own commercial
advantage. Barlow said they were not in the original
draft of the treaty submitted to him in April, 1797.
The Senate refused to ratify this article. Of the other
objectionable articles, the eleventh provided that a
barrel of gunpowder should be given to Tunis for
every gun fired in saluting a United States man-of-
war; and the twelfth that the bey might impress any
American merchant vessel into his service, paying such
freight as he should prescribe. The Senate resolved

[1] President's Message, June 23, 1797, St. Pap. x, p. 464; For. Rel.
ii, p. 65; Nav. Chron. p. 66.
[2] Cooper, i, p. 310; Pickering, vii, pp. 130, 580, 664; xxxvi, pp. 7,
124.

"that it be recommended to the President of the United States, to enter into a friendly negotiation with the bey and government of Tunis, on the subject of the said [fourteenth] article, so as to accommodate the provision thereof to the existing treaties of the United States with other nations."[1]

William Eaton had been appointed consul to Tunis in July 1797, but had not yet been ordered to his post. Eaton was an interesting character. He was born in Connecticut in 1764, and at the age of sixteen enlisted in the Continental Army. After the war he taught school, graduated at Dartmouth College in 1790, and two years later was appointed a captain in the army. December 22, 1798, he embarked on the United States brig Sophia, mounting twelve guns, commanded by Captain Henry Geddes of the navy, accompanied by James L. Cathcart, the former captive, now consul to Tripoli. The Sophia sailed in company with the ship Hero, the brig Hassan Bashaw, and the schooners Skjöldebrand and Lelah Eisha. The Hero was loaded with naval stores for Algiers, in payment of stipulations and arrearages. The others were armed vessels. The Hassan Bashaw and Skjöldebrand were the cruisers built for the dey at his expense, on the recommendation of President Adams. The Lelah Eisha, and the Hamdullah, a schooner that had sailed a year earlier, were to be delivered to the dey as a substitute for stipulated naval stores. The crews of the vessels to be left at Algiers were to return home in the Sophia.[2] The dey at this time was Mustapha, Hasan having died in 1798.

[1] Eaton, pp. 55, 56 ; Felton, pp. 185–190.

[2] Eaton, p. 54; Cathcart, II, p. 12 ; Pickering, vii, p. 664 ; ix, p. 505; x, p. 117.

WILLIAM EATON

The Sophia arrived at Algiers February 9, 1799, after a passage of thirty-six days from the capes of the Delaware, and the other vessels at about the same time, except the Hero, which was delayed. Eaton and Cathcart at once called on O'Brien. The three consuls had been appointed a commission to obtain the necessary alterations in the treaty with Tunis, and any two of them were authorized to act in this capacity.[1] February 22 they were presented to the dey of Algiers, and the interview is thus described by Eaton: " Consuls O'Brien, Cathcart and myself, Captains Geddes, Smith, Penrose, Maley, proceeded from the American house to the courtyard of the palace, uncovered our heads, entered the area of the hall, ascended a winding maze of five flights of stairs, to a narrow, dark entry, leading to a contracted apartment of about twelve by eight feet, the private audience room. Here we took off our shoes and, entering the cave (for so it seemed), with small apertures of light with iron grates, we were shown to a huge, shaggy beast, sitting on his rump, upon a low bench, covered with a cushion of embroidered velvet, with his hind legs gathered up like a tailor or a bear. On our approach to him, he reached out his fore paw as if to receive something to eat. Our guide exclaimed, ' Kiss the Dey's hand ! ' The consul-general bowed very elegantly and kissed it ; and we followed his example in succession. The animal seemed at that moment to be in a harmless mode ; he grinned several times, but made very little noise. Having performed this ceremony, and standing a few moments in silent agony, we had leave to take our shoes and other property, and leave the den, without any other injury than the humility of being obliged, in this involuntary

[1] For their instructions, see For. Rel. ii, p. 281.

manner, to violate the second commandment of God and offend common decency. Can any man believe that this elevated brute has seven kings of Europe, two republics, and a continent tributary to him, when his whole naval force is not equal to two line-of-battle ships? It is so!" [1]

The Sophia sailed with Eaton and Cathcart March 2, and anchored in the Bay of Tunis on the 12th. Two days later the consuls obtained permission to land, and proceeded up to the city, where they were welcomed by Famin. Flags were hoisted on the various consulates, and the new arrivals were soon occupied in receiving visits. The English consul warned them against putting any faith in Famin, said the situation was a critical one, and advised caution and firmness. The bey, he said, "was a man of acute discernment and generally of fair dealing, but that he was vain and avaricious." [2]

The next day they were presented to the bey, who asked: "'Is your vessel a vessel of war?' 'Yes.' 'Why was I not duly informed of it, that you might have been saluted, as is customary?' 'We were unacquainted with the customs.' (True cause, we did not choose to demand a salute which would cost the United States eight hundred dollars.) . . . 'It is now more than a year since I expected the regalia of maritime and military stores, stipulated by treaty; what impedes the fulfillment of the stipulation?' 'The treaty was received by our government about eight months ago. A malady then raged in our capital, which forced not only the citizens, but all the departments of the

[1] Eaton, p. 59.
[2] Eaton, pp. 60–62. The events of Eaton's consulate at Tunis are covered by Felton, ch. iii–ix.

government to fly into the interior villages of the country. About the time the plague ceased to rage, and
permitted the return of the government, the winter
shut up our harbors with ice. We are also engaged in
a war with France.'" The consuls then explained that
the treaty had not yet been ratified and that they had
come instructed to secure certain amendments. The
bey said: "'You have found no difficulty in fulfill-
ing your engagements with Algiers and Tripoli; and
to the former have very liberally made presents of
frigates and other armed vessels.' We told him these
facts had been misrepresented to him. Our government had, indeed, agreed to furnish to the dey of Algiers certain armed vessels for which he was to pay
cash." They then stated that they had also been instructed to offer him an armed vessel in lieu of naval
stores on account of the risk of sending the latter,
they being contraband of war. "Said he: 'I shall
expect an armed vessel from you gratuitously.' We
answered him he might not expect anything of the
kind; it was utterly impossible. We had business
enough for our naval force, in defending our commerce
against the depredations of our common enemy."[1]
Tunis was also at war with France.

Repeated interviews were held during the next ten
days, at which the amendments were discussed and
demands for presents persistently urged. A compro-
mise was reached on the twelfth article, which was
so modified that the bey might compel the service of
an American merchant vessel when needed to carry
dispatches or goods, paying a suitable freight. The
consuls tried to limit this service to couriers in case of
emergency, but were overruled. The eleventh article

[1] Eaton, pp. 62 66.

was made reciprocal, and so practically expunged : either nation might demand salutes for its own war vessels, which were to be paid for by a barrel of powder for each gun fired ; but if not demanded, salutes were not to be given. The fourteenth article was finally amended so that the commercial intercourse between the two countries should be substantially on the footing of the nations most favored in the United States. The treaty [1] was concluded March 26, 1799, and was ratified by the Senate January 10, 1800.[2]

Cathcart sailed for Tripoli April 2, 1799, and arrived on the 5th. The pasha refused to receive him unless he would agree to fulfill a promise said to have been made by O'Brien when the treaty was signed, which was to give up the brig Sophia to the pasha as a present. Cathcart declared that no such promise had ever come to the knowledge of his government. O'Brien appears to have entered into an engagement which he did not report to the state department ; he admitted to Captain Geddes having made "a kind of a promise by the way of 'greasing the ways.'" Finding it necessary to discharge this obligation, Cathcart offered the brig, to be delivered in nine months, in lieu of the stipulated stores which were on the Hero, not yet arrived ; it was feared that she had either been lost or captured by the French. He had been authorized to promise a small armed vessel, if it seemed indispensable, to preserve peace. Negotiations were carried on through the British consul, Bryan McDonough, who had a good deal of influence with the pasha and was of great assistance. He had formerly been very helpful to O'Brien and also to the crew of

---

[1] Appendix II.
[2] Eaton, pp. 67–80; Rep. Sen. Com. viii, p. 11.

the Betsy while in captivity at Tripoli, and had acted as chargé d'affaires for the United States. Within about a week it was finally settled that Cathcart should pay as a substitute for the stipulated naval stores ten thousand dollars, and eight thousand in lieu of the brig, and a consular present valued at four thousand. Upon the delivery of the consular present, consisting chiefly of jewelry, the flag of the United States was given a salute of twenty-one guns, which was returned by the Sophia. This settlement was considered a very favorable one, and was effected by the distribution of fifteen hundred dollars in bribes. The pasha gave Cathcart an acknowledgment that he had no further claims whatever on the United States. His prize, the Betsy, had been converted into a man-of-war mounting twenty-eight guns, and was the flagship of Murad Reis, her captor. The affairs of the United States and Tripoli now being adjusted, the Sophia was sent back to Tunis, and Cathcart entered upon the duties of his office. Tranquillity prevailed, and the first few months of his consulate were uneventful.[1]

At Tunis Eaton's situation was similar to Barlow's at Algiers three years earlier: waiting month after month for the stipulated naval stores, or regalia, as they were called, making excuses, striving to keep the bey in good humor while firmly resisting his claims; the latter getting more and more impatient, threatening to send out his cruisers for Americans, and demanding additional presents. He would not accept money, — of that he had plenty, — but he must have jewels; and all the other officials of the government must have presents. The sapitapa, or keeper of the seals, who was the second minister and closest

---

[1] Cathcart, II, pp. 2, 3, 7, 8, 18–27, 36, 59, 61.

to the bey, was constantly importuning Eaton for
presents for the bey, requesting for himself a double-
barreled gun and gold watch-chain. The prime minister, a very old man, was given some pieces of cloth,
but was offended at not receiving a more valuable
present and returned it. " A demand came from the
Admiral for a gold-headed cane, a gold watch and
chain, and twelve pieces of cloth : the usance on a
new consul's being received. Laid on the table. A
demand came from the Aga of the Goletta for his
usance on the occasion of the first vessel of war coming to anchor in the bay. To this I answered that
I would make him a present of a copy of the treaty.
. . . The Sapitapa informed me that the Bey had
rejected the proposal of a small cruiser in lieu of
the present in jewels. I told him, notwithstanding
the Bey had refused to listen to a cash proposition,
I would once more make him a tender, and proposed
fifty thousand dollars in full of all demands." This
also was rejected. To the state department Eaton
writes, April 3 : " It is hard to negociate where the
terms are wholly *ex parte*. The Barbary Courts are
indulged in the habits of dictating their own terms of
negociation. . . . To the United States they believe
they can dictate terms. . . . It is certain that there is
no access to the permanent friendship of these states
without paving the way with gold or cannon-balls ;
and the proper question is, which method is preferable. So long as they hold their own terms, no estimate can be made of the expense of maintaining
a peace. They are under no restraints of honor nor
honesty. There is not a scoundrel among them, from
the prince to the muleteer, who will not beg and steal.
. . . The United States set out wrongly and have

proceeded so. Too many concessions have been made to Algiers. There is but one language which can be held to these people, and this is *terror*." [1]

Eighty American ships entered the Mediterranean in the spring of 1799, and upon this increasing and unprotected commerce Tunis and the other Barbary powers turned greedy eyes. They were waiting only for a pretext and opportunity to break peace with the United States. Therefore Eaton believed that measures should be promptly taken to insure the future safety of our commerce and the stability of our relations with Barbary, and urged that the regalia already stipulated should be sent out at once and with a show of force; that a gratuity also should be offered, if thought expedient, by way of conciliation, and that then terms for the future should be made under our guns. In July war seemed imminent, but the bey finally consented to wait until January. In October Dr. Shaw of the Sophia was sent to England to consult with Rufus King, the American minister, as to procuring jewels there; he was then to proceed to America and report to the government. This had a good effect in convincing the bey that Eaton's intentions were sincere, and in December he was persuaded to grant an extension of time for sixty days in which to receive the regalia.[2]

Long before this Eaton had become convinced that Famin had all along been intriguing against him. He says: " I have uniformly treated this French pirate with polite attention, taking care to keep the commanding grounds, till I have finally defeated all his projects of mischief ; and if nothing interfere with

---

[1] Eaton, pp. 83–88.
[2] Eaton, pp. 103–107, 117–119; Felton, p. 214.

my present arrangements, have now a flattering prospect of ultimately terminating our affairs with this Regency more favorably to the interests of the United States and more conformably to the instructions of the government. Three things have operated to produce this change of projects at court: 1, Dr. Shaw's departure to America; 2, the Bey's persuasion that the United States, after obtaining a peace with France, will send a fleet into this sea; 3, the Sapitapa's desire to employ American carriers," they being considered the safest, as the vessels of other nations were more exposed to the belligerent powers. The sapitapa had an extensive trade with Spain. Six months later Eaton became so exasperated at Famin's intrigues and insults that he gave him a public horsewhipping. For this he was summoned before the tribunal. The bey was angry, and sympathy was with Famin; but after Eaton had thoroughly exposed his iniquity, the court was convinced, the bey was completely won over, and gave Eaton's hand a " cordial squeeze." [1]

Meanwhile, on March 24, 1800, the Sophia arrived with a letter from the President to the bey, assuring him that the stipulations would be fulfilled. The bey was pleased with the letter, but expressed solicitude about the jewels. Eaton replied that they were to be procured in England. A number of richly jeweled arms were ordered to be made for the bey in London. As an evidence of more kindly relations, the sapitapa pledged himself that the last clause in the twelfth article of the treaty,[2] which, though amended, was still objectionable and kept vessels away, should be suspended, except in emergencies, such as had been recognized by all other nations as conferring on the bey

[1] Eaton, pp. 118, 119, 146–149.   [2] Appendix II.

the right of exacting service. A circular to this effect
was at once sent to American consuls in Mediterranean
ports. At last, on April 12, the Hero arrived with a
portion of the long expected stores. The danger was
now averted, and the bey's corsairs, which had been
waiting for orders to cruise against Americans, were
turned upon the Danes. Eight Danish vessels were
captured, and Eaton purchased six of them on credit,
at the request of their captains, at risk of loss; and
after their difficulties had been settled, although he
had an opportunity to sell the vessels at a large profit,
he gave them up to their former owners on condition
of his credit being redeemed. For this he received the
thanks of the king of Denmark.[1]

Late in November, 1800, the American ship Anna
Maria arrived with another invoice of naval stores.
The bey found fault with some of these, and Eaton
says in his report: " I believe the facts to be, the
government are dissatisfied that *anything has come
forward*. If this opinion require evidence, I consider
it sufficient to state that the United States are the
only nation which have, at this moment, a rich, unguarded commerce in the Mediterranean ; and that
the Barbary Regencies are *Pirates*." [2] The sapitapa
demanded the Anna Maria for the service of the government, but Eaton refused, reminding him of the
pledge he had previously given. Then the sapitapa
offered a freight of four thousand dollars for a voyage
to Marseilles with a cargo of oil, which was accepted,
as it involved no concession of principle. Later, however, he broke his contract and insisted on sending
the vessel to London. To avoid this and " in order to

1 Eaton, pp. 130–139, 177–181, 185, 209, 210; Felton, p. 224.
2 Eaton, pp. 187, 188.

get the ship and people out of their hands," Eaton
became responsible for the cargo, which he purchased
of the sapitapa at a high price. He then sent the
ship to Marseilles, where the oil was sold. On account
of loss due to the vessel's long detention, the owners
subsequently made a claim for indemnity against the
United States government.[1]

In the spring of 1801 Eaton had a plan for a commercial convention between the United States and
Tunis which should promote the business interests of
both and thereby make peace more firm and lasting,
and at the same time more honorable, as he hoped to
get the treaty still further amended in favor of the
United States. The bey at first seemed favorably disposed, but suddenly dropped the subject. This was
due to the action of France, which not only seized and
disarmed two of his corsairs, but exercised protection
over all the other powers against which he could cruise.
He therefore once more began to turn his eyes towards
America with hostile intent, and projects of peaceful
trade no longer interested him.[2] The unsatisfactory
articles of the treaty which kept American commerce
away from Tunis or were otherwise objectionable
were finally amended by a convention in 1824.[3]

April 15, 1801, the bey wrote a letter to the President demanding forty 24-pound battery guns.[4] In
June a fire in the palace destroyed fifty thousand
stands of arms, and Eaton was informed that the bey
had apportioned the loss among his friends, and that
the quota of the United States was ten thousand

[1] Felton, p. 237; Amer. State Papers, Claims, pp. 300, 322, 337–341.
[2] Felton, pp. 245–248.
[3] For. Rel. v, pp. 430–432, 587–589; see Appendix II.
[4] Felton, p. 242; Nav. Chron. p. 189; Claims, p. 300.

stands of arms. Eaton positively refused to communicate this demand to his government, declaring " that the treaty stipulations were the conditions of a perpetual peace." This firm stand exasperated the bey and his minister, who vainly tried to browbeat him.[1] These repeated and insolent demands were a source of constant irritation and he began to long for home. He was also annoyed in other ways. He was no longer on pleasant terms with O'Brien, who was closely associated in business ventures with Bacri, the Jew of Algiers, who in turn was believed to be intriguing against American interests.[2]

The presence of an American squadron in the Mediterranean, on account of trouble with Tripoli, seems to have had a wholesome effect on the bey; especially the arrival at Tunis in July, 1801, of Commodore Dale with the frigate President and schooner Enterprise, followed by the third installment of naval stores in the ship Grand Turk under convoy of the frigate Essex. The fourth cargo of stores came December 1 in the ship Peace and Plenty, convoyed by the frigate George Washington. But in spite of all this naval display, the bey had so far regained courage in the spring that, immediately after the receipt of the long looked for jewels, a part in March, the rest in May, 1802, by the frigate Constellation, he made requisition for a corvette. In August this had become a demand for a thirty-six gun frigate. Eaton refused to communicate this to his government, and the bey wrote personally to the President acknowledging the receipt of the stores and jewels and demanding the frigate. He proposed to send this letter to America in a vessel called the Gloria, which be-

[1] Eaton, pp. 204–206.   [2] Felton, pp. 238, 239, 243, 244.

longed to Eaton ; but Eaton, rather than have his ship so used, sent her to Leghorn and sold her at a loss.[1]

Meanwhile Eaton's situation was complicated by the war between the United States and Tripoli, now in progress, and the attempts of the bey to give assistance to the latter. This will be noticed in a later chapter. It culminated in a quarrel with the bey, who ordered Eaton out of the country, and he accordingly departed from Tunis March 10, 1803.[2]

[1] Eaton, pp. 212, 219, 229–235, 251, 252 ; Felton, p. 255 ; Cathcart, II, p. 349 ; St. Pap. iv, p. 383 ; v, p. 392 ; x, p. 468; Claims, pp. 303, 306, 331, 332.

[2] Eaton, p. 242.

CHAPTER VI

THE VOYAGE OF THE GEORGE WASHINGTON TO CONSTANTINOPLE

WILLIAM BAINBRIDGE was born in New Jersey in 1774. He entered the navy as a lieutenant in 1798, having been in the merchant service since the age of fifteen. He was made a captain in 1800 and given command of the frigate George Washington, of twenty-four guns, a vessel which had been purchased in 1798, when the navy was greatly expanded on account of the difficulties with France then existing. The Washington was sent with tribute to Algiers, where she arrived in September, 1800, being the first United States man-of-war to enter the Mediterranean. This was a duty very repugnant to Bainbridge, as it must have been to any naval officer appreciating keenly the inglorious attitude assumed by his country towards barbarians.[1]

At this time the dey of Algiers, Mustapha, had incurred the displeasure of the grand seignior by making peace with France while Turkey, as the ally of England, was at war with Bonaparte in Egypt. In order to conciliate the sultan the dey determined to send an ambassador with valuable presents to Constantinople. For this purpose he requested of Consul O'Brien the service of the George Washington. The

---

[1] This chapter is based chiefly on Bainbridge, ch. ii; see also Cooper, i, pp. 377–388; Amer. Nav. Off. i, pp. 21–34; Nav. Chron. pp. 176–179; Adventures and Sufferings of Samuel Patterson (Palmer, 1817), ch. iii.

consul replied that the ship's orders would not admit
of such a long voyage, and urged that Captain Bainbridge could not protect the dey's property against
his enemies, the Portuguese and Neapolitans, as his
instructions allowed him to engage French vessels
only. Bainbridge obtained an audience with the dey,
and explaining his inability to perform the service,
he declined the honor, for such it was represented to
be, as the men-of-war of England, France, and Spain
had repeatedly undertaken similar missions. The dey
seemed surprised and displeased at the refusal, but
acquiesced, saying that he would send an English ship
of twenty-four guns which the English consul and
admiral had offered for the purpose. A little later he
suddenly changed his mind and declined the English
ship, apparently having determined to force the
Americans to yield to his demands what they had
declined to do at his request. They vehemently protested against his unwarranted assumption of authority,
and used every argument their ingenuity could sug-
gest to escape from their trying position, but in vain.
The dey was obdurate and had them at a great disadvantage. The George Washington was anchored
under his batteries, and escape would have been difficult and hazardous, if not impossible. Moreover, he
threatened instant war in case of refusal, and O'Brien
was convinced that this threat would be made good,
and that the large, unprotected American commerce
then in the Mediterranean would be at the mercy of
the dey's corsairs.[1]

Bainbridge writes of the situation as follows : "The
Dey of Algiers, soon after my arrival, made a demand
that the United States ship, George Washington,

[1] St. Pap. iv, pp. 354–358 ; For. Rel. ii, p. 353 ; Cathcart, II, p. 326.

WILLIAM BAINBRIDGE

should carry an ambassador to Constantinople with presents to the amount of five or six hundred thousand dollars, and upwards of two hundred Turkish passengers. Every effort was made by me to evade this demand, but it availed nothing. The light in which the chief of this regency looks upon the people of the United States may be inferred from his style of expression. He remarked to me, ' You pay me tribute, by which you become my slaves. I have, therefore, a right to order you as I may think proper.' The unpleasant situation in which I am placed must convince you that I have no alternative left but compliance or a renewal of hostilities against our commerce. The loss of the frigate and the fear of slavery for myself and crew were the least circumstances to be apprehended; but I knew our valuable commerce in these seas would fall a sacrifice to the corsairs of this power, as we have no cruisers to protect it. Inclosed is the correspondence between Richard O'Brien, Esq., consul-general, and myself on the subject of the embassy ; by which you will see that I had no choice in acting, but was governed by the tyrant within whose power I had fallen. I hope I may never again be sent to Algiers with *tribute*, unless I am authorized to deliver it from the mouth of our cannon. I trust that my conduct will be approved of by the President, for, with every desire to act right, it has caused me many unpleasant moments." [1]

Under the circumstances they felt obliged to yield, and it must have seemed, at the time at least, the best thing to do. The liability to such a predicament was simply one of the necessary consequences of the wrong policy that had been adopted towards the Barb-

[1] Bainbridge, p. 44.

ary States. Eaton, when he heard of it from O'Brien, was very indignant, and his comments were harsh and perhaps unjust.[1] Bainbridge was a man of great spirit and determination, as his career throughout life from boyhood amply testifies. Whether, with Eaton in place of O'Brien to back him up, he could have more successfully resisted the dey's demands, is an interesting question.

Another humiliation was now imposed upon these unhappy men. The dey insisted that the George Washington should carry the Algerine flag at the main. They urged that this would virtually put the ship out of commission and she should fly her own colors at the main and the Algerine flag at the fore; but on this point also they were obliged to yield. As soon as he got to sea, however, Bainbridge gave his own flag the precedence.

According to O'Brien's letter to Eaton, the Washington carried on this voyage, besides her own crew of one hundred and thirty-one, the ambassador and suite, one hundred in number; also a hundred negro women and children, four horses, one hundred and fifty sheep, twenty-five horned cattle, four lions, four tigers, four antelopes, twelve parrots, and funds and regalia amounting to nearly a million dollars.[2] O'Brien wrote to the secretary of state, October 22: "As the United States ship Washington, Captain Bainbridge, has proceeded *per force*, in fact to save the peace of the United States with Algiers, to prevent captivity and detention to the ship, officers, and crew, and prevent the pretense of a sudden war and pillage and slavery to the citizens of the United States, I calculate that if said ship goes and comes safe in five months, it will

[1] Eaton, pp. 189, 190, 221.   [2] Ibid. p. 189.

cost the United States forty thousand dollars. This, in comparison to what our losses might be if *war*, left me no time to hesitate in the choice of the evils and difficulties which presented fully in view; in surveying both sides of the coast and how we should stand on both tacks, I found there was no alternative but to proceed." [1] This was surely a practical business view of the situation. O'Brien's point of view may, not unnaturally, have been influenced by a lively recollection of ten years of slavery.[2]

The George Washington set sail October 19, 1800, and during the passage of three weeks there was much discomfort from overcrowding. The religious observances of so large a number of Mohammedans considerably hindered the working of the ship. At their prayers, which were performed five times a day, it was necessary to face towards Mecca; and whenever the ship tacked they were obliged to change direction accordingly, so that one of their number was stationed at the compass to insure correctness of position. These ceremonies afforded much amusement to the ship's crew.

The ship approached the Dardanelles with a fair wind. At a point where the strait is about a thousand yards in width are two castles, nearly opposite each other, which command the channel. Here ships were obliged to show their passports before proceeding to Constantinople. The batteries were composed of heavy guns, which, however, were stationary, and could not be trained on a vessel that had passed them. Bainbridge had no passport and feared a long detention be-

[1] St. Pap. iv, p. 358; For. Rel. ii, p. 354.
[2] The course pursued by Bainbridge and O'Brien is discussed in Cooper, i, pp. 380–383.

fore obtaining permission to proceed, if indeed it were granted at all. He therefore determined to attempt the passage by stratagem. As he approached the castles he began to take in sail and make preparations to anchor, at the same time firing a salute, which was promptly returned by the batteries on both sides of the strait. Taking advantage of the great quantity of smoke produced, the captain rapidly made all sail, bore off, and was soon out of range. He arrived at Constantinople November 9, and anchored in the outer harbor.

He was soon visited by an officer, who inquired under what flag the ship sailed, and having been told, went ashore to report. He soon returned, saying that the government had never heard of such a nation as the United States and wished a more explicit reply. Bainbridge explained that he came from the New World discovered by Columbus, and this was accepted as satisfactory. The officer returned again in a few hours, bringing with him a lamb and a bunch of flowers, tokens of peace and welcome. The sultan was friendly and had the ship brought into the inner harbor. As she passed the palace, she fired a salute of twenty-one guns. The sultan noticed the stars on the American flag, and from the fact that his own flag also bore one of the heavenly bodies, he inferred a similarity in the laws, religion, and customs of the two countries.

About a week after his arrival, Bainbridge was visited by the dragoman of the reis effendi or grand vizier, next in rank to the sultan, who stated that his master was offended by the neglect with which he had been treated, and that he ordered Captain Bainbridge to report to him the next morning at ten o'clock. This the captain declined to do, not recognizing the authority over him of the reis effendi. Thinking it best, however, to get advice on the subject, he applied to Lord Elgin, the British ambassador, who informed him that it was merely an attempt to extort money, and he kindly sent a message to the reis effendi which prevented further annoyance.

A few days later, the capudan-pasha, or admiral, arrived from Egypt with fifteen ships of the line, and several frigates; and as they sailed in, the George Washington saluted the capudan-pasha. Just then the flagship was struck by a squall and was with difficulty saved from going ashore; so the salute was not returned. The next day Mr. Zacbe, secretary to the capudan-pasha, came aboard and apologized for the omission, and the salute was later returned. Zacbe, who spoke English fluently, had known Franklin in Paris, and was well acquainted with American history. He showed Bainbridge great attention, and they became firm friends. The capudan-pasha, who was the brother-in-law and intimate of the sultan, also treated Bainbridge with great kindness and consideration, and invited him to his palace. He also visited the George Washington several times, and was much pleased with her fine appearance and the discipline of the crew.

At one of their interviews the capudan-pasha expressed his surprise that the Washington had passed through the Dardanelles without being stopped, remarking that she was the first foreign armed vessel that had ever reached Constantinople without a passport from the grand seignior obtained at the castle, if not previously. He did not hold Bainbridge responsible for this, supposing him to have been ignorant of this necessary formality. The governor of the castle, however, had been sentenced to death for his negligence. Bainbridge hastened to explain the manner of his passage, declared the innocence of the governor, and begged that he might be pardoned, and that he himself should be held responsible. The capudan-pasha accepted the explanation and pardoned the governor, while his friendship for Bainbridge was only strengthened by the captain's straightforward avowal.

Bainbridge also conversed with the capudan-pasha on the subject of a treaty between the United States and Turkey, and made the following report to the secretary of the navy: "On the 23d of December, 1800, I was requested by the Capudan-pasha to wait upon him at his palace. I was received in a very friendly manner, and had some conversation respecting the formation of a treaty with the Ottoman Porte; and he expressed a very great desire that a minister should be sent from the United States to effect it. I informed him that there was one already named, who at present was in Lisbon, and probably would be here in six months. He said he would write to the ambassador, which letter would be a protection for him while in the Turkish empire, and gave me liberty to recommend any merchant vessel to his protection which might wish to come here previously to the arrival of the ambassador. I thanked him in the name of the United States for the protection he had been pleased to give the frigate under my command and for his friendly attentions to myself and officers. I conceive it to be a very fortunate moment to negotiate an advantageous treaty with this government." [1]

[1] Bainbridge, p. 52.

While at Constantinople Bainbridge also made the acquaintance of Edward D. Clarke, the noted English traveler, who has left the following account of the visit of the George Washington: "On the arrival of an American frigate for the first time at Constantinople considerable sensation was excited, not only among the Turks, but also throughout the whole diplomatic corps stationed at Pera. The ship, commanded by Captain Bainbridge, came from Algiers with a letter from the Dey to the Sultan and Capudan-Pasha. . . . The order of the ship and the healthy state of the crew became topics of general conversation in Pera; and the different ministers strove who should first receive him in their palaces. We accompanied him in his long-boat to the Black Sea, as he was desirous of hoisting there for the first time the American flag; and upon his return were amused by a very singular entertainment at his table during dinner. Upon the four corners were so many decanters containing fresh water from the four quarters of the globe. The natives of Europe, Asia, Africa, and America sat down together at the same table, were regaled with flesh, fruits, bread, and other viands, while of every article a sample from each quarter of the globe was presented at the same time. The means of accomplishing this was easily explained by his having touched at Algiers, in his passage from America, and being at anchor so near the shores both of Europe and Asia." [1] The very favorable impression which Bainbridge made on both Turks and Europeans at Constantinople was due to his personal qualities, and was of advantage to him and to his country.

The reception of the Algerine ambassador was far

[1] Clarke's Travels, iii, pp. 77–79.

from friendly. The dey's peace with France and hostility towards nations at peace with the porte had given great offense to the grand seignior, who sent a message back to the dey demanding that he declare war against France and send him a million piastres within sixty days. The ambassador, who remained at Constantinople with the presents,[1] was anxious that the Washington should return as soon as possible with this message to Algiers, and Captain Bainbridge therefore made preparations to sail. The capudan-pasha gave him a firman which insured him respect and protection in all Turkish ports. He also ordered that the frigate should be saluted on passing the fortress of Tapana, which was an honor accorded only to the capudan-pasha himself and had never before been given a foreign vessel.

The George Washington sailed December 30. As she passed through the Dardanelles, salutes were exchanged with the castle, and the pardoned governor invited Bainbridge to his house, expressing the deepest gratitude to him for having saved his life. The ship arrived off Algiers January 21, 1801, and anchored out of range of the batteries. The dey suggested that she should come in closer for the convenience of the officers, but the object of his solicitude was soon disclosed when he requested Bainbridge, through the consul, to return to Constantinople with his messenger. This the captain promptly declined, declaring that he would run the risk of war rather than again submit to the humiliation. Indeed, he had written to the secretary of the navy to this effect, while at Constantinople. O'Brien in his report of the Washington's return, to the secretary of state, January 27, in

[1] St. Pap. iv, p. 361.

speaking of the sultan's demands and the losses of the dey and his probable measures to reimburse himself, says : " I hope we shall not be the victims ; we are nearly two and a half years in arrear ; no funds ; we have a valuable unguarded commerce in these seas ; we are threatened by all Barbary ; therefore we should act with energy, make good our stipulations and annuities, have consular friends (not to be depending on mercenary Jews), and show force in these seas." [1]

Before leaving Algiers in October, Bainbridge had borrowed some old cannon for ballast, to replace the stores he had brought from America, and he now wished to return these. He requested Consul O'Brien to send him ballast in lighters, that he might make the exchange. But the dey would not allow the consul to do this, and at the same time threatened instant war if the cannon were not returned. Bainbridge refused to run his ship into the mole unless the dey pledged himself that nothing further should be said about returning to Constantinople. To this the dey finally agreed, and the ship was brought in.

Bainbridge now had an audience with the dey, who was in a bad humor and soon flew into a violent rage. With his guard of janizaries ready to obey any command of the irresponsible despot on the instant, it seemed a perilous moment for the captain, and might have proved so, had he not suddenly thought of the capudan-pasha's firman. This he at once drew from his pocket, and the effect was magical. The ferocious pirate was transformed into a cringing supplicant, anxious to serve the man whom a moment before he had seemed ready to destroy.

The next day war was declared against France, the

[1] St. Pap. iv, pp. 361, 362; For. Rel. ii, p. 354.

French consul's flag-staff was cut down, and four hundred Venetians, Maltese, and Sicilians, who had been captured under British passports, were liberated. The exasperated dey, determined to wreak vengeance on some one, ordered all the French in Algiers, fifty-six in number, men, women, and children, including the consul, to be put in irons and held for ransom at a thousand dollars each. Bainbridge resolved to use his influence, now much increased by reason of the capudan-pasha's firman, in behalf of the unhappy French, and with O'Brien had an interview with the dey. They begged him to revise his verdict, and after much persuasion were so far successful as to obtain for them forty-eight hours within which to leave the country.

The French were filled with gratitude, but knew not how they were to escape, as there was no available vessel in port. As the only hope the consul begged Bainbridge to take them on the George Washington, to which he willingly acceded, although it was not yet known that peace had been restored between the United States and France. The ship was hastily prepared for the voyage, the old cannon were put ashore, other ballast taken in, the French embarked, and the ship got under way with scarcely an hour to spare. The French were landed at Alicante, whence they found their own way home. For this service Bainbridge received the thanks of Bonaparte.

He then sailed for home, and on his arrival reported in person to President Jefferson. His conduct was approved, and he was commended for the " judicious and skillful manner in which he had discharged his duties while under the pressure of such embarrassing circumstances." In the reduction of the navy which soon followed, in obedience to the act of March 3,

1801, and as a result of peace with France, when the number of captains was reduced to nine, Bainbridge was retained, although he had been twenty-seventh on the list.

The secretary of state, James Madison, in a letter to O'Brien dated May 20, 1801, instructs him to discourage as far as possible the use of American vessels as carriers for the Algerines, citing the case of the Fortune [1] as an instance of the disadvantage and loss likely to result from the practice; although in that case the flag only, and not the ship, was American. The sentiment of the administration respecting the impressment of the George Washington by the dey of Algiers is shown in the following extract from the same communication: "One subject of equal importance and delicacy still remains. The sending to Constantinople the national ship of war, the George Washington, by force, under the Algerine flag and for such a purpose, has deeply affected the sensibility, not only of the President, but of the people of the United States. Whatever temporary effects it may have had favorable to our interests, the indignity is of so serious a nature, that it is not impossible that it may be deemed necessary, on a fit occasion, to revive the subject. Viewing it in this light, the President wishes that nothing may be said or done by you, that may unnecessarily preclude the competent authority from animadverting on that transaction in any way that a vindication of the national honor may be thought to prescribe." [2]

[1] See above, p. 55.   [2] St. Pap. iv, p. 336; For. Rel. ii, p. 348.

CHAPTER VII

WAR WITH TRIPOLI

In 1762 Ali Karamanli became pasha of Tripoli. He had three sons, Hasan, Hamet, and Yusuf, who were inspired by mutual hostility and jealousy most bitter. Hamet was weak and vacillating and more despised than feared. Yusuf, the youngest, was determined to succeed his father, and in 1790, being then twenty years old, he murdered his brother Hasan. In 1796, on the death of his father, he got control of the army and had himself proclaimed pasha. Hamet happened to be away at the time, and a year later took refuge in Tunis, under the protection of the bey.[1] His wife and children remained in Tripoli, held as hostages by Yusuf.

One of Yusuf's first acts was the conclusion of the treaty with the United States. This was procured at far less expenditure, to the United States, of time, trouble, and money, than the treaties with Algiers and Tunis. The pasha seems soon to have come to appreciate this fact and to realize that he had not made as good a bargain as his fellow pirates. Accordingly, after a few months of apparent contentment following the settlement with Consul Cathcart in the spring of 1799,[2] he became dissatisfied, and not less so as he viewed the growing and unprotected American commerce in the Mediterranean. Under the circumstances the temptation to break the peace was doubtless strong

[1] Greenhow, pp. 11, 12.   [2] See above, p. 67.

to a barbarian who held the doctrine that treaties were
to be observed only so long as convenience dictated.
In this idea he was encouraged by his minister of
marine and naval officers, especially by Murad Reis,
the renegade Peter Lisle, who apparently had a particular aversion for Americans. The prime minister,
Mohammed Dghies, alone advised against war.[1]

In August, 1799, difficulties arose between the pasha
and Cathcart, first about passports and later about
certain goods which the pasha purchased of the consul and never paid for. The next year began the inevitable demands. In April Cathcart was requested
" to acquaint the President of the United States that
he [the pasha] is exceedingly pleased with his proffers
of friendship ; . . . that had his protestations been
accompanied with a frigate or brig-of-war, such as we
had given the Algerines, he would be still more inclined to believe them genuine." Cathcart called attention to the fact that in addition to the original sum
of forty thousand dollars paid for the treaty more than
that amount had subsequently been given in presents
not stipulated ; whereas, according to the tenth article
of the treaty,[2] no further payment or tribute was ever
to be expected. But the pasha was discontented. He
had made better terms with European nations, and
moreover complained that Algiers and Tunis were
treated by the United States more liberally than Tripoli. He therefore wrote a personal letter to President Adams, dated May 25, 1800, in which he acknowledges the friendly sentiments of the President,
communicated to him by Cathcart, and concludes :
" But, our sincere friend, we could wish that these
your expressions were followed by deeds, and not by

[1] Greenhow, p. 13.   [2] Appendix II.

empty words. You will therefore endeavor to satisfy us by a good manner of proceeding. We on our part will correspond with you, with equal friendship, as well in words as deeds. But if only flattering words are meant without performance, every one will act as he finds convenient. We beg a speedy answer without neglect of time, as a delay on your part cannot but be prejudicial to your interests." In September the brig Catharine of New York, Captain Carpenter, was brought in by one of the pasha's cruisers, and although the act was disavowed, she was detained a month, plundered of many valuable articles, and subjected to other annoyances. October 29, 1800, Cathcart issued a formal protest enumerating and complaining of the pasha's aggressions and referring the dispute to the dey of Algiers, in accordance with the twelfth article of the treaty.[1]

In November, 1800, and January, 1801, Cathcart sent out circular letters to American consuls in Mediterranean ports giving warning of probable trouble in the spring. In February the pasha repudiated the treaty, and demanded, as an alternative to war, a new treaty, without reference to Algiers, for which was to be paid two hundred and fifty thousand dollars and an annual tribute of twenty thousand. He had recently concluded a treaty with Sweden on these terms. It was the policy of the Barbary States always to be at war with some one, so as to give employment to the corsairs; as soon as peace was made with one nation it was necessary to pick a quarrel with another. The pasha expressed his willingness, for a consideration of a hundred thousand dollars, to allow the United States

[1] St. Pap. iv, pp. 342–354, 360, 364–374; For. Rel. ii, pp. 350–352, 354–357.

eighteen months within which to accept his terms. He finally reduced this last proposition to twenty thousand dollars and certain presents, which Cathcart agreed to in a letter dated February 19. The pasha then changed his mind and made further demands. The next day Cathcart wrote a letter to O'Brien and Eaton detailing all these circumstances, and sent out another circular warning American merchantmen of the danger. He also wrote a long letter to the secretary of state giving a full history of the transaction. Eaton considered the situation at Tripoli so critical as to justify him in chartering a Ragusan brig in April to convey the intelligence to the United States with the least possible delay.[1]

May 10, 1801, the pasha declared war against the United States, cut down the American flag-staff on the 14th, and Cathcart left Tripoli for Leghorn on the 24th, leaving the interests of the United States in the care of Nicholas Nissen, the Danish consul. On his way to Leghorn Cathcart was held up and plundered by a Tunisian corsair, for which Eaton demanded satisfaction of the bey of Tunis, and it was promised. The pasha of Tripoli sent out his corsairs at once in search of American prizes, but apparently without success,[2] as the timely warning which had been sent out had put the merchantmen on their guard. The two largest Tripolitan cruisers, under the command of Murad Reis, a ship of twenty-six guns and two hundred and sixty men, called the Meshuda, and a brig of

---

[1] Cathcart, II, pp. 197, 228, 264, 266, 274, 279; Eaton, pp. 191-204; Felton, p. 241.

[2] According to Greenhow (p. 13) and Blyth (p. 88), the Tripolitans took five prizes, but it seems doubtful, as there is no official mention of it, and the captives are not accounted for.

sixteen guns and one hundred and sixty men, proceeded to Gibraltar with the intention of cruising in
the Atlantic.[1]

Meanwhile the administration, in anticipation of
trouble, had determined to send a squadron of observation to the Mediterranean. Accordingly, four vessels, under the command of Commodore Richard Dale,
set sail from Hampton Roads about June 1, 1801.
Dale was a Virginian and in his forty-fifth year at this
time. He was Paul Jones's first lieutenant in the
famous fight between the Bon Homme Richard and
the Serapis in 1779, and was one of the six captains
appointed in 1794 at the establishment of the new
navy. His instructions[2] from the secretary of the
navy were dated May 20, 1801. He was directed to
proceed first to Gibraltar, which, with the governor's
permission, he was to make his base of supplies. He
was then to appear off Algiers, Tunis, and Tripoli
delivering letters from the state department to the
consuls. If he found affairs in a tranquil condition he
was to cruise in the Mediterranean not later than December, and then return to the United States. " But
should you find on your arrival at Gibraltar, that all
the Barbary powers have declared war against the
United States, you will then distribute your force in
such a manner, as your judgment shall direct, so as
best to protect our commerce and chastise their insolence — by sinking, burning, or destroying their ships
and vessels wherever you shall find them. . . . Should

---

[1] St. Pap. iv, pp. 362, 383; Felton, p. 253; Cathcart, II, pp. 317,
321–326.

[2] These instructions were written by General Samuel Smith, acting
secretary during the interim between the resignation of Benjamin
Stoddert and the appointment of Robert Smith, brother of Samuel.

RICHARD DALE

Algiers alone have declared war against the United States, you will cruise off that port so as effectually to prevent anything from going in or coming out, and you will sink, burn, or otherwise destroy their ships and vessels wherever you find them. Should the Bey [pasha] of Tripoli have declared war (as he has threatened) against the United States, you will then proceed direct to that port, where you will lay your ship in such a position as effectually to prevent any of their vessels from going in or out. . . . If Tunis alone, or in concert with Tripoli, should have declared war against the United States, you will chastise them in like manner. . . . Any prisoners you may take, you will treat with humanity and attention, and land them on any part of the Barbary shore most convenient to you. . . . But you will be careful to select from them such Christians as may be on board, whom you will treat kindly and land, when convenient, on some Christian shore. Should you have occasion, you may accept their services." [1]

Besides instructions to the consuls the commodore bore a letter from President Jefferson to the pasha of Tripoli. A circular from the state department was also sent to the United States ministers in England, Spain, Portugal, and Holland, and another to the consuls at Mediterranean ports, explaining the objects of the expedition. Lastly, Dale was given the form of a letter to be written by him to the dey of Algiers and the bey of Tunis declaring the object of his presence in the Mediterranean to be the protection of American commerce against the threatened attacks of Tripoli

[1] St. Pap. iv, pp. 379–382 ; For. Rel. ii, p. 359. For the operations of Dale's squadron, see Nav. Chron. pp. 190–198 ; Cooper, i, ch. xviii ; Bainbridge, ch. iii ; Decatur, ch. iii ; Porter, ch. iv.

and expressing the friendly disposition of the United States towards themselves. Dale also had thirty thousand dollars which the administration hoped to induce the dey to accept as a commutation for one annuity of naval stores.[1]

Jefferson, in a letter to W. C. Nicholas, dated June 11, 1801, mentions the expedition, and in speaking of the policy of subsidizing the Barbary States says he is "convinced it is money thrown away and that there is no end to the demand of these powers, nor any security in their promises. The real alternative before us is whether to abandon the Mediterranean or to keep up a cruise in it, perhaps in rotation with other powers, who would join us as soon as there is peace"[2] in Europe.

Dale's squadron consisted of the frigates President, 44 guns,[3] flagship, Captain James Barron, Philadelphia, 36, Captain Samuel Barron, and Essex, 32, Captain William Bainbridge, and the schooner Enterprise, 12, Lieutenant Andrew Sterrett. Bainbridge had returned home in the George Washington just in time to take the Essex back to the Mediterranean; his first lieutenant was Stephen Decatur, afterwards famous. David Porter, who was also to win a name for himself, was first lieutenant of the Enterprise. The commodore arrived at Gibraltar July 1. Here he found the two Tripolitan corsairs and by forestalling their passage into the Atlantic doubtless prevented severe losses to American commerce. Murad Reis declared there was no war, but Dale gathered

[1] St. Pap. iv, pp. 334–342; For. Rel. ii, pp. 347–349.
[2] Ford's Jefferson, viii, p. 62.
[3] The rates of all vessels are taken from Emmons, and occasionally differ slightly from the figures of Cooper. The number of guns actually carried was nearly always in excess of the rate.

enough information elsewhere to convince him of the contrary. He therefore directed the Philadelphia to cruise in the Straits and watch the Tripolitans. The Essex was ordered first to convoy the ship Grand Turk to Tunis; thence she was sent to Marseilles, Barcelona, and Alicante to collect American merchantmen in those ports and give them convoy through the Straits. The commodore cruised along the Barbary coast with the President and Enterprise, first putting into Algiers, where his appearance, according to Consul O'Brien, had a much better effect than a cargo of stores would have had. The ships arrived at Tunis July 17, the Essex coming in the next day, and here also they made a favorable impression.[1] On the 24th they appeared off Tripoli. The pasha was a good deal disturbed and anxious to treat for peace. He communicated with the commodore through Nissen, the Danish consul. Dale remained off Tripoli eighteen days, and during this time nothing of importance occurred. He then cruised westward a short distance and thence to Malta for water, where he arrived August 16.[2]

Meanwhile the Enterprise on August 1, while running for Malta, fell in with a Tripolitan polacca of fourteen guns and eighty men. As the Enterprise carried twelve guns and ninety-four men, the vessels were about evenly matched. They at once engaged at close range and fought for three hours. By his superior skill in manœuvring, Sterrett was able to avoid the enemy's attempts to board, and by choosing his position, to rake him repeatedly. Twice the Tripolitan struck his colors, and when he thought he had

[1] See above, p. 73.
[2] St. Pap. iv, pp. 383, 384; For. Rel. ii, p. 360.

his adversary at a disadvantage, reopened his fire, hoisting his flag again. The third time, there being no longer hope of making up for his poor seamanship and gunnery by treachery or stratagem, he threw his flag into the sea, and by supplicating gestures begged for quarter. Porter was then sent aboard the corsair to take possession. All her guns and small arms, with everything else of value, were thrown overboard, and she was sent back to Tripoli an empty hulk. Sterrett's report to Commodore Dale, dated at sea August 6, 1801, is as follows: " I have the honor to inform you, that on the 1st August I fell in with a Tripolitan ship of war, called the Tripoli, mounting fourteen guns, commanded by Reis Mahomet Sous. An action immediately commenced within pistol-shot, which continued three hours, incessant firing. She then struck her colors. The carnage on board was dreadful, she having twenty men killed and thirty wounded ; among the latter was the captain and first lieutenant. Her mizzen-mast went over the side. Agreeable to your orders, I dismantled her of every-thing but an old sail and spar. With heartfelt plea-sure I add, that the officers and men throughout the vessel behaved in the most spirited and determined manner, obeying every command with promptitude and alertness. We had not a man wounded, and sus-tained no material damage in our hull or rigging." Sterrett received the thanks of Congress and a sword, and his officers and men a month's extra pay. The Tripoli crept slowly home, and on her arrival the pasha was filled with rage and chagrin. The unfortu-nate Mahomet Sous was mounted on a jackass, paraded through the streets, and bastinadoed. The effect of this severity was that men were greatly discouraged

THE ENTERPRISE AND THE TRIPOLI

from serving in the corsairs then fitting out. For some time after this, very few Tripolitan cruisers ventured from port.[1]

Dale's orders did not allow him to take prizes, although he was directed by the secretary of the navy to "sink, burn, or otherwise destroy." The reason for this will appear from the following extract from the President's Message of December 8, 1801, in which, after relating the capture of the Tripoli, he says: "Unauthorized by the Constitution, without the sanction of Congress, to go beyond the line of defense, the vessel being disabled from committing further hostilities, was liberated with its crew. The legislature will doubtless consider whether, by authorizing measures of offense also, they will place our force on an equal footing with that of its adversaries." Jefferson's strict construction of the Constitution probably carried him too far; for while the Constitution vests in Congress alone the right to declare war, it seems reasonable to suppose that, when attacked, the Executive, without appeal to Congress, at least when not in session, may exercise all the rights and powers of belligerents. However, a few months later, February 6, 1802, Congress passed "an act for the protection of the commerce and seamen of the United States against the Tripolitan cruisers," giving the President full discretion in the employment of the navy and also authorizing him to commission privateers.[2]

Commodore Dale left Malta August 21, and on the 30th overhauled a Greek ship with forty-one Tripolitan passengers, including an officer and twenty soldiers. He took them on board the President, and

[1] St. Pap. iv, p. 385; Nat. Intell. Nov. 18, 1801.
[2] St. Pap. iv, p. 327; Nav. Chron. pp. 198, 199; Cooper, i, p. 414.

appearing before Tripoli opened a correspondence
with the pasha, through Mr. Nissen, on the subject
of the exchange of prisoners. The pasha expressed
small concern for his subjects in Dale's power, but
finally agreed to give three Americans for all the soldiers. This was in case he should capture any Americans, which fortunately he had not yet been able to
do. He now wished to make a truce, but Dale declined to talk on this subject. He landed the Tripolitans and sailed for Gibraltar September 3. On his
arrival he learned from Consul Gavino that Murad
Reis had sent most of his men in boats to Tetuan,
whence they were to journey to Tripoli overland.
Leaving the two vessels in charge of the captain of
the brig and twenty men, Murad had taken passage
himself in an English ship bound to Malta; from
there he passed over to Tripoli. The moral effect of
Sterrett's victory probably had much to do with this
abandonment of their ships by the Tripolitans. Of
the men who had been landed, two hundred and fifty
found their way to Algiers, where the dey requested
passports for them to Tripoli. This request was declined by Consul O'Brien. Tripoli was suffering
severely from the blockade and food was scarce. The
pasha was very desirous of the release of his ships at
Gibraltar and their employment as carriers of grain.
Both he and the bey of Tunis objected strenuously to
the blockade as an innovation in warfare, and they
appealed to the dey to support them in opposition to
a system so inimical to the interests of all Barbary.
If it had been possible to maintain a close blockade,
it is probable that the pasha might have been brought
to terms within a reasonable time.[1]

[1] St. Pap. iv, pp. 385-387, 455.

In the mean time the Essex had been cruising along the north shore in obedience to orders. At Barcelona her fine appearance attracted attention, and so excited the envy of certain Spanish naval officers that they behaved in an insulting manner to Bainbridge and his officers, and Decatur nearly became involved in a duel. The Essex collected a large fleet of American merchantmen, which she escorted through the Straits, and then, after cruising eastward along the Barbary coast, again visited the European ports and assembled another convoy. The Philadelphia,[1] after the desertion of the Tripolitan vessels, also cruised along the Barbary coast and blockaded Tripoli for a short time in September.

October 22, the President being off Gibraltar, one of her boats upset in the bay and two officers and eight men were lost.[2] During her cruising from port to port in the Mediterranean, the flagship had a narrow escape, about the first of December, while leaving the harbor of Mahon on the island of Minorca. The pilot misjudged the depth of water and the ship struck a rock while running six knots, rolled heavily, and slid off. The commodore took command, worked the ship through the narrow channel, and ran for Toulon. Although it blew a gale four or five days, she arrived safely December 6. She was there hove out, and it was found that her stem and keel were seriously injured, and but for the peculiar and skillful manner in which her planks had been fastened, she must certainly have been lost. Her return home was thereby delayed.[3]

---

[1] Eaton, p. 220.
[2] Dale to Sec. of Navy (Oct. 26, 1801), Nat. Intell. Jan. 29, 1802.
[3] Cooper, i, p. 417; Nat. Intell. March 22, 1802.

The frigate Boston, 28, Captain Daniel McNeill, was sent to France in October, 1801, with the United States minister, Robert R. Livingston, and after performing that duty her orders were to join the Mediterranean squadron. She arrived at Gibraltar December 22, and sailed the next day in search of the commodore, but apparently did not find him; and it has been thought that McNeill purposely avoided him and the other Americans, wishing to act independently. Hostilities had been renewed between Sweden and Tripoli, and a Swedish squadron arrived at Gibraltar about this time, under orders to coöperate with Commodore Dale.[1] In October Dale sent the Enterprise home, remaining himself in the Mediterranean until March, when he sailed for America in the President, arriving at Norfolk April 14, 1802. Meanwhile he had directed the Essex to blockade the two Tripolitan cruisers at Gibraltar, and the Philadelphia had gone into winter quarters at Syracuse, under orders to show herself occasionally off Tunis and Tripoli.[2]

During the blockade of Tripoli Consul Eaton at Tunis took an active interest in the course of events. He kept in communication with Commodore Dale, published a circular declaring Tripoli to be in a state of blockade, and refused passports to Tunisian vessels bound for Tripoli. He wrote to Samuel Lyman, member of Congress, October 12, 1801: "To avoid the expense of prolonging the war, Tripoli should be bombarded. This is a very practicable measure. Commodore Dale thinks that four frigates and three bomb-ketches are an ample force to do it effectually.

[1] St. Pap. x, pp. 467, 468; Cooper, i, p. 424; Amer. Nav. Off. i, p. 82; ii, p. 117.

[2] St. Pap. iv, p. 386; Morris, pp. 22, 25.

He also supposes a descent on the coast at the same time would have good effect. I am of the same opinion, and am so confident of its practicability, that I will volunteer in the enterprise, in any character consistent with my former military rank and my present station, with two thousand active light troops." [1]

This proposal of a land attack was associated with the project, first suggested by Cathcart, of espousing the cause of the rightful pasha of Tripoli, Hamet Karamanli, now an exile in Tunis. It was believed that the Tripolitans were disheartened by their reverses and the hardships of the blockade, and would welcome their lawful ruler if backed by sufficient force to assure success. Eaton conferred with Hamet, who entered willingly into the scheme, but his weak, irresolute character made him difficult to manage. The bey of Tunis, it was believed, would also give his approval. Eaton's first letter on the subject to the secretary of state is dated September 5, 1801. In December, being in poor health, Eaton took advantage of the opportunity for a sea voyage offered by the passage of the George Washington to Leghorn. The Washington, under the command of Lieutenant John Shaw, had again brought tribute to Algiers soon after her return to the United States with Bainbridge, and then had convoyed the ship Peace and Plenty to Tunis, with naval stores for the bey. After that she remained several months in the Mediterranean, giving convoy when needed. Eaton spent the winter in Italy, leaving his affairs at Tunis in the hands of Dr. William Turner of the navy, at this time surgeon of the frigate Philadelphia. At Naples he had interviews with the prime minister of Sicily and the king of Sardinia, and

[1] Felton, pp. 255–258; Cathcart, II, pp. 327–332, 341.

obtained from the latter permission for United States vessels to procure stores in his ports. At Leghorn, late in February, 1802, he learned that Hamet had received overtures from Yusuf, the reigning pasha, who, in order to defeat the scheme for his own expulsion, offered his brother the province of Derne. At the same time the bey of Tunis withdrew his protection from the exile. Eaton believed that the pasha's plan was to get Hamet within his grasp, which would quickly crush him. He at once returned to Tunis in a vessel of fourteen guns called the Gloria, which he had purchased. She was commanded by Captain Joseph Bounds and manned chiefly by Americans. She arrived at Tunis March 12. Eaton found Hamet about to embark for Derne, and succeeded in persuading him to abandon this plan. He then insisted on going to Malta, although Eaton wished him to go to Leghorn, where he would be under the eye of Cathcart. It was finally arranged that the exiled pasha should go to Malta and there await the arrival of the squadron, which he was to accompany to Tripoli, when it was hoped that the people would revolt and deliver the city into his hands; he accordingly sailed on a Russian ship bound for Malta. Meanwhile the Gloria was sent in quest of the Boston, which was blockading Tripoli at that time. Captain McNeill was found and informed of the situation, and he was prepared to arrest Hamet in case he should change his mind and attempt to pass over to Derne. Hamet, however, proceeded directly to Malta, where he arrived April 11. Eaton was assisted in his plans by the sapitapa, whose interest in the case was enlisted by a promise of ten thousand dollars in the event of success. The Gloria was taken temporarily into the service and placed at

Eaton's disposal, and he sent her to Gibraltar with dispatches.[1]

About this time the bey of Tunis was interested in an attempt to bring about peace between the United States and Tripoli, and on May 24, 1802, Eaton had an interview with his prime minister, who proposed peace through the mediation and under the guarantee of the bey. The minister observed that the pasha of Tripoli must have a present, and that it must surely be the interest of the United States to obtain peace for the security of their commerce and to save the expense of armaments. Eaton replied that the United States would always prefer peace to war, but the peace must be honorable; that the subject of a present to the pasha would not be considered; that American commerce in the Mediterranean was never safer than at that time; and that it was no more expensive to manœuvre a squadron in that sea than elsewhere, it being necessary always to keep a number of vessels in commission for the training of officers and men. The subject was therefore dropped. The pasha was also then endeavoring to bring about peace with the United States through the mediation of Algiers.[2]

According to a report made by Eaton to the secretary of state, June 8, 1802, the blockade of Tripoli during the previous winter and spring was very lax. He says that since October the Philadelphia had appeared but once before Tripoli, and then for six hours only, although she was under orders to make

[1] St. Pap. iv, p. 459; v, pp. 394–400; For. Rel. ii, pp. 699, 700; Claims, pp. 301–304, 330; Cathcart, II, pp. 349–353; Eaton, pp. 208, 212–214, 225–227; Felton, pp. 258–262; Amer. Nav. Off. i, p. 139.

[2] Eaton, pp. 216–219; St. Pap. iv, pp. 456, 457, 460.

occasional excursions from her station at Syracuse along the Barbary coast; and that the Boston was the only vessel that had done any blockade duty during that time. Captain Barron of the Philadelphia in his report says that he " was unable to look into Tripoli, or approach the coast, as the northerly winds are very common and excessively heavy." Eaton's plans for reinstating Hamet as pasha of Tripoli met with little encouragement from naval officers, and he complained that they " have undergone very severe criticism by Captains S. Barron and Bainbridge ; and by them reprobated in a style of most illiberal censure, and under their influence rejected by Captain Murray," who had recently arrived on the station in the Constellation. Eaton had a sharp tongue and little tact, and seems to have been unable to establish pleasant relations with these officers. He believed Bainbridge to have been offended at his outspoken animadversions on the George Washington's Constantinople mission and to have prejudiced the others against him.[1]

[1] Eaton, pp. 220-222; Morris, p. 64.

CHAPTER VIII

THE SECOND YEAR OF THE WAR

IN 1802 it was determined to prosecute the war against Tripoli with more vigor, and free scope was given the President by the act of February 6. As the terms of enlistment of Commodore Dale's men had nearly expired, it became necessary to send out a new squadron to relieve the vessels still remaining in the Mediterranean. After this, men were enlisted for two years instead of one. The command of the squadron was offered to Commodore Thomas Truxtun, who had won renown with the frigate Constellation in the war with France. On account of the scarcity of captains no officer of this grade was appointed to command the flagship, which Truxtun considered a descent in rank for him and therefore declined.[1] His action was interpreted by the navy department as a resignation from the service, and the navy thus lost one of its most valuable officers. The command was then given to Captain Richard V. Morris, who hoisted his pennant on the frigate Chesapeake, 36. The vessels of the squadron, being in various stages of preparation, sailed successively, as they became ready for sea. The Enterprise, which had just arrived home, was soon ready, and returned to the Mediterranean February 17, still under the command of Lieutenant Sterrett, followed by the Constellation, 36, Captain Alexander Murray, with Charles Stewart as first lieutenant, on March 14.

[1] Nat. Intell. June 16, 18, 20, 23, 1806.

The Chesapeake, flagship, with Lieutenant Isaac Chauncey as acting captain, sailed April 27; the Adams, 28, Captain Hugh G. Campbell, with Isaac Hull as first lieutenant, June 10; the New York, 36, Captain James Barron, with Stephen Decatur as first lieutenant, September 1; and the John Adams, 28, Captain John Rodgers, September 19. On board the Adams was Midshipman Oliver H. Perry, the future hero of Lake Erie. Great things were expected of this squadron, and it was thought that the pasha would soon sue for peace on any terms.[1]

Before he sailed Commodore Morris received orders dated February 18, March 20, April 1 and 13.[2] The first was his special commission, signed by the President and issued in accordance with the act of February 6, by which he was " authorized and directed to subdue, seize, and make prize of all " Tripolitan vessels and goods, " and to bring or send the same into port, to be proceeded against and distributed according to law." The other orders were signed by the secretary of the navy, Robert Smith, and conveyed specific instructions, at the same time allowing him ample discretion. He was to respect the rights of neutral nations, send his prizes to the United States when practicable, with all necessary papers, and to effect an exchange of prisoners if possible. He was to use his " best exertions to keep the enemy's vessels in port, to blockade the places out of which they issue, and prevent as far as possible their coming out or going in," and to aid and relieve American vessels and give them convoy when consistent with his naval oper-

[1] This chapter is based chiefly on Morris; see also Cooper, i, ch. xix, and Nav. Chron. pp. 199–203.
[2] Morris, pp. 14–23.

ations, and for these purposes was to distribute his
force to the best advantage, in his judgment. He was
to confer with Commodore Dale, who was supposed to
be still on the station, and was authorized to detain
one of the vessels ordered to return, until the Adams
should arrive. Funds were deposited in London subject to his draft, and a supply ship was to be sent
after him consigned to Consul Gavino at Gibraltar.
He was authorized to purchase gunboats for the
protection of American commerce in the Straits of
Gibraltar; and in case of a considerable amount of
sickness, he was instructed to establish a hospital at
some healthy port.

Shortly before Morris sailed, word came from Commodore Dale of threatening trouble with Morocco,
and Dale himself soon arrived at Norfolk with later
information which he believed would modify Morris's
orders. The secretary of the navy, however, would
allow him to wait no longer, but on April 17 ordered
him to proceed immediately, stating that he would
receive further instructions by the Adams, which
would be the next vessel to sail. Morris was detained
at Hampton Roads by contrary winds until April 27,
and the instructions which he received by the Adams,
three months later, were dated April 20.

In the mean time the Enterprise was the first of the
new squadron to arrive on the station, and she soon
sailed for the coast of Tripoli. There were still remaining in the Mediterranean from the previous year
the Philadelphia, which had spent most of the winter
at Malta, the Essex, the Boston, and the George
Washington. The Philadelphia and the Washington
soon returned to the United States. On the 5th of
May, off Tripoli, the Enterprise overhauled a Tuni-

sian xebec. After she had been boarded and examined, certain articles of small value were found to be missing. This was reported by her crew to the bey, who in a rage sent for Consul Eaton, and accused Lieutenant Sterrett of piracy. Shortly afterwards the Enterprise came into Tunis. It was an unpleasant affair, and the honor of the service was at stake. However, after diligent investigation, Eaton and the officers of the schooner were able to trace the theft to a private marine and two sailors, and to convince the bey that their shipmates, both officers and men, were innocent of any wrong-doing. The culprits were sent aboard the Boston for trial.[1]

The Constellation arrived at Gibraltar about May 1, and either there or at Algiers received a number of jeweled muskets and pistols which had been brought from London by an English frigate. They were a portion of the presents procured for the bey, and were turned over to Eaton at Tunis, May 28.[2] Captain Murray, having sent the Enterprise to Gibraltar with a convoy, proceeded in the Constellation off Tripoli, where he found the Boston and four Swedish frigates blockading the port. A short time before this the Boston had an engagement with three Tripolitan gunboats, one of which was sunk, while the others took refuge under the batteries. June 26 the Boston sailed for Malta to procure provisions and was to return at once, but did not. The eccentric Captain McNeill seems to have cruised elsewhere for several weeks, touched at Gibraltar in September, where he fell in with the Adams and took aboard her invalids, and then sailed for home, arriving at Boston in Octo-

---

[1] Felton, p. 265; Blyth, p. 97; Nat. Intell. Sept. 22, 1802.

[2] St. Pap. x, p. 468; Eaton, p. 219; Nat. Intell. Sept. 22, 1802.

ber. While in the Mediterranean he reported to neither Dale nor Morris. The Swedish vessels also went off for provisions in July, leaving the Constellation alone.[1]

One day, as she was lying about ten miles off the port, several Tripolitan gunboats were seen stealing along the shore from the westward. They had left Tripoli in the night to bring in an American prize which was expected from Tunis, but did not appear. In his report to the secretary of the navy, dated July 30, 1802,[2] Murray says: "On the 22nd instant we discovered their whole fleet of gunboats about three miles to leeward of the town, consisting of eight sail, with the Admiral's Galley, mounting long 24 and 18 pr. brass guns, full of men. We crowded all the sail we could to cut them off from the forts, and had nearly succeeded, but they plyed their oars and sails with such energy that by the time we got within gunshot of them we were within reach of the shot from their batteries, which began to fire upon us. However, we resolved to attack them, and stood on till we were within a mile and a half of the beach. Most of the boats had by this time got nearly on shore. The Admiral then began to fire upon us, as did the other galleys, when we rounded too in 12 fathoms of water (our pilot being much alarmed in standing in so near the land) and gave them a very severe fire for about half an hour, which must have done them considerable damage. At the same time they had an army of at least 6000 men drawn up along the beach to protect them, which our shot put to the route. As

1 Nat. Intell. Oct. 20, 1802 ; Misc. Letters, iii, nos. 36, 42, Murray and Campbell to Secretary of Navy (July 30, Sept. 7, 1802).

2 Misc. Letters, iii, no. 36.

the wind was in such a direction that we could not lay longer in our wanted position, we were obliged to haul off, when they got up under the walls of the town."

In the same letter Murray, in speaking of the difficulties of blockading Tripoli, says: "We cannot keep those small galleys in port, and they being in every respect so like all the small craft that navigate these seas and lurk so near the land, that the best security for our commerce will be to offer convoy from port to port to such vessels as wish to avail of our protection, and if we are still to carry on this kind of warfare, be assured, Sir, that it will be necessary to increase our force with brigs or schooners which will be fully adequate to any force they can have to encounter with belonging to Tripoli, and they can pursue their small craft in any direction where frigates cannot venture, provided they have sweeps to row after them, for few of their Galleys carry more than 8 guns and 40 men. In the Winter season they seldom venture out, nor will it be safe for us to be on this station in that season." August 14 he wrote: "I have turned off a number of merchant vessels since I have been on the station, but the little craft from Tunis will now and then get in, in defiance of me, by rowing close under the land, and furnish them with many supplies, and I am not satisfied in my mind that this blockade can answer any good purpose." Captain Murray was inclined to favor the policy of buying peace with the Barbary powers. July 31 three Danish frigates appeared and remained off the town twelve days; Murray was unable to ascertain what their business was. Shortly after their departure the Constellation was obliged to repair to Malta for a temporary supply of water and provisions. She had been blockading Tripoli as closely as possible for over two months, but as the Swedes had not yet returned, the town was now left entirely unguarded. Later it was necessary to proceed to Leghorn for further supplies. The Swedes soon made peace, and Tripoli was unmolested for the rest of the year.[1]

Both Eaton and Cathcart complained to the secretary of state of the reckless manner in which unarmed merchantmen navigated the Mediterranean at risk of capture. Eaton writes February 3, 1802: "The Mediterranean is covered with this kind of adventurers. If individuals will neither have regard to their own safety nor the general interests of the United States, should not the government interdict this loose manner of hazarding both by legal prohibitions to commerce here without convoy? One single merchantman's crew chained at Tripoli, would be of incalculable prejudice to the affairs of the United States in that regency." Cathcart says, July 2, 1802, "that positive instructions ought to be given to all consuls in the Mediterranean, in order that they may know whether they have power to retain the vessels of their nation in port, as the consuls of other nations have." Their apprehensions were justified June 17 by the capture of the brig Franklin of Philadelphia, Captain Andrew Morris, off Cape Palos, by one of two Tripolitan corsairs which had put into Algiers for supplies a week before, having recently, with three others, slipped out of Tripoli; another American escaped. These corsairs were described by Consul O'Brien as "row galleys, with three lateen sails, each having

[1] Misc. Letters, iii, nos. 36, 38, 48, Murray to Secretary of Navy (July 30, Aug. 14, Nov. 7, 1802).

four guns; one a crew of forty men, the other of thirty-five." On the 26th the captor returned to Algiers with the prize and with her crew of nine in chains. O'Brien demanded the release of vessel and crew on the ground that Algiers had guaranteed the treaty between the United States and Tripoli, but did not succeed in bringing the dey to his view of the matter; still the dey finally ordered the corsair and her prize away from Algiers. They then proceeded to Biserta, near Tunis. Eaton exerted himself zealously for the relief of the captives, but was not even allowed to see them. The bey, however, would not permit them to be transported by land through his dominions. The Franklin was left at Tunis and afterwards sold to the commercial agent of the bey. Presumably she was the American prize which the gunboats chased by the Constellation were expecting. The corsair returned to Tripoli with the captives, arriving July 19, apparently unobserved by the Constellation; but Captain Murray was promptly informed of the affair by Consul Nissen. Five of the prisoners were liberated, being foreign subjects. The captain and three seamen were held. Their release was claimed under the agreement in regard to exchange of prisoners between Commodore Dale and the pasha, when the Tripolitan soldiers were given up the year before; but this was not allowed. They were finally liberated in October, 1802, through the influence of Algiers, at an expense of sixty-five hundred dollars.[1]

Some merchantmen, however, were able to take

[1] St. Pap. iv, pp. 454–465; For. Rel. ii, pp. 461–463; Felton, p. 273; Morris, pp. 59–61; Nat. Intell. Feb. 18, 1803; Misc. Letters, iii, no. 35, Nissen to Eaton (July 27, 1802).

care of themselves. A few months after the capture of the Franklin, the ship Jason of Boston, Captain William G. Weld, was attacked by pirates off Tunis. She not only beat them off, but recaptured two American vessels that had previously been taken by them.[1]

Commodore Morris arrived at Gibraltar May 25, 1802. Having sprung his mainmast on the voyage, he was kindly allowed by the British admiral to refit at the navy-yard. He found the Essex blockading the Meshuda, the larger of the two Tripolitan cruisers at Gibraltar; what had become of the other does not appear. The Essex was detained until the repairs on the Chesapeake were completed, and sailed for the United States June 17. The trouble with Morocco was beginning to look serious. The emperor wished to send wheat to Tripoli, and for that purpose requested passports of James Simpson, the United States consul at Tangier, and also demanded the release of the Meshuda. He had been urging these measures for several months, and was now beginning to threaten. His naval force was insignificant, but he was fitting out a few new vessels on which he placed great hopes. Simpson had resisted the demands, but was now inclined to yield, and appealed to Morris, who refused to give his consent, pointing out the absurdity of blockading Tripoli and then giving passports to ships carrying wheat to that port. Thereupon the emperor declared war, and Simpson withdrew to Gibraltar June 25.[2]

The Chesapeake was now alone at Gibraltar, and nothing had been heard from Murray, McNeill, or Sterrett. Under the circumstances the necessity of

[1] MS. Record of Weld family.
[2] St. Pap. iv, pp. 465–471; For. Rel. ii, pp. 464–466; Morris, pp. 26–32.

remaining on the spot, watching the movements of Morocco, blockading the Tripolitan cruiser, and looking out for the safety of Americans entering the Mediterranean, seemed apparent to the commodore. He suggested to the United States ministers at London, Paris, and Madrid that American merchantmen should rendezvous at Cadiz, whence he might give them convoy from time to time through the Straits. The Enterprise arrived from the eastward about the middle of July, and was employed in convoying merchantmen. The Adams, which had been long expected, arrived at last, July 22, with orders for Morris, dated April 20,[1] to lay the whole squadron before Tripoli, accompanied by Consul Cathcart, who was authorized to treat for peace with the pasha. It was thought that the naval display would make a decided impression and aid in procuring favorable terms. The secretary, however, adds: "Although I have directed you to lay your whole force before Tripoli, you will yet consider yourself authorized, should you deem it necessary, to leave one vessel to watch the motions of the Emperor of Morocco, and to prevent the escape of the Tripolitan vessel at Gibraltar." The emperor had already assumed a less hostile attitude, evidently impressed by the proximity of the Chesapeake, which had visited Tangier, and he had invited Simpson to return. The consul thereupon returned to his post at Tangier on the Enterprise, as soon as the Adams arrived. The emperor now demanded annual presents, under the pretense that they had been stipulated, which Simpson proved to be untrue. It was clear that the hostility of Morocco would break forth again as soon as the Straits were left unprotected. August 17, leaving the

[1] Morris, p. 33.

Adams, Captain Campbell, at Gibraltar, Morris sailed
for Leghorn with the Chesapeake and Enterprise and
a large convoy bound to intermediate ports. Orders
were left with Consul Gavino for the Boston, which
had been reported to be at Malta in July, to sail
directly to America. Just after the commodore's departure the emperor of Morocco claimed the Meshuda
as his property and demanded that she be released
and given passports by Simpson and other consuls at
Tangier. The consuls refused. The emperor sent
thirty Moors from Tetuan to take possession of the
ship. Captain Campbell wrote to Simpson : " With
respect to the Emperor's pretensions to the Tripolean
ship, I have only to observe that unless they are
accompanied with vouchers sufficient to prove her his
property, I am determined to prevent her leaving this
place, nor can anything less than your passport alter
my determination ; " and he urged " the necessity of
coming to a better understanding with the Emperor
respecting the ship." [1]

Morris, having cruised along the north shore of the
Mediterranean, visiting several ports, arrived at Leghorn October 12, and there found the Constellation.
He received a letter from Cathcart, who was opposed
to any payment whatever for a peace with Tripoli.
The Constellation was ordered to Toulon for needed
repairs, thence to Gibraltar to procure supplies for
the squadron. Captain Murray was authorized to
instruct Simpson " to grant passports to vessels bound
to Tripoli laden with wheat." This retreat of the commodore from his former position in regard to passports

[1] St. Pap. iv, pp. 471–480; For. Rel. ii, pp. 466–469; Morris, pp.
35–38; Misc. Letters, iii, no. 42, Campbell to Sec. of Navy (Sept. 7,
1802).

was due to his fear of war with Morocco and to Murray's statement that provisions in Tripoli were plenty and cheap, which made the entrance of wheat into that port of less importance. Nissen had reported that the grain crop of Tripoli was unusually abundant that year.[1] Murray was instructed to proceed from Gibraltar to Malta with the Constellation and any other American vessels he might meet, except the Adams, which was to remain in the Straits. In a letter to the secretary of the navy, dated October 15,[2] Morris called attention to the necessity of a formidable force in the Mediterranean, and also of small vessels like the Enterprise, which could operate in shoal water and along shore. He doubted if gunboats could be purchased on account of the unwillingness of nations at peace with the Barbary powers to give offense by selling vessels to be used against them.

The Enterprise was directed to convoy merchantmen to Gibraltar, and the Chesapeake proceeded to Malta, arriving there November 20. She was again in need of repairs, it being found that her bowsprit "was decayed more than five inches in, and the rot extended thirty-five feet." The commodore was allowed to refit from the British stores at Malta. He here had an interview with an emissary of Hamet Karamanli, but was not favorably disposed toward the scheme for restoring the ex-pasha. Hamet had gone to Derne in August. In December the Enterprise arrived with dispatches, dated August 28,[3] which had come by the John Adams, and which gave Morris full powers to act with Cathcart, or independently in making peace with Tripoli and negotiating with any other Barbary power, if necessary. The sum of twenty

[1] Misc. Letters, iii, no. 35.   [2] Morris, p. 40.   [3] Ibid. p. 45.

thousand dollars was to be sent him to facilitate these
measures, but was to be used only if clearly indispensable. Eaton was not to be considered an authorized
agent of the government in affairs relating to Tripoli,
and whatever engagements he may have made with
Hamet were not to stand in the way of peace negotiations with his brother. Morris was "instructed to
protect our commerce by all the means in your power
against the armed vessels of any Barbary State that
may either declare or wage war against us," and was
given discretion in the distribution of his force. One
hundred gun-carriages, which the emperor of Morocco
had ordered and was to pay for, and which the President had decided to send to him as a present, were
to be withheld for a time, on account of his having
declared war.[1]

The New York, on arriving in the Mediterranean,
proceeded first to Algiers, where she delivered to
Consul O'Brien thirty thousand dollars, which it was
hoped the dey would take in payment of his annual
dues instead of naval stores. Being badly in need of
repairs, the frigate then put into Port Mahon to refit.
She finally arrived at Malta late in December, short
of provisions. The John Adams, on her arrival, was
detained at Malaga by Captain Murray, sent her dispatches to the commodore by the Enterprise, and at
last proceeded herself, arriving at Malta January 5,
1803. She brought a letter from the secretary of the
navy, dated October 23,[2] directing the Chesapeake
and Constellation to return to the United States at
once. The commodore was to transfer his flag to the
New York or John Adams. Captain Murray, who

[1] St Pap in, p 465
[2] Morris, p. 57.

read this letter at Malaga, soon sailed for home, in obedience to the order. The Chesapeake, however, was not in a fit condition for an Atlantic voyage in winter, and was detained. She had been to Syracuse for provisions, but without success, and returned to Malta the day the order arrived.

Commodore Morris now had with him at Malta his flagship the Chesapeake, Lieutenant Chauncey, the New York, Captain James Barron, the John Adams, Captain Rodgers, and the Enterprise, Lieutenant Sterrett. The Adams, Captain Campbell, was at Gibraltar. The court summoned a year later to inquire into Morris's conduct found no fault with his proceedings up to this time, and their first charge relates to his remaining at Malta from January 5 to 30, instead of blockading Tripoli. Morris says: "The John Adams, which had brought provisions from Gibraltar, wanted caulking, and it was necessary to distribute the provisions she brought. These things were not completed till the 25th. The persons employed to gain intelligence from Tripoli gave notice that their cruisers were returned to port and that they were about to haul up their gunboats. It was therefore useless to make the parade of blockading *partially* by three frigates a port which was blockaded *effectually* by the elements."[1] At this time disquieting news came from Algiers and Morocco, the former in a letter from O'Brien which stated that the dey was unwilling to take cash in place of naval stores, and refused to receive Cathcart as consul, O'Brien having resigned. Eaton also urgently desired the commodore's presence at Tunis. Morris's new responsibilities as negotiator with the various Barbary powers seem to

[1] Morris, p. 59.

have weighed heavily upon him, and these letters caused him uneasiness.

Having learned that a polacca called the Paulina, under the Imperial flag, had left Malta bound to Tripoli, the commodore sent out the Enterprise to cruise for her, and she was brought in January 17. The prize carried some Tunisian property in her cargo, which made trouble later, and the Imperial consul also took an active interest in the affair. Morris wished to have the prize tried at once, but as there was no admiralty court at Malta, it was necessary to wait for an opportunity to take the case to Gibraltar or to the United States. The question subsequently arose whether the owner of the alleged Tripolitan portion of the cargo, a Jew named Valenzin, was really a subject of Tripoli. His property having been sold, he went to America to urge his claim against the government. The Committee on Claims of the House of Representatives gave hearings, but before the matter was settled Valenzin became discouraged and committed suicide.[1]

January 30 the commodore sent the Enterprise to Tunis with a letter to Eaton, and sailed himself with the three frigates, intending to display the squadron before Tripoli; and then, if Cathcart's overtures of peace were unsuccessful, his plan was to send in the ships' boats and attempt to burn the shipping in the harbor. From the time he left port heavy gales from the northwest and southwest rendered approach to either Tripoli or Tunis impossible. On the 9th of February the ships were reduced to reefed foresails and storm staysails, and Morris feared that the Chesapeake

[1] Morris, pp. 62, 69; Claims, pp. 288, 292–296; Nat. Intell. Jan. 1, 1806.

would lose her masts. On the 10th, there being no
moderation of the weather, he returned to Malta. It
continued to blow heavily until the 19th.

During this stay at Malta a duel was fought between Midshipman Joseph Bainbridge of the New
York, a brother of Captain Bainbridge, and the secretary of Sir Alexander Ball, governor of Malta. The
Englishman had gone out of his way to insult Bainbridge, who knocked him down, and the next day
received a challenge. Decatur heard of the affair,
and, knowing that the Englishman was an experienced
duelist, offered to act as second to Bainbridge, who
was wholly ignorant of such matters. Decatur chose
pistols and prescribed the distance of four yards,
feeling sure that if they fought at the usual distance
of ten paces, Bainbridge would be killed. The Englishman's second objected to this, whereupon Decatur
offered to take Bainbridge's place and fight at ten
paces, but declared that he would not allow his prin-
cipal, an inexperienced boy, to be put at such a disadvantage. This offer was declined, and the duel took
place on Decatur's terms. After the order " Aim,"
they fired together at the word " Fire," and neither
was hurt. The Englishman was not satisfied, so they
fired again, and he was killed. The governor demanded
that Decatur and Bainbridge should be surrendered to
the authorities for trial in the civil courts, but the
squadron soon sailed and the matter was dropped.[1]
A few months before this, Captain McKnight of the
marines, of the Constellation, a brother-in-law of Decatur, was killed in a duel by one of the lieutenants of
that ship.[2]

By this time, February 19, the squadron was getting

[1] Decatur, pp. 55–59.   [2] Misc. Letters, iii, no. 48.

short of provisions, none could be procured at Malta
or Syracuse, and the store-ships from the United States
refused to bring supplies farther than Gibraltar. It
would also be necessary soon to send the Chesapeake
home, according to orders. The commodore therefore
felt obliged to give up his projected designs against
Tripoli, and decided to return to Gibraltar by way of
Tunis and Algiers. He believed that if he had had
provisions he could have remained longer, and in the
spring could have destroyed most, if not all, of the
cruisers of Tripoli. He was much disappointed when
the Constellation's orders compelled her to return to
America, instead of bringing him provisions, as he had
expected.

The squadron sailed from Malta February 19, and
arrived in Tunis Bay on the 22d. Eaton came aboard
and reported that affairs were in a critical state. The
bey was making trouble about the Paulina, captured
by the Enterprise in January. He insisted on the
immediate restitution of the Tunisian property carried
in her, and would not await the result of admiralty
proceedings. On the 28th the commodore, with Captain Rodgers, Cathcart, who had accompanied the
squadron, and Eaton, had an audience with the bey,
and finally agreed to give up any property which the
papers of the prize showed to belong to Tunis. The
bey's commercial agent examined the papers, and an
agreement was reached, but a few days later the agent
made fresh demands. The commodore yielded, and
then, to prevent further imposition, he proceeded to
embark without paying a farewell visit to the bey.
Thereupon the commercial agent detained him and
demanded the payment of a loan which had been advanced to Eaton. This sum, amounting to twenty-two

thousand dollars, had been used by Eaton in further-ing his plans with regard to Hamet Karamanli, and he had reported it to the state department four months before, hoping to have the expenditure allowed by the government. He had told the commercial agent that he had hopes of a remittance by the first United States vessel that appeared, and the agent now told Morris that Eaton had promised that he (Morris) would pay the loan. This Eaton emphatic-ally denied. The commodore was very angry at his detention, for which he blamed Eaton, and in his re-port of March 30, 1803, to the secretary of the navy, accused him of duplicity, with evident injustice. He paid the money, and for his security Eaton made an assignment to the government of the United States of his whole property. The next day they all had another audience with the bey, at which various affairs were warmly discussed, and which ended in Eaton's being ordered by the bey to leave his dominions. The commodore returned to his ship and sent ashore the twenty-two thousand dollars in charge of Dr. George Davis of the navy, who was to represent the United States at Tunis until a new consul should be appointed. March 10 the squadron sailed with Eaton and Cath-cart as passengers.[1]

The squadron arrived off Algiers March 19. The Enterprise ran in and brought off Consul O'Brien, who reported the condition of affairs and returned on shore with a letter from the commodore to the dey. The dey still refused to receive thirty thousand dollars in lieu of naval stores, although it was represented to him that there might be long delay in procuring the

[1] Morris, pp. 70–86; Eaton, pp. 235, 238–242; Claims, pp. 303, 304, 331.

latter. At the same time he would not allow the money to be returned to the commodore. He also refused to receive Cathcart as consul. The squadron then sailed for Gibraltar, and arrived March 23. All the vessels took in supplies, and a new crew was recruited for the Enterprise, Lieutenant Hull taking command of her. The claim of the emperor of Morocco to the Meshuda, the Tripolitan vessel at Gibraltar, as his property, was now allowed, and she was furnished with consular passports and permitted to depart. April 6 the commodore shifted his pennant to the New York, taking with him Captain Chauncey; David Porter was first lieutenant of the ship. Captain Barron of the New York took command of the Chesapeake, and the next day sailed for the United States with Sterrett, Decatur, and Bainbridge as passengers. It was considered inadvisable for the two latter to remain longer in the Mediterranean at that time on account of the duel at Malta. On the 8th the Adams sailed with a convoy of merchantmen, under orders to proceed to Malta by way of Leghorn. On the 11th the New York, John Adams, and Enterprise set sail, bound for Malta.

Eaton sailed for the United States March 30 in the ship Perseverance, and arrived in Boston May 5. The affairs of the exiled pasha, Hamet, had not made much progress up to this time. His presence at Malta had caused a good deal of uneasiness in Tripoli, but he finally decided to accept his brother's offer of the government of Derne, although Eaton continued to oppose it. Captain Murray became more favorably disposed towards Hamet, and in August, 1802, offered to take him across to Derne, but he preferred going in an English vessel that he had chartered, and did so. Commodore Morris had interviews with Hamet's agents at Malta and at Tunis. He declined to advance money, but offered to furnish twenty barrels of powder. He was informed that Hamet could raise thirty thousand men. The secretary of state, James Madison, had written to both Eaton and Cathcart on the subject in the summer of 1802, expressing the opinion of the administration that advantage might be taken of Hamet's claim to create a diversion in Tripoli and so force the pasha's abdication; or if an opportunity offered to make an advantageous peace with Yusuf, then Hamet must be treated with kindness and consideration, and if possible favorable terms in his interest must be extorted from his brother. Further than this the administration was not willing to involve itself in Hamet's affairs.[1]

[1] St. Pap. v, pp. 162, 397–401; Eaton, pp. 222, 223, 242; Morris, pp. 43, 47, 51, 69, 80, 81.

CHAPTER IX

OPERATIONS BEFORE TRIPOLI IN THE SUMMER OF 1803

ON the passage from Gibraltar to Malta an accident happened on board the New York which nearly ended in disaster. Through the carelessness of the gunner a quantity of powder was exploded near the magazine. Nineteen officers and men were injured, of whom fourteen died, including the gunner. Bulkheads were blown down and the ship was on fire and full of smoke below. The captain ordered the drummer to beat the crew to quarters, the men went quietly to their stations, and perfect discipline prevailed; but they were then thrown into confusion by an order of the commodore to hoist out the boats. It was a critical moment, and no one knew how soon the flames would reach the magazine. Captain Chauncey then bravely led the way below, and, assisted by Lieutenant Porter and other volunteers, succeeded in putting out the fire with wet blankets and buckets of water.[1]

The squadron arrived at Malta May 1, 1803, and the New York was there detained, repairing the damage done by the explosion and taking in fresh stores. The Enterprise also was hove out and newly coppered. These matters consumed nearly three weeks. The John Adams, however, was ready for service, and on the 3d was sent to cruise off Tripoli. Soon after reaching her

[1] For the events of this chapter, see Nav. Chron. pp. 203–212; Morris, pp. 92–98; Cooper, i, ch. xix; Porter, ch. iv.

station she captured the Tripolitan ship Meshuda, flying the colors of Morocco. This vessel, as soon as released from her long blockade at Gibraltar, had gone to Tunis, taken on military and naval stores, and was attempting to run into Tripoli when intercepted by the John Adams. Captain Rodgers returned to Malta with his prize on the 18th. Meanwhile the commodore had received a letter from Dr. Davis, chargé d'affaires at Tunis, dated March 24, stating that there was " a strong armament fitting out at Tunis, and that a junction was intended between the fleet of that power and the Algerines,"[1] apparently with the purpose of preying upon American commerce as soon as some pretext could be found for declaring war. This information caused him a good deal of anxiety, but Tripoli demanded his first attention, and on May 20 the New York, John Adams, and Enterprise sailed for their station off that port.

On approaching the town eleven small lateen-rigged coasting vessels, convoyed by several gunboats, were seen close in shore, making for the port. The New York immediately gave chase, and succeeded in cutting off the coasters, which put into the port of Old Tripoli, a short distance from the main town. The gunboats, by using their sweeps, escaped into the harbor and under the batteries of Tripoli. Preparations were at once made for the defense of the coasting vessels. A large stone building close to the shore was occupied by soldiers, and as soon as darkness came on the cargoes of the vessels, composed of sacks of wheat, were used in the construction of breastworks on each side of the building. They were manned by heavy reinforcements from the town, and at high tide the vessels

[1] Nav. Chron. p. 204.

were hauled up on the beach, close under these defenses.

Lieutenant Porter volunteered to take in a boat party that night, and attempt the destruction of the enemy's vessels, but the commodore was unwilling to risk what might be a serious loss of life, preferring an attack by day, when the ships' batteries could coöperate. He, however, permitted a reconnaissance, which Porter did in a single boat with muffled oars. He gained little information and did not discover the defensive operations of the enemy. He was seen and fired upon, but came off without injury. The next day an attack was made by the boats of the squadron under Porter's command. The enemy had a large force, including cavalry, and poured in a hot fire upon the boats as they approached, and being concealed behind the defenses, suffered little on their part. Boats in those days were not provided with howitzers, which would doubtless have been very effective against the improvised breastworks. The Americans landed on the beach so close to these works that they were pelted with stones by the Tripolitans, but they nevertheless set fire to all the coasting vessels. They then reëmbarked and withdrew in two divisions, to the right and left, so as to give the ships an opportunity to open fire. A heavy fire was thereupon thrown in, but the Tripolitans, with reckless courage, rushed out from behind their defenses, put out the fire, and saved their shipping. The Americans lost a dozen or fifteen in killed and wounded. Porter was shot through the left thigh and slightly wounded in the right. The conduct of officers and men was highly praiseworthy, Lieutenant James Lawrence and Midshipman John Downes being especially commended. The loss of the enemy was unknown, but was thought to be severe. Porter, although wounded, proposed another attack with the boats, but the commodore would not consent. It was believed that had the night attack been allowed and a force landed before the breastworks were built and the vessels hauled up, they could have been destroyed.

The Adams joined the squadron May 26. On the 28th an attack was made on the gunboats off Tripoli. These boats were lateen rigged. Some of the larger ones carried in the bow a brass gun eleven and a half feet long, throwing a twenty-nine pound shot, and two howitzers aft. They were moored behind the rocks at the entrance to the harbor and outside the mole. The John Adams was sent in first and opened fire. The New York and Adams were unable, on account of the lightness of the wind, to place themselves so as to fire without endangering the John Adams, and the gunboats withdrew with little injury. Commodore Morris was charged with mismanagement in the disposition of his force, and says in his justification : " It was my wish and intention to destroy the enemy and their boats, and if the disposition of the ships was not at one time exactly as I could have wished it to have been, still I cannot impute it to myself as an offense, but to causes that I could not control. The same might, and no doubt has happened to abler and better seamen than myself ; the escape of the enemy, under their batteries, was entirely owing to the calmness of the weather and the fast approach of night." [1]

The next day Commodore Morris opened negotiations through Mr. Nissen, the Danish consul. A few days later, on receiving assurances of his safety, he landed and had one or two interviews with the pasha's

[1] Nav. Chron. p. 211.

minister, Mohammed Dghies. Morris offered five
thousand dollars as a consular present and an additional sum of ten thousand at the end of five years.
The pasha demanded two hundred thousand dollars
and the expenses of the war. Negotiations were thereupon broken off, and the commodore returned to his
ship June 8. On the 10th he sailed for Malta with
the New York and Enterprise, leaving the John
Adams and Adams to blockade Tripoli. The Enterprise soon returned and joined the blockaders.

On the evening of June 21 some commotion was
noticed in the harbor which seemed to indicate that
preparations were being made to send off a cruiser or
to assist in running a vessel in. Accordingly Captain
Rodgers, the senior officer present, in order more effectually to control the approaches to the port, sent the
Adams to the westward and the Enterprise to
the eastward, while he himself in the John Adams
lay directly off the town. At six o'clock in the
morning Lieutenant Hull of the Enterprise discovered a large vessel running for Tripoli. The Enterprise at once ran in and intercepted the enemy, and,
although less than half her size, drove her into a small
bay for shelter. At half-past seven Captain Rodgers
saw the Enterprise flying a signal which he could
not distinguish, and making sail ran down to her,
when Hull communicated the state of affairs. The
two vessels then stood in close. In his report to the
secretary of the navy [1] Rodgers says: " At half-
past 8 A. M. shortened sail and prepared to anchor
with springs on our cables, discovering that the enemy
was anchored with springs on his cables in a deep,
narrow bay about five or six leagues to the eastward

[1] Nav. Chron. p. 208.

of the town and in a situation very advantageous to
the defense of their ship. At the same time observed
nine gunboats, close in with the shore, coming to her
assistance, and a vast number of cavalry and armed
men on the beach. At seven minutes before 9 A. M.,
being in seven fathoms water and supposing we were
within point-blank shot, commenced firing, which the
enemy returned and a constant fire was maintained
on both sides for forty-five minutes, when the enemy's
fire was silenced; at which instant the crew abandoned the ship in the most confused and precipitate
manner, such as her boats could not carry leaping
overboard. At this moment, being in a quarter less
than five fathoms water and the rocks appearing
under our bottom and in every direction around us,
I thought it would be prudent to wear and lay the
ship's head off shore, and in the mean time ordered
Lieutenant Hull to stand as close in as consisted with
safety and amuse the enemy on the beach until our
boats could be hoisted out to take possession. At a
quarter before 10 A. M., discovering one of the enemy's
boats returning to the ship whilst in the act of hoisting out ours, tacked and renewed our fire, and in a
few minutes after had the satisfaction to see the
enemy's colors hauled down, at the same time firing
both their broadsides, which was accompanied by the
ship's blowing up with a tremendous explosion which
burst the hull to pieces and forced the main and mizen
masts one hundred and fifty or one hundred and sixty
feet perpendicularly into the air, with all the yards,
shrouds, stays, &c. belonging to them. This ship was
polacre rigged, mounting 22 guns, and the largest
cruiser belonging to Tripoli, to appearance a very
fine vessel; and from the number of persons we saw

abandon her, her crew must have consisted of upwards of two hundred men. All the men who returned to the ship were blown up in her, and I have reason to believe her captain was among the number, as well as many lives lost before they abandoned her, as we saw several shot-holes through her. Immediately after the ship blew up I ordered the signal made to chase the gunboats, but was not able to approach them within gun-shot, owing to the water being very shoal a great distance seaward of them."

With the Meshuda and the cruiser just destroyed out of the way, Morris believed that Tripoli was no longer to be feared on the sea, and that the blockade was now unnecessary. Moreover, the squadron had no efficient means of attacking the enemy's gunboats, which, on their part, might be very dangerous to the frigates in case of these vessels becoming becalmed. On the other hand, in view of the activity of Algiers and Tunis, he considered the presence of the squadron in the western Mediterranean to be important. He feared also that the emperor of Morocco, out of resentment at the capture of the Meshuda, might declare war again, in the absence of any naval force in his vicinity. The term of enlistment of the Adams's crew had expired, which made it necessary, in his opinion, to send that ship home at once, and his fear of the united fleets of Algiers and Tunis was such that he dared not trust her to make the voyage alone. In view of all these considerations he raised the blockade of Tripoli June 26, and collected his whole force at Malta.

The squadron, with the Meshuda, left Malta July 11, proceeding to Messina and Naples. Here the commodore conferred with Sir John Acton, chief minister of the king of the Two Sicilies, and obtained certain concessions to American commerce, and permission to refit United States ships in some port of the kingdom, in case Malta should prove unsuitable for that purpose. He also made arrangements for the reception and maintenance of such prisoners as the Americans might capture. A request for the loan of ten gunboats and two bomb-ketches, to be used in attacking Tripoli, was declined on account of the uncertain relations of Sicily towards England and France, but it was promised that they should be loaned the next year if the king's neutrality could be preserved.[1]

Leaving Naples August 3, the squadron arrived at Leghorn on the 13th. Here the commodore learned that the corsairs of Algiers and Tunis were in port, and so no longer to be feared. The Enterprise was sent to Malta for dispatches said to have been forwarded there; the John Adams was sent with convoy to Gibraltar, and the Adams to Tunis with Consul Cathcart, and thence to Gibraltar. Cathcart had instructions from the secretary of state, dated April 9, 1803, to offer the bey of Tunis, but only if it seemed necessary for the preservation of peace, tribute not exceeding ten thousand dollars a year, to be paid biennially in cash and not in naval stores. The bey's demand for a frigate was to be refused. The sum of twenty thousand dollars was allowed for a peace with Tripoli, to be followed by the same periodical payments as in the case of Tunis. This was to be a private arrangement and not incorporated in the treaty. The secretary of state believed that tribute would be necessary to secure peace with the pasha of Tripoli,

[1] Morris, p. 96.

because "all the other nations at war with him have yielded to the customary terms of peace," and for the United States to hold out alone would entail "a very great expense." It was foreseen that such an arrangement with Tripoli would lead to demands from Tunis, and it was therefore thought that it might be best to make the offer first to Tunis, and that this would facilitate negotiations with Tripoli. This yielding of principle instead of sending increased armaments was only laying the foundation for future trouble; but fortunately it came to nothing, for the bey of Tunis rejected the terms. He also refused to receive Cathcart as consul. He continued his demand for the frigate, which called forth from the President, January 27, 1804, a letter which, although still resisting this demand, is expressed in language too deferential, and in which Cathcart's behavior, complained of by the bey, is disclaimed in an apologetic way.[1]

Commodore Morris left Leghorn in the New York, August 31, 1803, and reached Malaga September 9. On the 12th he received by the Nautilus a letter from the secretary of the navy, dated June 21, which announced his suspension and ordered him to return at once to the United States in the Adams, leaving the other vessels under the command of Captain Rodgers. The message was short and curt. Morris says: "The style of this letter and the manner in which it was transmitted are calculated to wound, as much as the occasion would permit, the officer to whom it is addressed."[2] The John Adams and the Adams arrived in the Straits soon after this. Rodgers

---

[1] St. Pap. v, p. 432; For. Rel. ii, p. 701; Eaton, pp. 256–260; Cathcart, I, pp. 287–293.

[2] Morris, p. 98.

hoisted his pennant on the New York, Campbell took the John Adams, and Morris sailed home in the Adams September 25, arriving November 21, 1803. Commodore Rodgers's command was of short duration. The squadron of Commodore Preble was already arriving, and Rodgers's orders were to return to the United States as soon as he was relieved.

After his return Morris was called to account for his proceedings in the Mediterranean, and his explanations not being satisfactory, a court of inquiry was called by an order of the secretary of the navy, dated March 10, 1804. The warrant set forth that "a close and vigorous blockade of the port of Tripoli hath not been made, and all practicable means have not been used to annoy the enemy, concerning the cause of which disobedience and neglect we think it necessary that inquiry should be made." The court was composed of Captain Samuel Barron, president, Captain Hugh G. Campbell, and Lieutenant John Cassin, members, all of whom were the juniors in rank of Commodore Morris. Walter Jones, Jr., Esq., was judge-advocate. The court reported April 13, 1804, "That the said Captain Morris did not conduct himself in his command of the Mediterranean squadron with the diligence or activity necessary to execute the important duties of his station; but that he is censurable for his inactive and dilatory conduct of the squadron under his command." [1] President Jefferson, having received this report, wrote to Secretary Smith, April 27: "I now return you the sentence of the court of inquiry in Morris's case. What is the next step? I am not military jurist enough to say. But if it be a court-martial to try and pass the proper

[1] Morris, pp. 9–13; Nav. Chron. pp. 205–207.

sentence on him, pray let it be done without delay, while our captains are here. This opportunity of having a court should not be lost." [1] The opportunity was lost, however, for what reason it is now difficult to say. May 16 the secretary of the navy wrote to Morris as follows: "With my letter to you of the 2nd instant I transmitted to you a copy of the opinion of the Court of Inquiry appointed to enquire into your conduct as commanding officer of the late squadron of armed vessels of the United States in the Mediterranean. This opinion having satisfied the President that it is not the public interest that you should be longer continued in command in the navy of the United States, I have it in charge from him to inform you that he has revoked your commission." [2] This abrupt dismissal from the service was arbitrary and out of proportion to his offense, which at the worst was inefficiency; and moreover he was fairly entitled to a court-martial.

Morris had a good reputation as an officer, and appears to have conscientiously performed his duty to the best of his ability, but he was not equal to the responsibility of flag rank. Doubtless he would have made a creditable record as captain of a frigate under Truxtun, if that officer had not declined the command of the squadron. It was unfortunate that he did decline, for the history of the squadron might have been a different one and the war have been brought earlier to an end with Truxtun at the head. Morris was not wholly to blame for the meagreness of the results. He had many difficulties to contend with. Most of his vessels were sent out in a state of imperfect prepara-

[1] Ford's Jefferson, viii. p. 301.
[2] Officers of Ships of War, vi, p. 432.

tion, and much time was wasted in repairs that should have been made and carefully supervised by responsible officers in the home navy-yards. He says in regard to the Chesapeake's mainmast: " It certainly was a shameful neglect in the carpenter employed at Norfolk not to have discovered the defect in that mast. There are also a number of smaller spars defective." [1] The arrangements for supplying the squadron also, making it necessary to return from Malta to Gibraltar for provisions, wasted much time; the captains of the store-ships refused to go beyond Gibraltar, because their contracts did not oblige them to. Furthermore, the squadron was seriously weakened by the recall of the Constellation and Chesapeake. After making due allowance, however, the fact remains that very little was accomplished. A commander of first-rate ability rises above difficulties and overcomes them.

Heretofore the Americans had been at a disadvantage for lack of small vessels, which were necessary to make the blockade more effective and to pursue and engage in shallow waters the gunboats of the enemy, which were very efficient vessels of their class. The Enterprise was the only vessel in the navy at that time below the frigate class. This want was appreciated by Captain Murray and by Commodore Morris also, but he does not seem to have made any effort to procure gunboats until after the blockade of Tripoli had been raised, when he made application to the king of the Two Sicilies. With the purpose of supplying the lack of light cruisers, Congress, on February 28, 1803, appropriated ninety-six thousand dollars for the construction of four vessels of this description. They were the brigs Siren and Argus, each carrying sixteen

[1] Morris, p. 26.

twenty-four pound carronades and two long twelve-pounders, and the schooners Nautilus and Vixen, with twelve eighteen-pound carronades and two long guns.[1] Carronades were short, light guns, able to bear only a small charge of powder.

A further defect of the frigates was that they were not equipped for bombarding the works of the enemy, as only the forty-fours carried long guns heavier than eighteen-pounders, and their carronades, though of large calibre, were entirely unfitted for assaulting fortifications.

[1] Cooper, ii, pp. 1, 2.

CHAPTER X

THE LOSS OF THE PHILADELPHIA

EDWARD PREBLE was born in Falmouth, now Portland, Maine, in 1761. When about sixteen he ran away to sea on a privateer. In 1779 his father, General Jedediah Preble, got him an appointment as midshipman in the Massachusetts State Marine. He saw a good deal of active service in the Revolution in Massachusetts cruisers, and was captured and confined for a time in the prison-ship Jersey. After the war he spent fifteen years in the merchant service. In 1798 he was appointed a lieutenant in the navy, and a year later was made a captain and served in the naval war with France. When it was decided, in the spring of 1803, to recall Morris, a new squadron was fitted out, the command of which was given to Preble. May 14 he was ordered to Boston to refit the frigate Constitution, which was to be his flagship. She required recoppering and other extensive repairs which consumed much time, and she was not ready for sea until August. Tobias Lear, who had been President Washington's private secretary and later his military secretary with the rank of colonel, had recently been appointed consul-general to the Barbary States, and took passage for Algiers in the Constitution, accompanied by his wife.[1]

Commodore Preble's instructions from the secretary of the navy, Robert Smith, are dated July 13, 1803,

[1] Preble, pp. 37–41.

EDWARD PREBLE

and differ in no essential particular from those of Commodore Morris, except that he was to establish a depot of stores at Malta or some other point near Tripoli, to avoid the delay and inconvenience of returning to Gibraltar for provisions. He received other letters from the secretary of later date authorizing him to hire one or more small vessels to be used against Tripoli and also to transfer to his squadron certain midshipmen from the vessels ordered home.[1] The vessels of the squadron sailed as they became ready for sea in the following order: Nautilus, 12, Lieutenant Richard Somers, June 30; Philadelphia, 36, Captain William Bainbridge, July 18; Vixen, 12, Lieutenant John Smith, August 3; Constitution, 44, flagship, Lieutenant Thomas Robinson, Jr., acting captain, August 14; Siren, 16, Lieutenant Charles Stewart, August 27; Argus, 16, Lieutenant Stephen Decatur, September 8. The Enterprise, 12, Lieutenant Isaac Hull, already in the Mediterranean, was to remain there as one of the new squadron, but on the arrival of the Argus, which was a larger vessel than the Enterprise, Hull, being senior in rank to Decatur, was to exchange commands with him.[2]

Preble at this time was personally known to very few of the officers ordered to serve under him. He had not happened to be thrown with them in the French war, had made a long voyage in 1800 to the East Indies in the Essex, and since then had been out of active service on account of sickness contracted on this voyage, from which he never fully recovered. His severe discipline and hot temper, not softened by ill

[1] Letter Book (1799 to 1807), p. 72; Preble Papers: Sec. of Navy to Preble (July 28 and Aug. 2, 1803).
[2] Nav. Chron. p. 213.

health, made him at first unpopular among his subordinates. Local prejudice, too, may have contributed somewhat to the feeling against Preble. Of his council of officers, the commanders of his vessels, Hull, from Connecticut, was the only New Englander besides himself; all the others, together with a majority of the junior officers, came from the Middle or Southern States. It was only after his great qualities were recognized that they learned to respect and admire him. They discovered under his rough exterior true kindness of heart and exact justice. He likewise did not appreciate his officers. Most of them were very young, even those in command all being under thirty, and he spoke complainingly of them as boys; but a year later he had acquired a real affection for them. This squadron was their training school for the struggle with the British navy a few years later; Preble was a great teacher, and they were worthy pupils. Hull, Bainbridge, and Stewart successively commanded the Constitution in her victories in the War of 1812, and Decatur also captured an English frigate. Chauncey was in chief command on the lakes, and among the officers of lower rank, Porter, Jones, Lawrence, Burrows, Warrington, Charles Morris, Macdonough, and Biddle all became famous in the war with England.

The Philadelphia arrived at Gibraltar August 24, just four weeks after the Nautilus, which was the first vessel out. Captain Bainbridge being informed that there were two Tripolitan cruisers off Cape de Gat, at once proceeded in search of them, and on the night of the 26th, when near the cape, fell in with a ship and a brig under foresails only. Bainbridge hailed the ship, and learning that she was a war vessel from Barbary, he ordered the commander to send his papers aboard the Philadelphia. In his report [1] to the secretary of the navy he says: "I now discovered that she was a cruiser belonging to the Emperor of Morocco and called the Mirboka, commanded by Ibrahim Lubarez, mounting twenty-two guns and carrying one hundred and twenty men." In another letter he makes the number ninety-eight. The brig turned out to be the Celia of Boston, which had been captured by the corsair August 17. The commander of the Mirboka at first attempted to conceal this fact, and would not allow his vessel to be searched; but upon an armed boat being sent he yielded, and the boarding officer found confined below Captain Bowen of the Celia, with seven of his crew. "After making this discovery I instantly ordered all the Moorish officers and crew on board the Philadelphia, for I had no hesitation in capturing the ship, after such proceedings on their part in violation of the faith of a passport which had been obtained from the United States consul at Tangier." While this was being done the Celia was lost sight of, and was not recovered until the following night. Bainbridge believed that Lubarez had acted under orders in capturing the Celia, but this he denied, declaring that he had taken the brig because, when he left port, war seemed inevitable. Bainbridge then observed that as he had made the capture while cruising with an American passport, he should be treated as a pirate, and hanged at the yardarm. This threat had the desired effect, and Lubarez promptly produced an order from the governor of Tangier to capture Americans. The Moorish prisoners were treated with kindness, and it made a marked impression upon them when the ship's corporal of the Philadelphia was punished in

1 Bainbridge, p. 73.

their presence for having struck one of them, although under great provocation. Bainbridge took the Mirboka to Gibraltar, there to await the arrival of Commodore Preble. The Celia was restored to her captain and crew, who thereupon resumed their interrupted voyage. Captain Bainbridge afterwards received the thanks of the President and secretary of the navy for the capture of the Mirboka. The Philadelphia next went in search of another cruiser of Morocco reported to be near Cape St. Vincent, but did not find her, and returned September 11 to Gibraltar.[1]

On the 7th of September, some distance off Cadiz, Commodore Preble in the Constitution fell in with a vessel, undoubtedly the one of which Bainbridge was in search. He cleared ship for action and then spoke the vessel and boarded her; Consul Lear was with the boarding party. She proved to be the Moorish frigate Maimona of thirty guns and one hundred and fifty men; she had passports signed by Consul Simpson at Tangier. As Lear reported her papers to be all right, and as the commodore had no reason to suspect the hostile intentions of Morocco, he let her go. On entering the Straits at night the Constitution suddenly found herself close by a British frigate. Preble showed great spirit in the parley that took place with the Englishman, who at first refused to answer his hail. This incident caused a change in the feeling towards Preble among his officers and marked the beginning of his popularity.[2]

[1] For this exploit of the Philadelphia and for the loss of the ship and captivity of her crew, see St. Pap. v, p. 5; For. Rel. ii, p. 591; Nav. Chron. pp. 214–217, 250–256; Bainbridge, ch. iii, iv, v; Porter, ch. v; Cowdery; Ray, ch. vii–xi; Cooper, ii, ch. i, ii; Amer. Nav. Off. i, pp. 38–51; Nat. Intell. March 26, May 16, 1804.

[2] Preble, p. 42; C. Morris, p. 21; Amer. Hist. Rec. i, p. 54; Preble Papers: Lear to Preble (Sept. 7, 1803), MS. Journal (Sept. 7, 1803).

The flagship arrived at Gibraltar September 12, and Lieutenant John H. Dent joined, becoming acting captain in place of Lieutenant Robinson, who was junior to Dent. The Vixen arrived on the 14th, and the New York and John Adams from Malaga the same day. Lieutenant Porter was transferred from the New York to the Philadelphia as first lieutenant, taking the place of Lieutenant John Cox, who wished to return home. Midshipman Macdonough of the Philadelphia had been left with the Mirboka as prize-master. All these vessels, with the Enterprise and Nautilus, were in the Straits about this time. The Adams came in from Tunis September 22, and sailed for the United States with Commodore Morris on the 25th.[1]

Upon his arrival at Gibraltar Commodore Preble at once perceived that affairs must be settled with Morocco before proceeding further. It was desirable to make as imposing a naval display as possible before the Moors; and Commodore Rodgers, although senior in rank to Preble, and feeling hurt at his junior's pennant flying in his presence, unselfishly agreed to postpone his departure for the United States and accompany him to Tangier with the New York and John Adams. In order that Tripoli should not be neglected the Philadelphia and Vixen were sent at once to establish the blockade of that port. The Nautilus and Enterprise were employed in convoying American merchantmen and in watching the Moors all along the coast, as far as Mogadore, with orders to capture their cruisers wherever found. The Siren and Argus had not yet arrived from the United States.

Preble set out in the Constitution for Tangier Sep-

[1] Amer. Hist. Rec. i, p. 54; Nav. Inst. v, p. 56; Amer. Nav. Off. i, p. 40; Cathcart, I, pp. 294, 295.

tember 20, having on board his ship the Moorish officers of the Meshuda and Mirboka; but owing to contrary winds he was several days in getting there. Meanwhile, on the 22d, he fell in with the Adams, just from Tunis. He was at Gibraltar again October 1, and the Siren arrived that day from America. Preble returned to Tangier on the 4th, where Rodgers with the New York and John Adams joined him on the 6th; the Nautilus was also in company. Consul Simpson came aboard the Constitution and consulted with the commodore. On the same day the emperor of Morocco, Muley Soliman, arrived at Tangier at the head of his army. The ships were cleared for action, and the emperor, impressed by the show of force, declared the most friendly sentiments. He was thereupon saluted with twenty-one guns. On the 8th the emperor paraded his army on the beach and was given another salute which was returned. During the following week negotiations progressed smoothly with the assistance of Commodore Rodgers, Colonel Lear, and Consul Simpson.

The emperor had chosen an inopportune moment for his naval demonstration, little expecting the simultaneous arrival in the Straits of two American squadrons. He was undoubtedly directly responsible for all the trouble, which resulted from his exasperation at the capture of the Meshuda. But he now disavowed the act of the governor of Tangier in sending out cruisers and removed him from office. As a token of good will he sent off to the squadron a present of bullocks, sheep, and fowls, and promised to give up the brig Hannah of Salem, which with her crew had been seized at Mogadore. October 10 Commodore Preble and Consul Simpson had an audience with the emperor, and on the 12th the treaty of 1786 was ratified and confirmed. This was accomplished without expense or presents at the time or engagements for the future. The Nautilus was sent the next day to Mogadore to release the Hannah and recall the Enterprise. Preble on his part released the Mirboka; and the Meshuda, with the consent of Commodore Rodgers, was also given up. These vessels were appraised and Congress afterwards granted prize-money to the captors. The Maimona had gone to Lisbon, where she remained until the trouble had blown over. The Siren was sent to Gibraltar with dispatches for the government and letters to different consuls announcing peace with Morocco. The John Adams returned to Gibraltar October 13, the New York the next day, and the Constitution on the 15th. On the 19th Commodore Rodgers, with the New York and John Adams, set sail for the United States.[1]

Meanwhile, on the 19th of September, the Philadelphia and Vixen had sailed from Gibraltar with orders, dated three days earlier, to go first to Malaga, holding up and sending in any vessels of Morocco that might be met on the way, and then to give convoy up the Mediterranean to any merchantmen bound east. Having touched at Malta, they were to sail at once for the coast of Tripoli and blockade that place. They left Malta October 5 and appeared before Tripoli on the 7th. About two weeks later Bainbridge was informed by the captain of an Imperial brig, coming out of Tripoli, that two Tripolitan vessels of war were out upon a cruise. Thereupon, thinking they were prob-

[1] For Preble's negotiations with Morocco, see St. Pap. v, p. 8 ; For. Rel. ii, p. 592; Nav. Aff. i, pp. 115–117 ; Nav. Chron. p. 215; Nav. Inst. v, pp. 55-62 ; Preble, pp. 41–46; Preble Papers : Preble to Simpson (Sept. 13, 1803), Simpson to Preble (Sept. 14, 1803), Emperor to Simpson (Sept. 11, 1803).

ably to the westward, he sent the Vixen to cruise off
Cape Bon, "as the most likely place of falling in with
them should they be returning from that quarter, and
at the same time a safer situation for the schooner
than off Tripoli,"[1] as the season for heavy storms
was approaching. The Philadelphia thenceforth maintained the blockade alone. For several days nothing
of importance occurred.[2]

Towards the end of October the frigate was driven
some distance to the eastward by a heavy blow from
the west; but the wind having shifted to the east, she
was running back before it to her station on the last
day of the month, when the events occurred which are
narrated by Captain Bainbridge in his report to the
secretary of the navy, dated November 1, 1803, as
follows: " Misfortune necessitates me to make a communication the most distressing of my life; and it is
with deep regret that I inform you of the loss of the
United States frigate Philadelphia, under my command, by being wrecked on rocks between four and
five miles to the eastward of the town of Tripoli. The
circumstances relating to this unfortunate event are:
At 9 A. M., being about five leagues to the eastward of Tripoli, saw a ship inshore of us standing
before the wind to the westward. We immediately
gave chase; she hoisted Tripolitan colors and continued her course very near the shore. About 11
o'clock had approached the shore to seven fathoms
water, commenced firing at her, which we continued
by running before the wind until half-past 11, being

---

[1] Bainbridge's testimony before Court of Inquiry, Nat. Intell. Sept.
25, 1805.

[2] Preble Papers : Preble to Bainbridge (Sept. 16, 1803) ; Bainbridge
to Preble (Oct. 22, and Nov. 1, 1803).

then in seven fathoms water; and finding our fire
ineffectual to prevent her getting into Tripoli, gave
up the pursuit and was bearing off the land when we
ran on the rocks in twelve feet water forward and
seventeen feet abaft. Immediately lowered down a
boat from the stern, sounded and found the greatest
depth of water astern. Laid all sails aback, loosed
topgallant sails and set a heavy press of sail canvas on
the ship, blowing fresh, to back her off. Cast three
anchors away from the bows, started the water in the
hold, hove overboard the guns excepting some abaft
to defend the ship against the gunboats which were
then firing on us; found all this ineffectual. Then
made the last resort of lightening her forward by cutting away the foremast, which carried the main-top-
gallant mast with it. But labor and enterprise were
in vain, for our fate was direfully fixed. . . . Striking
on the rocks was an accident not possible for me to
guard against by any intimation of charts, as no such
shoals were laid down in any on board, and every
careful precaution, by three leads kept heaving, was
made use of on approaching the shore to effect the
capture of a Tripolitan cruiser. And after the ship
struck the rocks all possible measures were taken to
get her off and the firm determination made not to give
her up as long as a possible hope remained, although
annoyed by gunboats which took their position in such
a manner that we could not bring our guns to bear
on them, not even after cutting away part of the
stern to effect it. When my officers and self had not
a hope left of its being possible to get her off the
rocks and having withstood the fire of the gunboats
for four hours, and a reinforcement coming out from
Tripoli, without the smallest chance of injuring them

by resistance, to save the lives of brave men left no alternative but the distressing one of hauling our colors down and submitting to the enemy whom chance had befriended. In such a dilemma the flag of the United States was struck. . . . The gunboats in attacking fired principally at our masts ; had they directed their shot at the hull, no doubt but they would have killed many. The ship was taken possession of a little after sunset and in the course of the evening myself and all the officers, with part of the crew, were brought on shore." [1]

To Preble Bainbridge wrote : " Had we been able in our situation to have injured our enemy in the least, never would I have surrendered, while such means were in my power." [2] Before striking his flag Captain Bainbridge destroyed his signal books, and gave orders to throw overboard all the small arms and everything else of value. The gunner and carpenter were sent below to flood the magazine and scuttle the ship. As it afterwards turned out, the latter operation was imperfectly done. According to William Ray, a marine on the Philadelphia, several of the crew begged the captain not to surrender the ship, believing that she could be got off the reef.

Before the court of inquiry [3] into the loss of the Philadelphia, composed of Captains James Barron, Hugh G. Campbell, and Stephen Decatur, with William Eaton as judge-advocate, and held on board the Constitution at Syracuse June 29, 1805, Lieutenant Porter testified : " The ship had about eight knots

[1] Nav. Chron. p. 250 ; Nav. Aff. i, p. 123.

[2] Preble Papers (Nov. 25, 1803).

[3] Nav. Chron. pp. 254–256. There is a full report in Nat. Intell. Sept. 25, 1805.

way upon her. This witness was ordered into the mizen top to look into the harbor of Tripoli and observe if any cruisers were in port. At this instant the water shoaled and the helm was put down. He had got about halfway up the mizen rigging when he felt the ship strike. He immediately returned on deck. . . . The ship lifted at times abaft and the helm was then clear. The enemy's gunboats were already seen coming out of port, nine in number, as nearly as the witness recollects." Porter speaks of the various expedients tried on the recommendation of a council of officers and mentioned by the captain in his report. " In the mean time the enemy passed under the fire of the frigate's stern guns and took a position on the starboard and weather quarter, where no guns could be brought to bear on them by reason of their advantageous position and the deep heel to port and fixed position of the ship. . . . It had now already been determined that the flag must be struck, as no hopes remained of saving the ship and no possible means of defending her." Porter estimated the position of the wreck at three and a half miles from the town and a mile and a half north of the nearest point of land. No attempt had been made to carry out one of the ship's anchors for the purpose of warping her off the reef. In regard to this Porter stated that in his opinion the ship had no boat able to bear an anchor, and Lieutenant Hunt testified " that in the river Delaware he made an experiment in carrying out an anchor in the Philadelphia's launch, when she was obliged to be buoyed by casks." All the other witnesses supported the testimony of Lieutenant Porter. The verdict of the court was : " The Court having deliberated on the evidence deduced from the testimony of the witnesses heard in this case, are decidedly of opinion that Captain William Bainbridge acted with fortitude and conduct, in the loss of his ship the United States frigate Philadelphia, on the 31st October, 1803; and that no degree of censure should attach itself to him from that event." In this opinion the government and the people concurred.

The Philadelphia had struck and run up on a shelving rock forming part of an extensive reef called Kaliusa, not shown on the ship's charts. The reef was divided into two parts with deep water between them, and the ship was wrecked on the eastern reef. If she had continued a short distance farther before bearing off she would have run clear, between the two reefs, and if she had followed the chase up to the mouth of the harbor, she would have cleared the western reef. The absence of the Vixen at this time was particularly unfortunate. If she had been on hand the Philadelphia would not have run so close in shore. Or if she had appeared after the wreck she could have defended the frigate, prevented her surrender, and saved her, or could have destroyed her to prevent her capture, after taking off the crew.

After the surrender the Tripolitans swarmed over the ship, plundering everything they could lay their hands on, stripping officers and men, and leaving most of them nearly naked. They were then tumbled into boats and taken ashore, the Philadelphia's men manning the oars. They were landed about ten o'clock in the evening; the officers were landed, while the men were thrown out of the boats when within a few rods of the shore, as the surf made it difficult to beach the boats. They were conducted between rows of armed men to the castle gate, through which they passed into a narrow passage leading by many turns to a great hall paved with marble and sumptuously furnished. Here they were received by the pasha, surrounded by his ministers and guards, richly dressed. He was in a gracious mood and asked many questions in regard to the capture. The officers were then led to another apartment where supper was served for them, and about midnight were conducted by the pasha's prime minister, Sidi Mohammed Dghies, through the town to the late American consul's house, which for the present was to be their abode. Dghies treated the officers with consideration and kindness, and was always friendly in his feeling towards Americans. He introduced Captain Bainbridge to the Danish consul, Nicholas C. Nissen, who exerted himself in every way for their relief. The men were led from the audience hall to another room in the castle, where they were given dry rags in exchange for their wet clothes, which were not returned to them. They were then taken to an open balcony, where they spent the night supperless, and suffered severely from the cold. The next day they were set to work cleaning out an old warehouse. This was to serve as their prison and was too small to afford them all room to lie down; several months later they were transferred to a larger and cleaner prison. Towards evening of the day after the capture they were given their first food, a small loaf of bread to each man.

Captain Bainbridge was greatly depressed in spirits over the calamity which the fortune of war had brought upon himself and his officers and men, as well as upon his country, and for which he felt responsible. His officers sympathized deeply with him, and in a letter, signed by all of them, November 1, 1803, expressed their feelings in the following words: "We, late officers of the United States frigate Philadelphia, under your command, wishing to express our full approbation of your conduct concerning the unfortunate event of yesterday, do conceive that the charts and soundings justified as near an approach to the shore as we made, and that after the ship struck, every exertion was made and every expedient tried to get her off and to defend her, which either courage or abilities could have dictated." [1] In view of the fact that these officers were necessarily to be summoned as witnesses in the official inquiry always held in such cases, the propriety of their thus formally committing themselves might be questioned; but under the circumstances they could hardly be criticised for a spontaneous act of kindness, and no one could grudge the captain the comfort he derived from this letter, which was very great.

November 2 a heavy blow from the northwest piled the water up on the shore so that the stern of the Philadelphia floated. The Tripolitans with boats, anchors, and cables, and an army of men at work, succeeded in pulling her off the reef the next day. The anchors, guns, and other articles that had been thrown overboard, being in shallow water, were easily recovered. The scuttling of the ship had been so hastily and imperfectly done that the Tripolitans were able to pump her out and make her tight. She was then brought into the harbor, amid the rejoicings of the people and to the great mortification of the Americans. In his letter of November 25 to Preble, Bainbridge says: "The gale of wind which came on about forty hours after we surrendered to the rocks, raised the

[1] Nav. Chron. p. 252; Nav. Aff. i, p. 123; Bainbridge, p. 82.

waters on this coast so as to get the ship off, much damaged, her keel, etc. broke; this added to our distress, but feel conscious that it was morally impossible for us to have effected it."

These unfortunate captives, three hundred and seven in number, had a long bondage before them. The officers were well treated at first, and were allowed to take the air on the roof of the house, but this privilege was denied them after three or four days. A week later, a report having come to the pasha of the ill treatment of the Tripolitan prisoners on the Meshuda, Captain Bainbridge and his officers were removed to the prison of the men and kept there a day without food. Bainbridge insisted that the report must be false. Through the influence of the minister, Dghies, the officers were sent back to their quarters in the evening.[1] After the destruction of the Philadelphia in February they were removed to the pasha's castle, where they remained during the rest of their stay in Tripoli, closely confined most of the time, though occasionally allowed some liberty. Dr. Jonathan Cowdery, one of the surgeon's mates, attracted the attention of the pasha, who employed him as his physician, and he was allowed more freedom than any other officer. He kept a journal during his captivity, which gives much information about the condition of the prisoners.[2] Part of the time he was permitted to care for the men when sick, but was often denied this privilege. Dr. Cowdery lived to be many years the senior surgeon of the navy.

Very soon Consul Nissen, finding that the officers missed occupation, sent them a large number of books,

[1] Preble Papers: Bainbridge to Preble (Nov. 15, 1803).
[2] See also letter of Cowdery in Nat. Intell. Aug. 5, 1805.

and then purchased for them their own books that were offered for sale at a moderate price, which was promptly and cheerfully refunded. After this, time not only passed more quickly, but was greatly improved. The captain and Lieutenant Porter organized a school of instruction for the younger officers, which kept them busy during the rest of their stay; and they learned much that they never otherwise would have been able to, in the press of professional duties. The captain was allowed a room by himself, and spent much time alone. He was permitted to write to Commodore Preble when in need of money or supplies, which were sent when opportunity offered. Besides this he kept up a secret correspondence with Preble through Nissen and the Danish consul at Malta, writing these letters in cipher or with lime juice, which made an invisible mark that became legible on heating. Several projects for escape were discussed by the officers, and one or two plans were partially carried out, but in each case insurmountable difficulties were met with.

The men fared much worse than the officers. The different classes of mechanics were put to work at their various trades, and the others employed in all sorts of hard labor, chiefly on the fortifications. They were beaten and maltreated by many of their taskmasters and keepers, and sometimes bastinadoed. At night they were locked up in their dismal prison. Whenever anything happened to exasperate or enrage the Tripolitans, they took their revenge on the unhappy captives, who were subjected to insult and hard usage greatly exceeding their usual allowance. This was especially the case just after the destruction of the Philadelphia and during the attacks on the town by

Commodore Preble's squadron in 1804. They occasionally complained to the pasha, and he forbade their being beaten, but apparently with little effect. Their diet was scanty and poor, consisting chiefly of coarse black bread and olive oil. When the blockade was closest, food was necessarily scarce, not only with them but with the whole population. A few escaped their sufferings by death, and a few by adopting the Mohammedan faith. Most of these renegades, especially a Swede named Wilson, and some of the others, were bad characters. There were many Englishmen among the crew, and the captain wished that Admiral Nelson might claim them and so liberate them.[1] The men as well as the officers meditated escape, and formed a plan to surprise the castle when the gates were opened in the morning, liberate their officers, seize the pasha with his family and guards, and put the castle in a state of defense. The plan was never attempted, and in the absence of the squadron must necessarily have failed.

At the request of Captain Bainbridge and with the help of Consul Nissen, extra food was provided for the sick, and later provisions and clothing for the crew were sent by the commodore. By this means the men had occasional supplies of good food. Now and then, on holidays, recreation was allowed and their dreary lives brightened. In celebration of Christmas, 1804, they feasted on fresh beef and vegetables and wine provided by order of the captain through Nissen, who was untiring in his attention to the men no less than to the officers. On New Year's Day the same entertainment was provided, and William Ray, who kept a journal, says : " I was told to take eight men, go to the

[1] Preble Papers : Bainbridge to Preble (Nov. 25, and Dec. 5, 1803).

Danish consul's, and get the wine. Our men were the tapsters and the consul requested me to keep an account of the measure. The good-natured, benevolent man told us to drink as much as we wanted. . . . The tapsters accepted of his liberal invitation with such unreserved cordiality that . . . they were not able to carry the cask to the prison. Another set of bearers was collected and the consul made them drink, until they were nearly as much intoxicated as the first ; and when we were departing, he distributed a handful of money amongst the whole. Our tars pronounced him the best fellow they had ever met with, and swore he must have been a sailor." [1]

After his return to America, at the request of the secretary of the navy, Captain Bainbridge wrote a letter setting forth the services of Mr. Nissen at Tripoli, for the information of Congress ; and that body passed a resolution, approved April 10, 1806, expressing " the high sense entertained by Congress of his disinterested and benevolent attentions, manifested to Captain Bainbridge, his officers and crew, during the time of their captivity in Tripoli." [2] The officers of the Philadelphia presented Nissen with a silver urn.[3]

In spite of poor food and hard usage there were but six deaths out of the whole number of three hundred and seven in nineteen months. When the captives were finally liberated, the pasha called together the renegades among the crew, five in number, " and told them that peace was now concluded, the Americans were about to leave Tripoli, and if they or either of them chose to go, it was left at their option. Unaware of the artifice, all except Wilson expressed their wish

[1] Ray, p. 151.   [2] Nav. Chron. p. 260.
[3] Nat. Intell. Oct. 9, 1805, June 3, 1807.

and anxiety to relinquish the turban and accompany us to America. Wilson, jealous of the Pasha's sincerity and perhaps afraid of the threatened halter, thanked his majesty for this generous offer, but told him that he preferred Tripoli to America and Mahometanism to Christianity, and that he chose to remain and would ever continue firmly attached to his service. Wilson was honored and caressed by the Pasha and his Divan for his singular fidelity, while the other four were sent into the country with a formidable guard. We had a glance at them as they passed our prison and could see horror and despair depicted in their countenances." [1]

The loss of the Philadelphia was a severe blow to the American cause. The squadron, with two frigates only, was already too small for the work in hand, and it had now lost a very large proportion of its strength. On the other hand, the enemy gained a better vessel than they had ever owned before, though fortunately for a short time only. Moreover, the large number of captives in the power of the pasha greatly complicated matters, and of course gave him an immense advantage in treating for peace. Preble, when he heard the news, wrote to the secretary of the navy that "it distresses me beyond description." It may be said with some confidence that if Bainbridge with his ship and men had been with his chief the following summer, the commodore's vigorous campaign would probably have been decisive, and peace, uncomplicated with the question of ransom, would have come earlier.

[1] Ray, p. 158.

CHAPTER XI

THE DESTRUCTION OF THE PHILADELPHIA

COMMODORE PREBLE sailed from Gibraltar for Cadiz October 23, 1803, with the Constitution and Enterprise,[1] in order to obtain water and other supplies which could not be got at Gibraltar just at that time, as the British fleet required everything then on hand. He had lost an anchor and cable at Tangier which he wished to replace, if possible. He returned in about two weeks, stopping at Tangier on the way, to show himself once more to the Moors. The Argus arrived from America November 1, and Lieutenant Hull took command of her, turning the Enterprise over to Decatur. November 12 the commodore issued a circular proclaiming the blockade of Tripoli, which he sent to the United States ministers at London, Paris, and Madrid, and to a number of American consuls. He afterwards received instructions from the secretary of the navy, dated February 4, 1804, not to seize neutral vessels attempting to enter Tripoli without knowledge of the blockade, but to turn them back. Such, however, as had been warned, and those having knowledge of the blockade were to be sent into port for adjudication. The blockade must, moreover, be an actual one.[2] November 13 the commodore sailed up the

---

[1] For the operations of Preble's squadron up to July, 1804, see Preble, ch. iii, iv; Cooper, ii, ch. ii, iii; Nav. Chron. pp. 218-220; Amer. Hist. Rec. i, pp. 55, 56; Preble Papers.

[2] Nav. Chron. p. 213; St. Pap. vii, p. 397.

Mediterranean with the Constitution and Nautilus. The Argus, after a cruise to the eastward, remained at Gibraltar to watch Morocco and look after American interests in the Straits.[1] The Siren, with ex-Consul Cathcart on board, had already been sent, October 24, with a convoy to Leghorn, where Cathcart was to turn over to Stewart certain public property to be delivered to Consul Lear at Algiers. The Enterprise was sent to Syracuse with the supply ship Traveler, after which she was to join the Philadelphia and Vixen off Tripoli. On the 19th the Constitution arrived at Algiers and landed Colonel Lear, proceeding on her way the next day. On the 24th, off the coast of Sardinia, "at 9 A. M. spoke His B. M. ship Amazon on a cruise, the captain of which gave me the melancholy and distressing intelligence of the loss of the U. S. ship Philadelphia." [2] Putting into Malta three days later, Preble found a letter from Bainbridge giving details of the disaster. He sailed at once for Syracuse, where he arrived the next day.

Syracuse was made the base of supplies for the squadron. It had certain advantages over Malta, among which was the smaller number of desertions. One of Preble's difficulties had been that of enlisting crews for the squadron, by reason of the small pay in the navy as compared with the merchant service.[3] The crews were therefore made up largely of foreigners, principally English; Preble states, however, that to the best of his knowledge and belief they were naturalized Americans and not British subjects. When they deserted they sought the protection of the British

[1] Preble Papers : Preble to Hull (Nov. 7).
[2] Preble Papers, Journal.
[3] Preble Papers : Sec. of Navy to Preble (June 25, 1803).

flag, and the English commanders would not give them up. There had been trouble on this account at Gibraltar, where three deserters took refuge on an English frigate, the captain of which refused to surrender them to Lieutenant Stewart, then the senior American officer at Gibraltar. Preble feared the same difficulty at Malta. This state of things was subsequently remedied by order of Admiral Nelson. It was also often impossible, on account of the existing war between England and France, to procure supplies, particularly in the ports most frequented by the British and French fleets. The supplies sent out from home were apt to be irregular and delayed in their arrival, and the provisions were sometimes spoiled.[1]

The Vixen had first heard of the loss of the Philadelphia at Malta November 19, in a letter [2] from Captain Bainbridge dated the first of that month. Lieutenant Smith at once set sail for Gibraltar, in obedience to this letter, to notify the commodore; but meeting with bad weather and contrary winds and being short of provisions, he was forced to turn back, and reached Syracuse December 12. On the 16th Preble sent the Nautilus to Gibraltar with dispatches to be forwarded to the navy department. The Vixen was employed on convoy duty. The next day the commodore sailed on a cruise in his flagship, with the Enterprise in company, to reconnoitre off Tripoli. On the 23d the Enterprise captured the ketch Mastico, under Turkish colors and without passports, bound from Tripoli to Constantinople. "She is armed with two cannon and some muskets, pistols &c., has on board

[1] Preble, p. 137 ; C. Morris, pp. 22–24 ; Port Folio, Dec. 1810; Preble Papers : Corres. between Stewart, Preble, and Gore (Oct. 1803).
[2] Preble Papers.

a Turkish master, seven Greeks and four Turks, sailors, a Turkish officer, two Tripoline officers, ten Tripoline soldiers as passengers and forty-two negro men, women and children," [1] who with other presents, were to be given to the capudan-pasha. " She had on board also two cannon in the hold." She had formerly been a French gunboat. " An Italian doctor who came on board [the Constitution] at Malta and who was in Tripoly when the Philadelphia was captured," told Preble that the Tripolitan officers were of high rank and that the soldiers had served in the gunboats which attacked the wrecked frigate, as did also the Turkish captain of the Mastico, who " was among the first that boarded her and was extremely active in taking the officers out and carrying them to the Bashaw of Tripoly, as well as plundering them of their cloathing. Conceiving it improper to let her pass under all these circumstances with officers, soldiers, guns and other property all belonging to the Bashaw of Tripoly and bound from one of his ports, I ordered all the crew and passengers on board " the flagship, except the slaves and a few others, and " sent off the Prize under convoy of the Enterprise " to Syracuse. Preble afterwards learned that the Mastico had taken part in the attack on the Philadelphia, under Tripolitan colors. The Constitution reconnoitred Tripoli until the 26th, when a heavy northeast gale threatened to drive her ashore, but she succeeded in getting back to Syracuse on the 30th. The Mastico was renamed the Intrepid, and was taken into the United States service.

The Constitution remained at Syracuse until March, but the smaller vessels, except the Enterprise, which

[1] Preble Papers : Journal (Dec. 24, 1803) ; see also Preble to Sec. of Navy (Feb. 3, 1804).

was undergoing repairs, were actively cruising all
winter. The Siren, in obedience to orders, had landed
Cathcart at Leghorn November 12, was detained until
the 26th, received the public property which was
delivered to Lear at Algiers December 21, and after
a very stormy passage arrived at Syracuse on the 28th.
She was then found in need of repairs, and her mainmast was shifted farther aft to improve her sailing.[1]
Preble went to Malta in the Vixen January 12, 1804,
to arrange for sending letters and supplies to Bainbridge. He was shown attention by the English army
and navy officers, and formed a pleasant acquaintance
with Sir Alexander Ball, the governor. He returned
to Syracuse on the 24th, and on the 27th the Nautilus
arrived from Gibraltar, leaving the Argus still in the
Straits.

In the mean time the commodore had been carrying
on a correspondence with Captain Bainbridge. His
earlier letters were delayed in delivery through the
negligence of the American consul at Malta. In a
long, sympathetic letter dated off Malta, December
19, 1803, Preble says: " Your zeal for your country
has occasioned the loss of a frigate and, for a time, of
a valuable commander, officers and crew. I have not
the smallest doubt, but that you all have done everything which you conceived could be done to get the
ship off and extricate yourself from the unhappy
situation in which you were placed. . . . You may
rest assured that in me you have a friend whose exertions shall never be wanting in endeavors to relieve
you; and in the mean time you may command such
supplies of money for the comfort of yourself, officers
and crew as you may require. I have only to request

[1] Preble Papers: Stewart to Preble (Jan. 1, 1804).

your requisition for such supplies. . . . I have been furnished by the governor of Syracuse with every convenient accommodation for the deposit of provisions and stores, masts, spars, boats, etc. I have formed an establishment at that place and made it the general rendezvous of the squadron, although in the winter I shall keep a vessel at Malta for information and occasionally visit it myself. I am now on my way for a cruise off Tripoli. The weather has been extremely stormy since our arrival at Syracuse; for many days it blew a gale and prevented us from putting to sea. . . . I shall lodge funds for you at Malta and will make such arrangements that you can receive a regular supply from thence, until I can make a better arrangement at Tunis. God bless and preserve you. May you have health and live to enjoy the smiles of the fickle goddess. . . . The first consul of France, the much celebrated Bonaparte, has interested himself deeply in your situation." [1]

From Syracuse, January 4, 1804, Preble wrote in regard to sending money and supplies for the captives, mentioned the capture of the Mastico, and added: "A gale of wind drove me from off Tripoly or I should have sent a Boat on Shore. I shall soon be off there again." [2] During his stay at Malta Preble wrote again, January 23: "You will receive a present supply of money from here through the British consul, B. McDonough, Esq., forwarded by Mr. Higgins. Any letters you will direct to the care of William Higgins, Esq., whom I have appointed Agent at this port for the squadron of the United States in these seas, and I am confident that he will pay you every attention. The clothing and other stores, which ought to have

[1] Bainbridge, p. 93.   [2] Preble Papers.

been with you six weeks since, were detained by Mr. Pulis [United States consul at Malta, who turned out to be an unworthy representative]; and for what reason I know not. Your drafts on Mr. Higgins will be duly honored. Keep up your spirits and despair not; recollect there's a sweet little cherub that sits up aloft." [1]

In January Preble began negotiations for peace with Tripoli through the agent of the pasha at Malta, who was ready to agree that no money should be demanded for peace or tribute, but merely a small consular present with the first consul, that the Philadelphia should be exchanged for a schooner, that the Tripolitan prisoners in Preble's hands, sixty in number, should be exchanged for as many Americans, and that the remaining Americans, two hundred and forty in number, should be ransomed at five hundred dollars each, or one hundred and twenty thousand in all. The agent later expressed the opinion that the pasha would reduce the ransom to one hundred thousand dollars, the other terms being the same. The commodore wrote to Consul Lear for his advice on the subject. Before hearing from him, however, an event happened which changed the aspect of affairs.[2]

The destruction of the Philadelphia was suggested by Bainbridge in a letter to Preble dated December 5, 1803. He says: " By chartering a merchant vessel and sending her into the harbor with men secreted, and steering directly on board the frigate, it might be effected without any or a trifling loss. It would not be possible to carry the frigate out, owing to the difficulty of the channel." On the strength of this letter

---

[1] Nav. Inst. v, p. 65.

[2] Preble Papers: Preble to Sec. of Navy (Feb. 3, 1804).

it was claimed that the idea of burning the frigate
originated with Bainbridge ; the plan is again urged
in his letters of January 18 and February 15, 1804.[1]
But long before he received the letter, Preble announced to the secretary of the navy, December 10,
his intention of doing this very thing, and he subsequently wrote to others that he had formed this intention as soon as he had heard of the frigate's capture.
Years afterwards several naval officers ascribed the
credit to Decatur. No doubt the idea of attempting
to save or destroy the Philadelphia occurred independently to many of the officers of the squadron, and
men too, as would be only natural ; and as Bainbridge
knew of the ship's being in the hands of the enemy
three weeks before Preble did, he probably had the
plan well matured in his mind correspondingly early.
His suggestion bears a striking resemblance to the
plan finally carried out. As the Constitution and
Enterprise were cruising together about this time,
Preble discussed the matter freely with Decatur, who
offered to attempt cutting out the Philadelphia with
the Enterprise. Soon after this, Stewart, returning
from a cruise, requested to be allowed to do the same
thing with the Siren. The commodore, however, had
given his promise to Decatur, but rejecting the attempt
at cutting out, believing it impossible to save her,
proposed to destroy the frigate, and to utilize for the
purpose the recently captured ketch Intrepid. The
letters of Bainbridge were of great assistance, giving
information of the exact situation of the Philadelphia
and of the strength and disposition of the Tripolitan
batteries and gunboats. During the month of January
the plan was fully matured. The Intrepid, whose

[1] Preble Papers.

Mediterranean rig would not excite suspicion, was to sail boldly into the harbor and run alongside the frigate, when her crew, previously concealed, were to board and fire the ship. Stewart in the Siren was to accompany Decatur and give what aid he could, particularly in covering the retreat of the Intrepid.[1]

In his instructions to Decatur, dated Syracuse, January 31, 1804, Preble says : " It is my order that you proceed to Tripoli in company with the Siren, Lieutenant Stewart, enter that harbor in the night, board the Philadelphia, burn her and make good your retreat with the Intrepid, if possible, unless you can make her the means of destroying the enemy's vessels in the harbor, by converting her into a fire-ship for that purpose, and retreating in your boats and those of the Siren. You must take fixed ammunition and apparatus for the frigate's eighteen-pounders, and if you can, without risking too much, you may endeavor to make them the instruments of destruction to the shipping and Bashaw's castle. You will provide all the necessary combustibles for burning and destroying ships. The destruction of the Philadelphia is an object of great importance and I rely with confidence on your intrepidity and enterprise to effect it. Lieutenant Stewart will support you with the boats of the Siren and cover your retreat with that vessel. Be sure and set fire in the gun-room berths, cockpit, storerooms forward and berths on the berth deck. After the ship is well on fire, point two of the eighteen pounders, shotted, down the main hatch and blow her bottom out." [2]

[1] Preble, pp. 60-63 ; Mrs. Decatur, pp. 46-50.
[2] For the destruction of the Philadelphia, see Decatur, ch. iv and app. iv ; Cooper, ii, ch. ii ; C. Morris, pp. 25-31 ; Mrs. Decatur, pp. 27-

STEPHEN DECATUR

Everything being ready and the weather favorable, on February 3 Decatur mustered the crew of the Enterprise, explained the object of the expedition, and called for volunteers. Every officer, man, and boy immediately stepped forward. Five officers, Lieutenants James Lawrence, Joseph Bainbridge, and Jonathan Thorn, Surgeon Lewis Heermann and Midshipman Thomas Macdonough, and sixty-two men, were selected. These were joined by Midshipmen Ralph Izard, John Rowe, Charles Morris, Alexander Laws, and John Davis from the Constitution ; and Salvadore Catalano, a Sicilian pilot familiar with the harbor of Tripoli, was also taken. Catalano was afterwards for many years a sailing-master in the navy.

The Siren and Intrepid sailed in the evening of February 3, and were off Tripoli on the 7th. To avoid suspicion, the Intrepid drew ahead and anchored after dark about a mile to the westward of the town. Bad weather was just setting in, and although Decatur was extremely anxious to go in that night, he took the precaution to send in a boat with the pilot and Midshipman Morris to reconnoitre. They found the sea breaking across the western entrance, and advised against going in. The vessels therefore stood off shore, and were driven far to the eastward by a violent gale which lasted several days. The situation of the Intrepid's crew was most uncomfortable. Morris says : " The commander, three lieutenants, and the surgeon occupied the very small cabin. Six midshipmen and the pilot had a platform laid on the water casks, whose surface they covered when they lay down for

81 ; Nav. Chron. pp. 256–260 ; Nav. Aff. i, p. 128 ; iii, pp. 180–188 (containing Preble's orders to Stewart and Decatur, and official reports of Preble, Stewart, and Decatur).

sleep, and at so small a distance below the deck that their heads would reach it when seated on the platform. The marines had corresponding accommodations on the opposite side, and the sailors had only the surface of the casks in the hold. To these inconveniences were added the want of any room on the deck for exercise and the attacks of innumerable vermin which our predecessors the slaves had left behind them. The provisions proved to be decayed and offensive." [1]

On the 16th they again approached Tripoli. The weather was fine, with a light wind. The Intrepid stood slowly in towards the town, using drags to prevent her too early arrival. The Siren, disguised as a merchantman, held back to give the appearance of not being associated with her consort. Both vessels were seen from Tripoli. Dr. Cowdery believed them to be English merchantmen, and William Ray thought they were Americans coming to treat for peace. At dark Decatur was two miles from the eastern entrance. The sea was still breaking in the western entrance, and the Intrepid entered the harbor by the eastern or main channel. The plan had been for the Siren's boats to join the Intrepid at ten o'clock; but as the wind was very light, Decatur feared that he might not be able to reach the frigate, and decided not to wait for the boats, and the drags were taken in. Stewart had, the day before, sent him one boat under Midshipman Thomas O. Anderson with nine men. This would seem to make the total number on board the Intrepid eighty-four.[2]

[1] C. Morris, p. 27.
[2] A list is given in Nav. Aff. ii, p. 776, and iii, p. 126, of those on board the Intrepid February 16, 1804, which contains 70 names,

As the ketch crept towards the harbor final arrangements were made and officers and men again instructed in the duties that had been already assigned and explained to them. Firearms were to be used only in case of urgent necessity. The boarders were to carry first the spar deck, next the gun deck, and then divide into parties with combustibles for the rest of the work in hand. The commander, with Midshipmen Rowe and Izard and fifteen men, was to hold the spar deck; Lieutenant Lawrence, with Midshipmen Laws and Macdonough and ten men, was to take the berth deck and forward storerooms; Lieutenant Bainbridge, with Midshipman Davis and ten men, the wardroom and steerage; Midshipman Morris, with eight men, the cock-pit and after storerooms. Lieutenant Thorn, with Dr. Heermann and fourteen men, was to remain on the ketch. Midshipman Anderson in the Siren's boat was to secure the Philadelphia's boats and prevent, if possible, the enemy's escape by means of them or by swimming. The watchword was "Philadelphia."

The Intrepid drifted slowly into the harbor by the faint light of a young moon, and by half-past nine was within two hundred yards of the Philadelphia. The frigate had her topmasts housed; she was stripped of her sails, and her lower yards were on the gunwales. The foremast, which had been cut away at the time of the wreck, had not been replaced. She had forty guns, all loaded and double-shotted, and appears to have been well manned. The little ketch of sixty tons and four small guns was face to face with this force and also within easy range of the pasha's castle and several

besides the pilot, including 14 commissioned and warrant officers, 12 petty officers, 28 able seamen, 8 ordinary seamen, and 8 marines. See Appendix V.

other batteries, mounting in all one hundred and fifteen heavy guns. The floating defenses, anchored close by, consisted of two or three cruisers and a few galleys, all fully manned. The gunboats were hauled up on shore for the winter. If the slightest suspicion of the Intrepid's character had been aroused, she would have been blown out of the water and not a man could have escaped.

As she approached, the crew were kept concealed, except six or eight men in Maltese dress. The pilot, Catalano, had the helm, and Decatur stood beside him. At a distance of about a hundred yards the Intrepid was hailed and ordered to keep off. The pilot replied that she had lost her anchors in the recent gale, and requested permission to make fast to the frigate for the night. This was granted, and the Tripolitan asked what the brig outside was. Catalano replied that it was the Transfer, a vessel recently purchased at Malta by the Tripolitans, and which the pilot knew was expected about that time. He then kept up a conversation at the dictation of Decatur, in order to distract, as much as possible, the attention of the Tripolitans. The Intrepid was now close under the port bow of the Philadelphia; " but just as the ketch was about coming in contact with the frigate the wind shifted, blowing lightly directly from the frigate, and it left us at rest abeam and about twenty yards from her. This was a moment of great anxiety. We were directly under her guns, motionless and powerless, except by exertions which might betray our character. The Siren's boat was, however, in tow, and was leisurely manned, and took a rope to make fast to the ship. She was met by a boat [from the Philadelphia] with another rope, when both were united, and each boat returned to its vessel.

This rope was passed along the deck and hauled upon by the crew as they lay stretched upon it, and the vessels gradually brought nearer each other. When nearly in contact the suspicions of the enemy appeared to be aroused, and the cry of ' Americanos ! ' resounded through the ship. In a moment we were near enough, and the order ' Board ! ' was given ; and with this cry our men were soon on the decks of the frigate." [1] Morris was the first to reach the deck, followed in an instant by Decatur. Most of the Tripolitans were huddled together in confusion on the forecastle. The Americans were quickly formed and charged forward, with their commander in the lead. The enemy made little resistance and no firearms were used. The lower decks were also soon cleared. Decatur says in his report : " I can form no judgment as to the number of men on board ; but there were twenty killed. A large boat full got off and many leaped into the sea. We have made one prisoner." The combustibles were then passed up from the ketch and distributed, and the men scattered to the various parts of the ship that had been assigned to them. The commodore's orders were positive not to attempt to save the Philadelphia. There was, then, no alternative to the painful necessity of destroying her. The thing was done quickly and exactly according to arrangement. Morris was a trifle late in receiving his combustibles, but he remained at his post until he had a fire well started, and then had some difficulty in reaching the deck, on account of fire and smoke above him. In a few minutes the ship was in flames, and the men had barely time to regain the Intrepid, cut the fasts, shove off, and save her from the fire. The ketch still had on deck a large quantity of

[1] C. Morris, p. 28.

combustibles in barrels, covered only by a tarpaulin, ready for use in case she should be converted into a fire-ship for the destruction of the enemy's shipping. The danger of her taking fire, therefore, was very great. Decatur was the last to leave the frigate, and leaped into the rigging of the ketch just as she swung off. The whole affair had taken less than twenty minutes. No one was killed and only one slightly wounded.

The sweeps were manned, and the Intrepid began her retreat from the harbor, favored by a light breeze off shore. Her situation was still a perilous one. The town had by this time become thoroughly aroused. Morris says: "Up to this time the ships and batteries of the enemy had remained silent, but they were now prepared to act; and when the crew of the ketch gave three cheers in exultation of their success, they received the return of a general discharge from the enemy. The confusion of the moment probably prevented much care in their direction and, though under the fire of nearly a hundred pieces for half an hour, the only shot which struck the ketch was one through the top-gallant sail. We were in greater danger from the ship, whose broadside commanded the passage by which we were retreating and whose guns were loaded and were discharged as they became heated. We escaped these also, and while urging the ketch onwards with sweeps, the crew were commenting upon the beauty of the spray thrown up by the shot between us and the brilliant light of the ship, rather than calculating any danger that might be apprehended from the contact. The appearance of the ship was indeed magnificent. The flames in the interior illuminated her ports and, ascending her rigging and masts, formed columns of fire, which, meeting the tops,

DESTRUCTION OF THE PHILADELPHIA

were reflected into beautiful capitals; whilst the occasional discharge of her guns gave an idea of some directing spirit within her. The walls of the city and its batteries and the masts and rigging of cruisers at anchor, brilliantly illuminated and animated by the discharge of artillery, formed worthy adjuncts and an appropriate background to the picture." [1] The starboard battery of the Philadelphia was discharged towards the town and into the shipping of the enemy, and was supposed to have done some damage. After a while the frigate's cables burned off, and she drifted ashore and soon blew up. At the entrance to the harbor the Intrepid was met by the Siren's boats. The brig herself was found outside, and Decatur went aboard and reported his success to Stewart. The wind was still light, but it soon began to blow and rapidly increased to a gale. It was favorable for their course, however, and they were soon running for Syracuse.

"The success of this enterprise," says Morris, "added much to the reputation of the Navy, both at home and abroad. Great credit was given and was justly due to Commodore Preble, who directed and first designed it, and to Lieutenant Decatur, who volunteered to execute it and to whose coolness, self-possession, resources and intrepidity its success was in an eminent degree due." When Admiral Nelson, who was at that time blockading Toulon, heard of it, he is said to have called it "the most bold and daring act of the age."

As to whether the Philadelphia could have been saved and brought away in triumph, opinions differ. The belief of Bainbridge, already quoted, was that it was impossible, and Preble, in his official report of

[1] C. Morris, p. 29.

February 19, 1804, says: "I was well informed that her situation was such as to render it impossible to bring her out; and her destruction being absolutely necessary to favor my intended operations against this city, I determined the attempt should be made." More than twenty years later Jacob Jones, one of the Philadelphia's captive officers in Tripoli, wrote to Mrs. Decatur: "I know of nothing which could have rendered it impracticable to the captors to have taken the Philadelphia out of the harbor of Tripoli." At the same time the pilot Catalano certified: "That he is and always was of opinion, that in the state of the wind at the time and his knowledge of the current and the soundings of the harbor, that the ship might have been brought out with safety had not orders been peremptorily given to destroy her. That he gave this opinion to Commodore Decatur on board the Philadelphia at the moment of her capture, who was only prevented by his orders from making the attempt." Mrs. Decatur said: "It was, moreover, the opinion of my husband that he could have towed the ship out, the distance being only two miles, if the wind had been adverse; that her guns, which were all loaded, would have protected the ketch while engaged in that operation; that it being dark, they had nothing to apprehend from the batteries; and that it was the flames of the frigate that exposed them to the view of the enemy and greatly increased the peril of the enterprise." [1] Mackenzie and Cooper believed it to have been impracticable on the ground that the ship's own motive power was lacking and that Decatur had not men enough to afford the attempt to tow her out the probability of success. The removal of the frigate

[1] Mrs. Decatur, pp. 10, 12, 30.

from the hands of the enemy was of supreme importance, and Commodore Preble doubtless felt that he would not be justified in increasing the risk of failure or in leaving the question to be decided at a critical moment.

The Siren and Intrepid reached Syracuse on the morning of February 19, to the great relief and joy of the commodore and of every other officer and man in the squadron, the vessels then in port being the Constitution, Vixen, and Enterprise. The log of the flagship records that " at 10 appeared in the offing the United States Brig Siren and the Intrepid. . . . The wind being light we sent boats out to assist in towing them in. . . . At ½ past 10 they passed through our squadron in triumph, receiving three cheers from each as they passed." [1]

In a letter [2] of the same date to the secretary of the navy, Preble earnestly recommended Decatur's promotion. This was promptly accomplished and the secretary wrote a letter dated May 22, 1804, addressed to Stephen Decatur, Esq., Captain in the Navy of the United States, in which he says : " The achievement of this brilliant enterprise reflects the highest honor on all the officers and men concerned. You have acquitted yourself in a manner which justifies the high confidence we have reposed in your valor and your skill. The President has desired me to convey to you his thanks for your gallant conduct on this occasion, and he likewise requests that you will in his name thank each individual of your gallant band for their honorable and valorous support, rendered the

---

[1] Preble Papers; Hollis, The Frigate Constitution (Boston, 1900), p. 98.

[2] Mrs. Decatur, p. 33.

more honorable from its having been volunteered. As a testimonial of the President's high opinion of your gallant conduct in this instance, he sends you the enclosed commission." [1] Decatur was the youngest captain ever appointed in the United States navy, being a little over twenty-five years of age. He was promoted over the heads of seven other officers, which caused some dissatisfaction, as is always the case under such circumstances. This was foreseen by Charles W. Goldsborough, chief clerk of the navy department, who wrote a confidential letter to Preble on the subject. After expressing great admiration for Decatur he says : " Suppose Capt. Decatur was to decline accepting the promotion given him, upon the principle of regard for the feelings of those who were appointed Lieutenants before him. Such a measure would immortalize him. The deed would justly bear the character of sublimity — rare instance of the most noble disinterestedness. . . . It would be the means of avoiding those bickerings & heart-burnings which his promotion will create among those who were his senior Lt. officers, & of fixing him with their cordial consent in the commission. If he were to act his part, they would feel the same noble sentiment & make to the government a declaration of their wishes that he might be placed over their heads." [2]

At nearly the same time the grade of master commandant, now known as commander, which had been abolished by the naval reduction act of 1801, was revived, and Lieutenants Charles Stewart, Isaac Hull, Andrew Sterrett, John Shaw, Isaac Chauncey, John Smith, Richard Somers, and George Cox were pro-

[1] Nav. Chron. p. 259.
[2] Preble Papers (June 6, 1804).

moted to the new rank. Several midshipmen were appointed acting lieutenants by Commodore Preble.

In November, 1804, Congress resolved: "That the President of the United States be requested to present in the name of Congress to Captain Stephen Decatur a sword, and to each of the officers and crew of the United States ketch Intrepid, two months' pay." [1] The officers would not accept this extra pay, but, with reason, felt that they were entitled to prize-money. The matter was brought up several years later, and Congress, with great injustice, declined or neglected to grant prize-money to the officers and men of the Intrepid, although it was recommended by committees both of the Senate and the House, and a bill providing for it passed the Senate. [2]

Meanwhile the squadron had not been idle. Early in February the Vixen and Nautilus were sent to Tunis to communicate with Dr. Davis, the American chargé d'affaires, and the former was to proceed to Algiers with dispatches for Consul Lear. She was next to search for Tripolitan cruisers, if any were reported to be to the westward, then stop again at Algiers, take on board Lear or O'Brien or both of them, and return to Syracuse. O'Brien had remained in Algiers after his resignation. The Vixen performed this duty, and returned with O'Brien early in April. The Nautilus proceeded from Tunis to the coast of Tripoli, and on February 16, the same day the Philadelphia was burned, she captured the brig Fortunata Barbara, under English colors, trying to run into

---

[1] Nav. Chron. p. 259.

[2] Decatur, app. iii; Mrs. Decatur, pp. 35–45; Nav. Aff. ii, pp. 483–486, 776–779; iii, pp. 25–35, 122–127, 178–189, 459–461; iv, pp. 84, 269, 301, 398, 816.

Tripoli. The Nautilus returned to Malta with the prize, which was afterwards ordered to the United States for adjudication, but not being seaworthy put back to Malta, and was finally given up to her former owners for a small sum, to avoid litigation.[1]

Lieutenant Dent was sent in the Enterprise to Messina to see what arrangements could be made for the purchase or charter of gunboats and mortar-vessels. Decatur, after his return, was sent to Messina to superintend necessary repairs to the Enterprise. The Constitution sailed March 2 for Malta, and returned to Syracuse on the 17th. March 9 the Siren and Nautilus sailed for the coast of Tripoli, and soon after their arrival the Siren captured a polacca called the Madona Catapoliana, under the Russian flag, from Tripoli bound to Malta. Lieutenant Stewart sent her to that place as a prize. She was of little value, and later was given up, in view of the friendly interest of the czar in American affairs at Tripoli. March 20 the Siren ran foul of the Nautilus, and the latter went back to Syracuse for repairs, but soon returned to the blockade. Some days later she encountered a severe gale, was obliged to throw overboard four guns, and received such severe damage as to compel her to go to Messina for a thorough overhauling.[2]

One morning towards the end of March, an armed brig was discovered lying to off Tripoli. She had just left that port bound for Malta, and attempted to get back into the harbor ; but the Siren succeeded in cutting her off and she at once surrendered. She proved to

[1] Preble Papers: Preble to Sec. of Navy (Feb. 3, April 19, and July 5, 1804) ; to Smith and to Somers (Feb. 3) ; certificate (Apr. 23).

[2] Preble Papers: Preble to Sec. of Navy (April 19 and July 5, 1804) ; Reed to Somers (March 20) ; Somers to Preble (April 16).

be the Transfer, before mentioned as having been
expected at Tripoli,[1] and had been carrying on a contraband trade between Malta and Tripoli for some
time. She had been a British privateer and had been
purchased at Malta by the Tripolitan consul. She was
undoubtedly the property of the pasha. The prize had
a crew of eighty men. Lieutenant Stewart sent her to
Syracuse, and the commodore took her into the service
April 17. He says in his journal: "I have named
her the Scourge. She mounts sixteen six-pounders
and is a good cruiser." He gave the command of her
to Lieutenant Dent, at that time acting captain of the
Constitution.[2]

The commodore sailed from Syracuse March 21,
and arrived off Tripoli on the 26th. He had letters
for the French consul, M. Beaussier, which Mr. Livingston, the United States minister to France, had
received from Talleyrand by order of Bonaparte. He
delivered them the next day through Midshipman
Izard, who went ashore with a flag. Izard was allowed
to see Captain Bainbridge, to whom Preble obtained
permission to send supplies by neutral vessels, but not
in boats of the squadron. Bainbridge advised Preble
to be on the lookout for Tripolitan vessels which might
attempt to enter Syracuse harbor in disguise. He
suggested that the commodore should endeavor to
exchange all his Tripolitan prisoners for one or two of
the Philadelphia's officers, whose knowledge of Tripoli
would be very useful to him. For offensive measures
he advised an attack on the Tripolitan gunboats by
eighteen or twenty of the ships' boats; also a land

[1] See above, p. 170.
[2] Preble Papers: Preble to Sec. of Navy (April 19, 1804); Journal
(April 17). See also Claims, p. 479.

attack by three or four thousand men. On the 28th Preble had a conference with the French consul on board the flagship, but nothing was accomplished. The pasha, exasperated at the loss of the Philadelphia, now demanded, according to the consul, two hundred and fifty thousand dollars for peace and ransom, and would not consider an exchange of prisoners ; this demand was soon raised to half a million. Preble was convinced that the French consul was acting in the interest of the pasha, and that all the other consuls, except Nissen, were intriguing against peace with the United States, in the belief that in such event the pasha would go to war with some of their own governments. March 30 a northeast gale set in, and the Constitution and Siren ran over to Tunis and from there to Malta, where they arrived April 12. The next day the Vixen arrived from Algiers with O'Brien, who soon sailed for Tunis in the Enterprise with dispatches for Davis from the secretary of state.[1]

During the whole spring the commodore was constantly cruising about from port to port, arranging for the needs of the squadron, the relief of the captives in Tripoli, and for the summer campaign. His activity and energy were untiring. Incidentally he found it necessary to keep his eye on the bey of Tunis, who was getting restless and still demanding a frigate. O'Brien and Davis had a conference with the sapitapa on the subject and made a report.[2]

In the mean time the Argus had searched in vain for a Tripolitan cruiser reported to be in the western

[1] Preble Papers: Preble to Sec. of Navy (April 19, 1804); Bainbridge to Preble (March 26) ; Journal (March 28) ; Preble to Livingston (June 29).

[2] Preble Papers : O'Brien and Davis (April 29, 1804).

Mediterranean. In March she was ordered to leave her station in the Straits of Gibraltar, and join the squadron. She convoyed a store-ship to Syracuse, and arrived off Tripoli in April. On the 30th she captured a small sloop.[1] The blockading force now consisted of the Siren, Argus, Vixen, and Enterprise, with Stewart as senior officer present in command. They were later joined by the Scourge. During May and June they had several unimportant encounters with the batteries and gunboats of Tripoli.[2]

In the course of his cruising in the Constitution Preble arrived at Naples May 9. Here he obtained from the king of the Two Sicilies, who was also at war with Tripoli, an order for six gunboats and two bomb-vessels, with their equipment, " under the title of a friendly loan." The gunboats were twenty-five ton, flat-bottomed vessels, difficult to handle under sail or oar, and unseaworthy, being intended only for harbor defense; each carried a long twenty-four pounder in the bow. The bomb-vessels were thirty-ton boats, similar in construction to the gunboats, and each carried a thirteen-inch brass mortar. The commodore also borrowed six long twenty-six pounders, which he mounted on the upper deck of the Constitution, in the waist. As the squadron was short-handed, the king also allowed ninety-six Neapolitan bombardiers, gunners, and sailors to enter the United States service ; they helped to man the gunboats and bomb-vessels, being equally distributed among these craft. Preble then proceeded to Messina, where the boats

[1] Officers' Letters, i, no. 32 : Hull to Sec. of Navy (March 3, 1804) ; Preble Papers : Log of Argus (April 30).

[2] Preble Papers : Decatur to Preble (May 26) ; Stewart to Preble (June 13).

were, and thence conveyed the gunboats to Syracuse, arriving May 31; the mortar-boats were not ready.[1]

The commodore left Syracuse June 4, stopped over three days at Malta, and appeared before Tripoli on the 13th. He had with him on the flagship ex-Consul O'Brien, who had returned from Tunis, and whom he now sent ashore to treat for ransom and exchange of prisoners, but he was unable to make satisfactory terms. Preble offered to pay two hundred dollars for each prisoner, but "not a cent for tribute or peace." He had been advised by Lear to offer six hundred, but this he would not do. The pasha would not abate his previous demands.[2]

At this time the bey of Tunis was making threats on account of one of his vessels being detained by the blockaders off Tripoli, although she had been subsequently released. A Spanish vessel also, from Tunis bound to Tripoli, with material for Spanish carpenters who were building gunboats for the pasha, had been stopped and sent back to Tunis. The bey had sent several cruisers to sea and was fitting out others. But on the appearance of the Constitution, Argus, and Enterprise in Tunis Bay, June 19, he became quiet and professed friendship. The commodore then sailed for Syracuse, arriving on the 25th.[3]

June 28 Preble sent two thousand dollars and provisions and clothing to Captain Bainbridge in a neutral vessel convoyed by the Argus. In his letters of July 7 and 8, Bainbridge again suggested sending a land force against Tripoli, and believed that in attacking

[1] Preble Papers: Acton to Preble (May 13, 1804).

[2] Preble Papers: Preble to Sec. of Navy (June 14); to Cathcart (July 5); Journal (June 13 and 14).

[3] Nav. Chron. p. 219; Nav. Inst. v, p. 69, note; Preble Papers: Preble to Sec. of Navy (June 14).

the enemy's gunboats, the ships' boats would prove more efficient than the borrowed gunboats. He advised bombarding Tripoli at night, and said that in his opinion throwing shells into the town occasionally would drive all the inhabitants into the country, and that if it were kept up a month or two the distress of the people would incline the pasha to more moderate terms.[1]

July 7 the Siren, Argus, Vixen, and Scourge were on the blockade. "At daybreak a large Galliot was discovered standing for Tripoly," from the westward. The squadron immediately gave chase with a good breeze. The enemy made for the shore and reached a point about nine miles west of the town. " At 6 the wind left us, then about gun-shot from the chase, which we observed them hauling on shore. Several shots were fired, but without producing any effect, and they continued unloading her. I then made the signal for armed boats and immediately dispatched the Syren's launch with a 12 lb. Carronade and barge with a heavy swivel under the command of Lt. Caldwell & Mr. Dorsey, Midshipman, who advanced with the greatest expedition & spirit to the reef, where they both grounded and were momentarily exposed to a severe fire from the Enemy (who were posted in great numbers behind the rocks and ridges of Sand hills) ; however, they soon extricated themselves & took a position from whence they kept up a brisk fire with the carronade & swivel untill the schooner [Vixen] by the assistance of some boats towing & her sweeps gained a position to cover them. The rocks formed too strong a breastwork to admit of the Enemy's being

[1] Bainbridge, p. 89 ; Preble Papers. For correspondence between Preble and Bainbridge, see also Sabine's Preble, ch. viii.

dislodged, but from the fire of the Vixen & boats the vessel was cut to pieces. Seeing nothing farther could be effected I made the signal of recall that the boats might return to tow off the respective ships." In this attack one man was killed and three wounded, one of them mortally. All of them were marines. Lieutenant Stewart believed that the enemy suffered severely.[1]

Commodore Preble sailed from Syracuse for Messina June 29, and arrived July 1. On the 8th he sent the Nautilus, whose repairs were just completed, to Syracuse with the two mortar-boats, which were now ready. The commodore followed in his flagship the next day. On the 14th everything was ready, and he left Syracuse with the Constitution, Nautilus, and Enterprise, the six gunboats and two mortar-boats. After being detained five days at Malta by bad weather they sailed for Tripoli, and joined the blockading force July 25. The squadron was accompanied by a store-ship.

[1] Preble Papers: Stewart to Preble (July 8, 1804).

CHAPTER XII

COMMODORE PREBLE BEFORE TRIPOLI

COMMODORE PREBLE now had his squadron assembled before Tripoli, prepared to do all that could be done with the means at his disposal. Besides his two thirteen-inch mortars he had forty-two heavy guns : thirty long twenty-four pounders on the gun deck of the Constitution and one on each of the six gunboats, and the six borrowed twenty-six pounders on the spar deck of his ship. The remaining force comprised the brigs Siren, Argus, and Scourge, and the schooners Vixen, Nautilus, and Enterprise, commanded respectively by Lieutenants Charles Stewart, Isaac Hull, John H. Dent, John Smith, Richard Somers, and Stephen Decatur. All these officers, except Dent, had been promoted, but the fact was unknown in the squadron at this time. The first two brigs carried sixteen twenty-four pound carronades, the first two schooners twelve eighteen-pound carronades, while the Scourge had sixteen and the Enterprise twelve six-pounders. On the Constitution's quarter-deck and forecastle were mounted a number of long twelve-pounders ; and each of the two heavier brigs had two of the same. To make up the total strength of the squadron, a few other lighter pieces must be added. Of all these guns the only ones fit for assaulting the enemy's batteries were the twenty-four and twenty-six pound long guns. The squadron was manned by one thousand and sixty officers and men.[1]

[1] This chapter is based on Preble's Report of Sept. 18, 1804, to the

Tripoli was a walled city protected by forts and batteries mounting one hundred and fifteen guns, most of them heavy. One of the batteries had been built by the crew of the Philadelphia and was called Fort America; another was known as Vixen Battery, from having first fired on that vessel. The enemy's force for the defense of the city and fortifications was estimated at twenty-five thousand Arabs and Turks. Their floating defenses comprised a ten-gun brig, two eight-gun schooners, two large galleys, and nineteen gunboats, each carrying an eighteen or twenty-six pounder, some a twenty-nine pounder, in the bow, and two howitzers aft. The brig, schooners, and galleys were manned by about one hundred men each, while the gunboats carried from thirty-six to fifty men each, making a considerably larger number of men afloat than Preble had under his command. These vessels were disposed behind the long line of reefs extending two miles from the northeast corner of the town, and forming the northern side of the harbor, through the numerous openings in which their light craft could sally forth for attack and quickly retire under their batteries when pursued. On account of the shoal water and reefs the Constitution could not get near enough to destroy them.

The day before arriving off Tripoli the first matter attended to was filling the water casks of the gunboats, and as soon as the squadron was assembled arrangements were made for towing these small ves-

Sec. of the Navy, Nav. Aff. i, p. 133 ; Nav. Chron. p. 220. It is a long document in the form of a journal. All quotations, not otherwise specified, are from this report. See also Preble, ch. v ; Decatur, ch. v, vi; Cooper, ii, ch. iii, iv, v; Amer. Nav. Off. i, pp. 89–122, 208– 232 ; Nav. Inst. v, p. 83; Mag. Amer. Hist. iii. p. 182; **Preble Papers.**

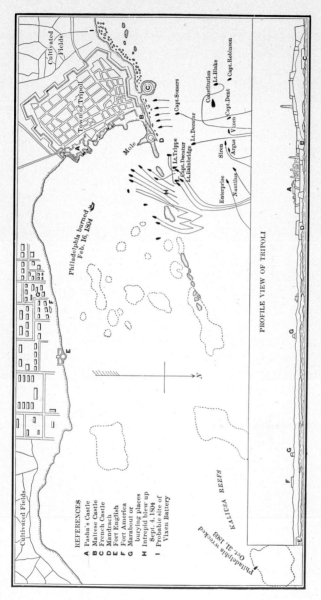

REFERENCES

A Pasha's Castle
B Maltese Castle
C French Castle
D Mandrach
E Fort English
F Fort America
G Marabout or
   burying places
H Intrepid blew up
   Sept. 4, 1804
I Probable site of
   Vixen Battery

Cultivated Fields

Town of Tripoli

Mole

Philadelphia burned
Feb. 16, 1804

Capt. Somers

Constitution   Lt. Blake
              Capt. Robinson
Capt. Dent
Vixen
Lt. Decatur

Lt. Trippe
Capt. Decatur
Lt. Bainbridge

Siren   Argus
Enterprise
Nautilus

KALUSA REEFS

Philadelphia wrecked
Oct. 31, 1803

PROFILE VIEW OF TRIPOLI

MAP OF TRIPOLI

sels to sea in case of northerly gales. To the Constitution were assigned the two mortar-boats, to the
Argus two of the gunboats, and to the Siren, Vixen,
Nautilus, and Enterprise one each. The commodore
also gave orders for anchoring before Tripoli in two
columns, parallel with the shore. July 28 the weather
for the first time appeared favorable for beginning
operations, and at 3 P. M. Preble anchored his squadron two miles and a half north of the town. No sooner
was this done, however, than the wind, which had been
east-southeast, shifted to north-northwest and then to
north-northeast, and soon began to blow hard, making
it necessary at six o'clock to weigh anchor and stand off
shore. The wind increased and blew a gale until the
31st. Fortunately it continued to haul to the eastward, so that the sea did not rise in proportion to
the wind, otherwise the difficulty of clawing off a lee
shore with the gunboats in tow might have been more
than the squadron was equal to. As it was, it split
the reefed foresail and close-reefed main topsail of the
Constitution. August 1 the wind subsided, and the
squadron stood in again towards Tripoli. Notwithstanding all the bad weather, opportunities had been
found to discharge from the store-ship and distribute
to the squadron water, provisions, and the naval and
military stores necessary for the active service ahead.
The store-ship was then sent to Malta under convoy
of the Scourge, with Lieutenant Izard in charge.

August 3 was a fine day with an easterly breeze.
Several of the enemy's gunboats were seen outside
the harbor, and the commodore determined to make
an attack. Signaling his commanders at 12.30 P. M.
to come within hail, he issued his orders. The two
mortar-boats were assigned to Lieutenants John H.

Dent and Thomas Robinson. The gunboats were marshaled in two divisions of three boats each, under the command of Lieutenants Richard Somers and Stephen Decatur in No. 1 and No. 4 respectively. In the first division with Somers were Lieutenants James Decatur of the Nautilus and Joshua Blake of the Argus in No. 2 and No. 3; while No. 5 and No. 6 in the second division were in charge of Lieutenants Joseph Bainbridge of the Enterprise and John Trippe of the Vixen. Each gunboat had a crew of about thirty.

The squadron stood in until two o'clock, when the gunboats and bombs were cast off and ordered to advance under cover of the larger vessels. All then approached to within point-blank range of the batteries. At quarter before three the mortars began the battle by throwing shells into the town. The enemy immediately opened a hot fire from all their guns, ashore and afloat. The Tripolitan flotilla consisted of their nineteen gunboats and two galleys, and was arrayed in three divisions: an easterly division of nine boats outside the rocks, a reserve division of seven boats, including the galleys, in the centre behind the rocks, and a westerly division of five boats outside and close under the western batteries.

The American gunboats were ordered to attack the easterly division of the enemy; but Somers, being the senior officer, had the right of the line, which was to leeward, and he was unable to bring his division into action with Decatur's. His own boat in particular, being a dull sailer, could not be brought up, even with the aid of sweeps. James Decatur, however, was able to get up to windward and to join his brother's division. Blake, owing to a misunderstanding about signals, did not close with the enemy, but maintained his fire from a distance, accomplishing little. Of his own movements Somers says: "I found it impossible to join the division to windward, which had commenced firing on the weather line of the enemy, who lay close under the rocks. By this time there was five of the enemy's gunboats of the lee line under way, advancing and firing. When within point-blank shot I commenced firing on the enemy with round and grape. They still advanced until within pistol-shot when they wore round and stood in for the batteries. I pursued them until within musket-shot of the batteries, which kept up a continual fire of round and grape. Three of their boats had got in behind the rocks. I then wore and stood off. The boat has received no damage, and but two of the men slightly wounded." [1] It was thought that if Blake had supported Somers they could have captured some of the enemy's gunboats.

Meanwhile Decatur's division, reinforced by his brother's boat, attacked the eastern division with spirit. Bainbridge had his lateen yard shot away at the outset and was unable to close, but getting as near as he could, kept up a heavy fire; at one time he grounded for a moment under the batteries. The other three boats, No. 4, No. 6, and No. 2, reserved their fire until close upon the enemy, when they poured in a heavy discharge of grape and canister. They were now closely engaged with three times their number of Tripolitan gunboats, which were larger and better boats than their own and most of them more heavily armed and manned. Moreover, they were too near the enemy to receive longer the support of the squadron's fire. The elder Decatur, having delivered his fire, ran along-

[1] Preble Papers: Somers to Preble (Aug. 4, 1804).

side the nearest gunboat and boarded her, followed by
Lieutenant Thorn, Midshipman Macdonough, and the
Americans of his crew, leaving the Neapolitans in the
boat. They at once engaged in a desperate hand-to-
hand encounter on the deck of the Tripolitan gunboat
with pistols, cutlasses, pikes, and axes. In the centre
of the boat was a large hatchway, to the further side
of which the enemy retreated, followed by the Americans around both ends. The fight was soon ended by
the surrender of the Tripolitans. Of their crew of
thirty-six they had lost sixteen killed and fifteen
wounded, the other five being made prisoners. The
prize was then taken in tow.

James Decatur also had singled out an enemy and,
after pouring in his fire, had run alongside to board,
when the Tripolitan at once surrendered ; but as Decatur was about to step aboard to take possession, the
captain drew a pistol and shot him through the head.
Midshipman Brown, next in command, thereupon drew
off, and running under the stern of No. 4 informed
Stephen Decatur of what had happened. According
to Preble, Somers, and Morris, the gunboat engaged
by James Decatur escaped after killing him ; but Mackenzie, apparently on the authority of Stephen Decatur
himself, states that upon learning of his brother's
murder he left his prize in charge of Thorn, with
a large part of his crew, and immediately pursued and
overtook the assassin. Stewart also, in a letter written
at the time, says that Decatur took the boat first
attacked by his brother.[1]

[1] Nav. Chron. p. 223 ; Preble Papers : Somers to Preble (Aug. 4,
1804) ; C. Morris, p. 32 ; Decatur, p. 93, note ; Nat. Intell. Dec. 5, 1804 ;
see also statement of Stewart quoted in Chautauquan, July, 1898,
p. 414.

At all events, after the capture of his first prize, Decatur engaged a second gunboat, armed with a long eighteen-pounder and two howitzers and manned by a crew of twenty-four. He ran alongside, and at once boarded with Macdonough and the remnant of his crew. Decatur singled out the captain, a man of great size and strength, and attacked him furiously. The Tripolitan made a thrust with his boarding pike and, in attempting to parry the blow, Decatur's cutlass was broken off at the hilt, leaving him for the moment unarmed. Another thrust of the pike wounded him in the arm. Decatur seized the weapon, wrenched it away, and grappled with his antagonist. After a short struggle they fell to the deck with Decatur on top. Meanwhile the two crews were fighting fiercely about their leaders, and a Tripolitan aimed a blow at Decatur's head with his scimitar; when a seaman named Daniel Frazier, having both arms disabled by wounds, interposed his head and received the blow, which laid open his scalp. The Tripolitan captain, being much more powerful than Decatur, soon turned him underneath and holding him down with his left hand, drew a knife and was about to plunge it into his breast. Decatur seized the uplifted arm with his left hand while he managed to get his right into his pocket, where he had a pistol. Giving it the proper direction, he fired through the pocket; the giant relaxed his hold and fell dead. Having lost seventeen killed, including their leader, the seven surviving Tripolitans, four of whom were wounded, soon gave up the fight. In his official report of August 3, 1804, Decatur gives a very brief account of his day's fighting. He speaks of bearing down on the enemy's gunboats and only adds: " I boarded and carried two of them and was successful in bringing them off." Accompanying this is Surgeon Heermann's report for the day, which gives four wounded on board gunboat No. 4, including "Capt. Decatur, wounded slightly in the arm," and "Dnl. Frashier, two incised wounds on the head, one of them severe; one bad wound across the wrist and seven slightly about his hands."[1] Of James Decatur's crew two were wounded.

In the mean time Lieutenant Trippe had been well occupied. Running alongside a heavy gunboat with a crew of thirty-six, he boarded her, followed by Midshipman Henley and nine men. The boats then drifted apart, and no others could get aboard the enemy. In this case, also, there was a hand-to-hand contest between the commanders, the Tripolitan being much the more powerful. Trippe received eleven sabre wounds, but finally succeeded in thrusting his boarding pike through the Tripolitan's body and brought him down. With the loss of their leader the enemy surrendered, having had fourteen killed and seven wounded; the remaining fifteen were made prisoners. Trippe had three wounded besides himself.

For centuries the Barbary pirates had inspired terror by their fierce attacks and their mode of boarding and sweeping the decks of an enemy. It was supposed that the only hope for an adversary lay in keeping them at a distance by superior seamanship and gunnery; in hand-to-hand fighting they were believed to be invincible. But they had now met their peers and had been overcome by numbers far smaller than their

[1] Preble Papers. According to most accounts Reuben James was the seaman who risked his life for Decatur (see Decatur, app. ii), but the surgeon's report would seem to settle it. Reuben James does not appear in the list of wounded; a Thomas James received a "superficial puncture in the face."

FIGHT OF THE GUNBOATS

own. In future actions they did not allow the Americans to get within boarding distance, and no more prizes were taken from the Tripolitan gunboat flotilla.

"Five of the enemy's gunboats and two galleys, composing the centre division and stationed within the rocks as a reserve, joined by the boats that had been driven in and supplied by fresh men from the shore to replace those they had lost, twice attempted to row out to endeavor to surround our gunboats and their prizes. I as often made the signal to cover them, which was promptly attended to by the brigs and schooners, all of which were gallantly conducted and annoyed the enemy exceedingly; but the fire from this ship kept their flotilla completely in check. Our grape-shot made great havoc among their men, not only on board their shipping, but on shore. We were several times within two cables' length of the rocks and within three of their batteries, every one of which in succession were silenced so long as we could bring our broadside to bear upon them. But the moment we passed a battery it was reanimated, and a constant heavy fire kept up from all that we could not point our guns at. We suffered most when wearing and tacking; it was then I most sensibly felt the want of another frigate."

The mortar-boats were actively engaged during the whole time, throwing shells into the town, and although so near the batteries that the men were wet through with the spray caused by the enemy's projectiles falling in the sea near them, the crews came off uninjured. Most of the shells appear not to have exploded. They had been obtained at Messina and were of poor quality. The house of Nissen, the Danish consul, was struck several times. He was the only consul that remained in town during the bombardment, all the others, with many of the inhabitants, having fled into the country. The Philadelphia's officers were able to see, from the window of their prison, the attack of Decatur's division on the Tripolitan gunboats. The Philadelphia's men were employed in carrying ammunition to the Tripolitan batteries and were severely beaten and maltreated.

"At half-past four, the wind inclining to the northward, I made the signal for the bombs and gunboats to retire from action, and immediately after, the signal to tow off the gunboats and prizes, which was handsomely executed by the brigs, schooners, and boats of the squadron, covered by a heavy fire from the Constitution." The fire of the flagship just at this time is described more in detail in Preble's journal: "Tacked ship and fired two broadsides in stays, which drove the Tripolines out of the castle and brought down the steeple of a mosque." As soon as the gunboats had been towed to a safe distance, the Constitution took the bomb-vessels in tow. This was at a quarter before five, and the action had lasted two hours.

The vessels of the squadron had their sails and rigging a good deal cut by shot, and a twenty-four pound ball passed nearly through the Constitution's mainmast. The only man wounded, not in the gunboats, was a marine on the flagship; the marines worked the twenty-six pounders on the spar deck. "We must impute our getting off so well to our keeping so near that they overshot us, and to the annoyance our grape-shot gave them; they are, however, but wretched gunners. . . . The enemy must have suffered very much in killed and wounded, both among their shipping and on shore. Three of their gunboats were sunk in the

PREBLE'S SQUADRON ATTACKING TRIPOLI

harbor, several of them had their decks nearly cleared of men by our shot, and a number of shells burst in the town and batteries."

In his official report and in general orders,[1] published the next day, the commodore praises the conduct of the officers and men of his flagship, of the smaller vessels, and of the flotilla, including the Neapolitan gunners and bombardiers. It has sometimes been said that Preble was dissatisfied with the result of the day's work and thought that more prizes should have been taken, but there is not the slightest hint of such a feeling on his part in his report or in his private journal, where it might be expected if anywhere. There is only praise, except the mildest sort of reprehension of Lieutenant Blake.[2]

Lieutenant James Decatur was taken aboard the Constitution as soon as the action was over and died almost immediately. He was buried at sea the next day. He was the only American killed, and thirteen were wounded. The wounded Tripolitans were also brought aboard the flagship and cared for by the medical officers of the squadron.

August 5 a French privateer, which had been in Tripoli some days, came out, and Preble induced her captain to return to the port with letters to the prime minister and the French consul, and with fourteen badly wounded prisoners, who were thus restored to their friends. It was thought that this act of humanity might produce a pleasant impression upon the pasha and perhaps affect favorably the welfare of the American prisoners in his power, but apparently no such result was brought about. When the privateer returned she brought a letter from the French consul intimat-

[1] Preble Papers.   [2] Nav. Inst. v, p. 71, note.

ing that the pasha was more disposed to peace upon
reasonable terms; but as no definite proposition was
made, Preble paid no attention to it. Meanwhile all
hands were occupied in repairing damages and in fitting out the prize gunboats, which were altered from
lateen-rigged boats to sloops. They were called No. 7,
No. 8, and No. 9. Each carried a heavy brass or
copper gun in the bow and two brass howitzers aft.
Two of these bow guns, according to Preble's official
report, weighed sixty-six hundred pounds each, were
eleven and a half feet long, and threw a twenty-nine
pound shot. The other, mounted on No. 9, was an
eighteen-pounder.

On the 7th everything was ready for another attack.
Gunboat No. 2 was commanded by Lieutenant Charles
Gordon of the Constitution, No. 3 by Sailing-Master
Samuel B. Brooks of the Argus, No. 6, No. 7, No. 8,
and No. 9 by Lieutenants Henry Wadsworth of the
Constitution, William M. Crane of the Vixen, Jonathan Thorn of the Enterprise, and James R. Caldwell
of the Siren; the others had the same commanders
as on the 3d. The two bomb-vessels, under Dent and
Robinson, took a position in a small bay to the westward of Tripoli, where they were not much exposed to
the enemy's fire, and bombarded the town. The gunboats advanced in two divisions, under Somers and
Decatur, and opened fire on one of the western batteries mounting seven heavy guns, and also on the
town. They received a hot fire in return. The action
began at half-past two in the afternoon. The wind was
north-northeast, and being on shore, the commodore did
not venture very close with the Constitution, fearing
that if the ship were disabled she might be lost. She
remained to windward with the Enterprise and Nautilus,

which were commanded by Lieutenants James Lawrence and George W. Reed, in the absence of their captains. They stood ready to cut off the enemy's gunboats and galleys, fifteen in number, should they come out to attack the American gunboats, which they seemed to be threatening to do. "The seven-gun battery in less than two hours was silenced, except one gun. I presume the others were dismounted by our shot, as the walls were almost totally destroyed. At a quarter past three P. M. a ship hove in sight to the northward, standing for the town ; made the Argus signal to chase." The Siren and Vixen remained near the gunboats to cover them in case of need. At half-past three gunboat No. 9, in Decatur's division, received a hot shot in her magazine and blew up. Out of her complement of twenty-eight, Lieutenant Caldwell, Midshipman Dorsey, and eight men were killed, and six men wounded, two of them mortally. At the time of the accident Midshipman Spence was superintending the loading of the gun. This was finished, the gun was fired, and the men gave three cheers as the boat sank under them. Spence, who could not swim, and the other eleven men who were unhurt, together with the wounded, were picked up by the Siren's boats or the nearest gunboats. Those who were able immediately went to work with the crews of the other boats. Spence's father was purser of the Philadelphia and a prisoner in Tripoli at this time.[1]

At half-past five, as the wind began to freshen, the commodore signaled to the gunboats and bombs to retire, and they were taken in tow by the other vessels. " In this day's action No. 4 had a twenty-four

[1] Nav. Chron. p. 228, note ; Nat. Intell. Dec. 5, 1804 (Stewart's letter).

pound shot through her hull; No. 6, her lateen yard shot away; No. 8, a twenty-four shot through her hull, which killed two men. Some of the other boats had their rigging and sails considerably cut. We threw forty-eight shells and about five hundred twenty-four pound shot into the town and batteries. All the officers and men engaged in the action behaved with the utmost intrepidity. At half-past six all the boats were in tow and the squadron standing to the northwest."

The strange sail turned out to be the frigate John Adams, Captain Isaac Chauncey, from the United States, who brought out the new commissions for Captain Decatur and the other officers who had been promoted. To Commodore Preble he brought a letter from the secretary of the navy, dated May 22, 1804, less pleasing in its import, announcing as it did the coming of Commodore Samuel Barron with four frigates to supersede him in command. This act of the administration, however unfortunate, would appear from the secretary's letter to have been unavoidable. When the news of the loss of the Philadelphia reached Washington, it was decided to push the war with increased vigor. The secretary writes: " The President immediately determined to put in commission and to send to the Mediterranean a force which would be able, beyond the possibility of a doubt, to coerce the enemy to a peace on terms compatible with our honor and our interest. A due regard to our situation with Tripoli, and precautionary considerations in relation to the other Barbary powers, demanded that our forces in that quarter should be so far augmented as to leave no doubt of our compelling the existing enemy to submit to our own terms, and of effectually

checking any hostile dispositions that might be entertained towards us by any of the other Barbary powers.
. . . Your good sense will perceive that we have thus
been unavoidably constrained to supersede you in a
command in which you have acquitted yourself in
a manner honorable to yourself, useful to your country, and in all respects perfectly satisfactory to us.
The only captains in the country, junior to yourself,
are Captains James Barron and H. G. Campbell;
and as the frigates cannot be commanded but by captains, agreeably to law, we of necessity have been
obliged to send out two gentlemen senior to yourself
in commission. Be assured, sir, that no want of confidence in you has been mingled with the considerations which have imposed upon us the necessity of
this measure. You have fulfilled our highest expecta-
tions; and the President has given it, in an especial
charge to me, to declare to you that he has the highest confidence in your activity, judgment, and valor.
Through me he desires to convey to you his thanks
for the very important services which you have rendered to your country; and I beg you to be assured,
sir, that it affords me great personal satisfaction to be
the medium of conveying to you his sentiments in
relation to your conduct." [1] The force expected consisted of the frigates President, 44, Captain George
Cox, flagship of Commodore Samuel Barron; Congress, 36, Captain John Rodgers; Essex, 32, Captain
James Barron; and Constellation, 36, Captain H. G.
Campbell.

As Chauncey expected the new squadron to arrive
very soon, Preble was greatly disappointed at the
prospect of not being able to carry out to the end

[1] Nav. Chron. p. 245.

the campaign he had planned, as well as chagrined at his displacement from the command. In his private journal he wrote, under the date of August 8 : " How much my feelings are lacerated by this supersedure at the moment of victory cannot be described and can be felt only by an officer placed in my mortifying situation." In his official report he acknowledges the secretary's letters " approbating my conduct and conveying to me the thanks of the President for my services. I beg you, sir, to accept my warmest thanks for the very obliging language in which you have made these communications, and to assure the President that to merit the applause of my country is my only aim, and to receive it the highest gratification it can bestow. . . . I cannot but regret that our naval establishment is so limited as to deprive me of the means and glory of completely subduing the haughty tyrant of Tripoli, while in the chief command. It will, however, afford me satisfaction to give my successor all the assistance in my power." However, owing to delay in the arrival of the new squadron, Preble was not called upon immediately to surrender his command.

After the news of Preble's assaults on Tripoli in August had reached home, the administration could better appreciate his true worth, and the secretary of the navy wrote to him : " This information furnishes additional testimony of your energy and judgment. We sensibly feel the value of your services and take pleasure in acknowledging them. Be assured that your Country will never prove ungrateful. I most ardently hope that you will have accomplished the reduction of Tripoli before the arrival of Commodore Barron's squadron, so that the whole glory of its reduction may be attributed to you. Nothing, however, can deprive you of the reputation which you have justly acquired by the preparatory arrangements made by you for this object and by your conduct in carrying those arrangements into effect, and although your successor may give the final blow to the enemy, the credit will, I trust, justly attach to you." [1]

The John Adams was loaded with stores for the squadron, and, to make room, most of her gun-carriages had been put aboard the other vessels, to be brought out later. She was therefore of little use to Preble in attacking Tripoli; but her men and boats made a welcome addition to the resources of the squadron, which was short-handed and taxed to its utmost to man the flotilla. Preble waited several days for Barron, believing that one vigorous assault by the united squadrons would end the war. On the 9th he reconnoitred the harbor in the Argus. The brig had a narrow escape, being struck under the water-line by a large shot which cut half through her planking. The Scourge returned from Malta the same day.

The next day, in answer to a signal from the French consul, a boat with Mr. O'Brien was sent in, under a flag of truce, with letters and an offer to pay eighty thousand dollars for ransom and ten thousand for a consular present. [2] The boat returned with information that the pasha would accept five hundred dollars ransom for each prisoner, amounting to about one hundred and fifty thousand dollars, waiving all claim to payment for peace and tribute. These were substantially the same terms proposed by the pasha six months before and less by three hundred and fifty thousand

[1] Preble Papers (Nov. 28, 1804).
[2] Preble Papers: Preble to Beaussier (Aug. 9, 1804).

dollars than his later demands. They were rejected.
Preble states in his journal that the next day he authorized "the French consul to offer the pasha one
hundred thousand dollars for ransom of the prisoners,
ten thousand as a consular present, nothing for peace,
and no tribute. These terms were rejected."

As Barron's squadron did not appear, Preble made
preparations for a night attack on Tripoli; but there
was a heavy sea, and he considered it inadvisable to
make the attempt while it continued. On the 16th
the Enterprise, Lieutenant Lawrence, was sent to
Malta "with orders to the agent there to hire transports and send off immediately a supply of fresh water,
provision, and other stores." Fresh vegetables were
especially needed, as scurvy had made its appearance
in the squadron. Some of the vessels had been five
months on the coast without visiting port. On the
evening of the 18th, Decatur and Chauncey were sent
in to reconnoitre in small boats. They found the
Tripolitan gunboats "anchored in a line abreast from
the Mole to the Pasha's castle, with their heads to the
eastward." The next morning it blew a gale from
the north-northwest and the squadron was obliged to
weigh anchor and get an offing. During the next few
days, while it was still blowing hard, the Intrepid and
another vessel from Malta with water and provisions
joined the squadron. On the 22d the Enterprise also
returned, bringing no news of Barron's squadron. On
the 24th the conditions were favorable for a night
attack. At midnight the bombs and gunboats were
towed in by the boats of the squadron. From two to
six o'clock they bombarded the town and were then
towed out. They received no fire in return. Apparently little damage was done by the bombardment.

After another delay on account of bad weather, the next attack was made on the night of August 28. The evening was spent in preparation. The bomb-vessels were disabled and could not take part; one leaked, and in the other the mortar-bed had given way. The John Adams, Scourge, transports, and bombs were anchored seven miles out. Captain Chauncey, with several of his officers and seventy of the crew of the John Adams, and Lieutenants Dent and Izard of the Scourge, joined the Constitution. The gunboats were in two divisions as before, under Decatur and Somers. Lawrence relieved Bainbridge in No. 5; the others were commanded as on the 7th. At half-past one in the morning they went in, accompanied by the Siren, Argus, Vixen, Nautilus, and Enterprise, and the boats of the squadron, and at three anchored close to the rocks. The brigs and schooners kept under way just outside, ready to support the gunboats; their guns were too light to make any impression on the batteries. The ships' boats remained with the gunboats, to give assistance if needed. The gunboats kept up a heavy fire for two hours and a half, throwing four hundred round shot, besides grape and canister. At daylight, from her position two miles off Fort English, the Constitution stood in towards the harbor, receiving a heavy fire from the fort, the castle, and the batteries. When within two cables' length of the rocks, she opened a hot fire with round and grape-shot on the thirteen Tripolitan gunboats and galleys engaged with the American flotilla. One boat was sunk, two driven ashore disabled, and the others retreated. The frigate advanced to within musket-shot of the mole battery, and was there brought to, and holding this position for three quarters of an hour, fired over three hundred round shot, besides grape and canister, into the batteries, the castle, and the town; she fired nine broadsides. One twenty-four pound shot entered the room occupied by the Philadelphia's officers and fell close to Captain Bainbridge's head. He was nearly buried in a mass of stone and mortar, and his ankle was injured. By quarter-past six the gunboats had withdrawn and were in tow, and the Constitution hauled off. The commodore believed that he had inflicted severe damage on the enemy by this attack. One of the John Adams's boats, in company with the gunboats, was sunk by a shot which killed three men and wounded one. These were the only casualties on the American side. All the vessels and gunboats were cut up more or less in their sails and rigging, but otherwise suffered little injury.

The next few days were spent in preparing for another attack. On the 31st another supply ship arrived from Malta, but brought no news of Commodore Barron. September 2 a Spanish vessel coming out of Tripoli reported that great damage had been done in the city and harbor by the last bombardment and that many people had been killed, also that three of the gunboats that had been sunk had been raised and refitted.

On the 3d the squadron was ready for the fifth attack, which proved to be the last. The bombs were in commission again under their former commanders, Lieutenants Dent and Robinson. The two divisions of gunboats were, as usual, commanded by Captains Decatur and Somers. No. 3 was put in charge of Lieutenant Morris, while Lieutenant Trippe, having recovered from his wounds, returned to No. 6. Captain Chauncey and a number of his officers and men again volunteered for duty on the flagship. " At two P. M. Tripoli bore south-southwest two and a half miles distant, wind east by north. At half-past two the signals were made for the gunboats to cast off, advance and attack the enemy's galleys and gunboats, which were all under way in the eastern part of the harbor, whither they had for some time been working up against the wind. This was certainly a judicious movement of theirs, as it precluded the possibility of our boats going down to attack the town without leaving the enemy's flotilla in their rear and directly to windward. I accordingly ordered the bomb-vessels to run down within proper distance of the town and bombard it, while our gunboats were to engage the enemy's galleys and boats to windward. At half-past three, our bombs having gained the station to which they were directed, anchored and commenced throwing shells into the city. At the same time our gunboats opened a brisk fire on the galleys, and within point-blank shot, which was warmly returned by them and Fort English and by a new battery a little to the westward; but as soon as our boats arrived within good musket-shot of their galleys and boats, they gave way and retreated to the shore within the rocks, and under cover of musketry from Fort English. They were followed by our boats and by the Siren, Argus, Vixen, Nautilus, and Enterprise as far as the reefs would permit them to go with prudence. The action was then divided. One division of our boats, with the brigs and schooners, attacked Fort English, whilst the other was engaged with the enemy's galleys and boats. The Pasha's castle, the mole, crown and several other batteries kept up a constant fire on our bomb-vessels, which were well conducted and threw shells briskly into the town, but from their situation they were very much exposed and in great danger of being sunk. I accordingly ran within them with the Constitution, to draw off the enemy's attention and amuse them whilst the bombardment was kept up. We brought to within reach of grape and fired eleven broadsides into the Pasha's castle, town and batteries, in a situation where more than seventy guns could bear upon us. One of their batteries was silenced. The town, castle and other batteries considerably damaged. By this time it was half-past four o'clock. The wind was increasing and inclining rapidly to the northward. I made the signal for the boats to retire from action, and for the brigs and schooners to take them in tow, and soon after hauled off with the Constitution to repair damages."

The mortars threw fifty shells. The gunboats were an hour and a quarter in action, and fired four hundred round shot, besides grape and canister. The brigs and schooners were able to get near enough to Fort English to make their carronades effective. The fort was considerably damaged, and several of the Tripolitan gunboats were disabled. All the vessels of the squadron and the gunboats were a good deal cut up in their sails and rigging, but suffered no serious injury. Lieutenant Robinson's mortar-boat was disabled, and came near sinking, but was finally towed off. There were no casualties on the American side. The commodore commended the services of Captain Chauncey on the Constitution during the last two actions.

For several days Commodore Preble had been maturing a plan to send into the harbor a fire-ship, or floating mine, to be exploded in the midst of the enemy's shipping, in the hope that many of their gun-

boats might be destroyed and that possibly injury
might be done to the castle and town, if the fire-ship
could be brought near enough. The ketch Intrepid
was chosen for the purpose. A compartment was built
in the hold just forward of the mainmast, in which
were placed one hundred barrels, or about fifteen
thousand pounds, of powder in bulk. From this led
a tube in which a train was laid connected with a fuse
calculated to burn fifteen minutes. This communicated with another room aft, which was filled with
splinters and other combustibles. When the vessel
had been brought into position, this was to be ignited,
and it was thought that the fire produced would keep
off boarders and that the crew would have time to
escape while the fuse was burning. On the deck just
over the powder were placed one hundred thirteen-
inch and fifty nine-inch shells, with a large quantity
of solid shot and kentledge. Captain Somers volunteered to take in the Intrepid and Lieutenant Wadsworth to accompany him. As usual there was no lack
of volunteers for this service, although the desperate
nature of the expedition was pointed out to them. Six
men were selected from the crew of the Constitution
and four from the Nautilus. Two of the fastest rowing
boats in the squadron were taken, — a six-oared boat
from the Constitution, and one of four oars from the
Siren, — in which the crew were to make their escape.
On the evening of September 4 there was a light
breeze from the east, and it was decided to go in.
Everything seemed favorable for the enterprise except
that three Tripolitan gunboats were seen near the
western entrance, by which they were to go in. The
ketch was convoyed as far as the rocks near the
entrance by the Argus, Vixen, and Nautilus, and these

vessels remained in the vicinity, so as to pick up the boats when they came out. It was between nine and ten o'clock when they parted company. Just before going in Lieutenant Joseph Israel of the Constitution went aboard the Intrepid, it is said to deliver a message from the commodore, and as he begged earnestly to be allowed to join the expedition, Somers consented.

It was a dark night and the Intrepid was soon lost to view, but Lieutenant Ridgely [1] of the Nautilus believed that he saw her with a night-glass up to the last moment, and that she was still advancing. As she entered the harbor she was seen by the Tripolitans and the batteries at once opened on her. Suddenly, at 9.47 P. M., [2] there was a blinding flash and a terrific explosion. The vessels outside plainly felt the concussion. The masts rose high in the air with sails and rigging on fire, with fragments of wreckage and many shells, some of which exploded. Cries of terror and drums beating to arms were heard in the town for a few minutes. The batteries ceased their fire. Then followed profound silence and darkness. The vessels hovered about the entrance until sunrise, keeping a sharp lookout for the boats, which never appeared.

It is certain that the explosion was premature, because there was no preceding blaze of the combustibles ; and it was also evident that the ketch had not had time to reach her destination. The exact manner of the explosion has always been a mystery. It may have been caused by one of the enemy's shot passing through the magazine, as was the case with gunboat No. 9 on August 7. Or it may have been an acci-

[1] See article by Ridgely, A Naval Reminiscence, in Naval Magazine, i, p. 172, March 1836.

[2] Preble Papers : Log of Constitution.

dent; some of the watchers said they saw a light pass rapidly across the deck of the ketch just before the catastrophe, and thought that possibly it was being carried to ignite the combustibles and that a spark found its way into the powder. Preble believed that the Tripolitans attempted to board the Intrepid from their gunboats, and that the magazine was fired by Somers rather than surrender to the enemy and allow them to get possession of the powder, of which they were in great need. In support of this theory Preble states that one of the largest Tripolitan gunboats was missing the next day, and that three others were seen to be shattered and drawn up on the beach. But this fact has been doubted, and an error in observation, at a little distance, would have been possible. Another theory was that so many of the crew were killed or disabled by the enemy's fire that escape became impossible and that the magazine was therefore intentionally exploded, rather than allow the vessel to be captured. It has always been believed that Somers and his companions were capable of this act of self-devotion, and it is known that they had expressed the determination not to allow the capture of themselves or the ketch.[1]

All of the thirteen bodies were recovered, two days later, by the Tripolitans. Two were found in the bottom of the ketch, which grounded on the rocks at the north side of the western entrance, one was in the six-oared boat, which drifted ashore to the westward, four were floating in the harbor, and six were picked up on the beach southeast of the town. All were so mangled as to make identification impossible. Captain Bainbridge saw six of the bodies. He believed that

[1] See statement of Stewart in Chautauquan, July, 1898, p. 414.

no damage whatever was done to the enemy by the explosion and no Tripolitan was injured. This view has become the most generally accepted one, and, if true, Preble must have been mistaken in supposing that any gunboats had been sunk or injured. On the other hand, Eaton, a few months later, met a Turk in Egypt who had been in Tripoli at the time of the explosion, and who affirmed that the Intrepid blew up "after having been boarded by two row galleys."[1] If the Intrepid had been boarded, many Tripolitans would have been blown up. If their bodies had been found and could have been distinguished from Americans, the fact might have been concealed by their countrymen, but the case is perhaps hardly supposable. However, Dr. Cowdery distinctly states in his journal that he saw fourteen bodies and heard of six others. He was able, as he thought, to pick out three of them as officers, although of course it was not known in Tripoli how many officers there were in the party, or how many in all. His opinion was based on the softness of their hands and a few fragments of clothing. There was a rumor that several showed wounds of grape-shot, but this is mentioned by neither Bainbridge nor Cowdery. The bodies were buried south of the town, the three supposed officers by themselves.[2]

This event and the mystery surrounding it cast a gloom over the squadron. Decatur in particular, having so recently lost his brother, was deeply affected. Somers had been his dearest friend from boyhood; they had been schoolmates in Philadelphia and entered the navy together in 1798. A monument to the memory of Somers, Caldwell, James Decatur, Wadsworth,

[1] Eaton, p. 287.   [2] See Heston's Absegami, pp. 213–217.

Israel, and Dorsey, erected by their fellow officers of the squadron, stands in the grounds of the Naval Academy at Annapolis. The total number of casualties in Preble's squadron, during its operations before Tripoli, was thirty killed and twenty-four wounded, of whom two died of their wounds.

September 5, preparations were made for another attack, but the weather became threatening; and as it was getting to be too late in the season for the safety of the gunboats and bomb-vessels, the commodore decided to dismantle them. Their guns, mortars, and ammunition were accordingly taken on board the Constitution and John Adams, and on the 7th the boats were sent to Syracuse, towed by the John Adams, Siren, Nautilus, Enterprise, and Scourge. The Constitution, Argus, and Vixen remained before Tripoli, blockading the port. The ammunition of the squadron had been so far expended that there was no more than enough for these three vessels.

At last, September 10, the frigates President, Commodore Barron, and Constellation, Captain Campbell, appeared, and Commodore Preble turned over the command of the squadron to his successor, with the customary ceremonies. On the 12th the President and Constitution captured two Greek ships, loaded with wheat, bound for Tripoli. The Constellation and Argus chased a third, which was also taken.[1] The first two of these prizes were sent to Malta under convoy of the Constitution, arriving September 17, after a stormy passage. Here Preble learned that the gunboats and bombs had arrived safely at Syracuse two days before. Those that had been borrowed were returned to the Neapolitan government.

[1] St. Pap. v, p. 164.

In his report to the secretary of the navy, after calling special attention to Decatur's high qualities, Preble says: "The other commanders merit the highest commendations for their prompt obedience to orders on all occasions and for the zeal, spirit, and judgment which they displayed in the several attacks on the enemy's shipping and batteries, as well as for the general good order and discipline, at all times observed on board their respective vessels. The officers of the squadron have conducted themselves in the most gallant and handsome manner; and the conduct of the different ships' companies has merited my warmest approbation, since I have had the honor to command them. It affords me much satisfaction to observe that we have neither had a duel nor a court-martial in the squadron since we left the United States. I most sincerely regret the loss of our gallant countrymen who have sacrificed their lives to the honor of the service, and that it has not been in my power, consistent with the interest and expectation of our country, to liberate Captain Bainbridge and the unfortunate officers and crew of the Philadelphia."

CHAPTER XIII

THE WINTER OF 1804-1805

FROM Malta Commodore Preble proceeded to Syracuse, September 22, in the Argus. The Constitution was undergoing repairs, and with the consent of Commodore Barron, Captain Decatur was now ordered to take command of her. Preble was for some time occupied in settling his accounts at Malta, Syracuse, Messina, and Palermo. October 29 he joined the John Adams, and proceeded to Naples early in December. He there tried to arrange for the loan or hire of another flotilla of mortar-vessels and gunboats for the next year's operations, but was unsuccessful. December 23 he sailed for home in the John Adams, Captain Chauncey, with James Lawrence as first lieutenant and ex-Consul O'Brien as passenger. They touched at Gibraltar and Tangier, and arrived at New York February 26, 1805.[1]

When Preble first received notice of his recall, in August, he feared that the cause of it might be misunderstood, and therefore sent copies of the secretary's letter of May 22 to his many friends in the Mediterranean. In reply he received many sympathetic letters from American consuls and others, regretting his departure and congratulating him upon his achievements in the war. Among the acquaintances he had made were several English officers, who had shown him great attention, and had done him many favors; es-

[1] Nav. Chron. p. 244; Amer. Hist. Rec. i, p. 57; Nat. Intell. Mar. 4, 1805.

pecially Captain Schomberg of the British navy, and Sir Alexander Ball, governor of Malta, who was also a naval man, having formerly been one of Nelson's captains. The governor wrote two or three very friendly letters. The war had excited the interest of the pope also, who declared that " the American commander, with a small force and in a short space of time, has done more for the cause of Christianity than the most powerful nations of Christendom have done for ages." [1]

Preble received a letter of regret November 4, signed by fifty-three of his officers, which was very gratifying to him. This letter and his reply show the warm feeling between the commodore and his subordinates.[2] His official report was sent to Congress February 20, 1805, with a message from the President, in which he says: "The energy and judgment displayed by this excellent officer, through the whole course of the service lately confided to him, and the zeal and bravery of his officers and men in the several enterprises executed by them, cannot fail to give high satisfaction to Congress and their country, of whom they have deserved well." [3] March 3, Congress voted the commodore a gold medal, swords to the officers who had distinguished themselves, and a month's extra pay to all petty officers, seamen, and marines. The medal was presented to Preble in May, 1806, and the men received their extra pay; but the President, embarrassed at being called upon to decide as to which officers had distinguished themselves, deferred action on the matter of swords. In 1812 the subject was brought up in Congress by Josiah Quincy. He was made

---

[1] Preble, ch. ix; Nav. Chron. pp. 246, 247.
[2] Nav. Chron. p. 242.   [3] Ibid. p. 220.

chairman of the committee to which it was referred, and had some correspondence with the secretary of the navy. The committee reported in favor of giving swords to all the officers. Being in the midst of war with England, however, more important business prevented further consideration.[1]

When he first arrived in the Mediterranean in 1803, Preble feared that his force was inadequate, and before the loss of the Philadelphia he wrote to the secretary of the navy urging that two or three additional vessels be sent out, and he repeated this recommendation at every opportunity.[2] It might have been better if the administration had not been so forcibly impressed with the idea that large reinforcements were necessary. At least, if two frigates, under the junior captains, had been sent promptly, so as to reach Tripoli in the spring of 1804, it would have been far better than the arrival of four at the end of the season. With the help of two additional frigates the operations before Tripoli in the summer of 1804 would very likely have resulted in bringing the pasha to terms, and in the release of the prisoners without ransom. If Preble's great efficiency had been fully appreciated at home, the importance of retaining him in the chief command would have been recognized as paramount, and would probably have suggested some way of reinforcing without superseding him.

The difficulties with which Preble was forced to contend would have overcome most men. Naval administration in the United States was still in its

[1] Nav. Chron. p. 248; Nav. Aff. i, pp. 281, 282, 291–293; Amer. Hist. Rec. i, pp. 58–60; Palmer, Hist. Register of U. S. (Phil. 1814), i, p. 88; Preble Papers: Preble to Sec. of Navy (June 17, 1806).

[2] Preble, ch. vii.

infancy, and the needs of the navy were little understood and excited little interest in Congress or among
the people. There was still, moreover, a widespread
prejudice against the service, especially in the domi-
nant political party. The difficulty of inducing Congress to make appropriations for the navy was such
that in order to carry on the Tripolitan war additional duties were laid on imports, and the money thus
raised was known as the Mediterranean Fund.[1] Robert Smith, the secretary, was a man of ability, energy,
and zeal, but the department was not thoroughly organized and could not be while it received such grudg-
ing support from Congress. There was great delay in
fitting out ships, the work was imperfectly done, and
they were sent to sea without a proper supply of
naval stores. The scarcity of all commodities in the
Mediterranean ports, due to the war between England
and France, made it necessary to send out from the
United States most of the supplies and provisions.
Those sent were of poor quality, and large quantities
of beef and pork were spoiled and had to be thrown
overboard. An insufficient amount of clothing was
sent, and there was much suffering from cold. An instance of the difficulty in providing stores is furnished
by the case of the ship Huntress, which occurred,
however, at a later date. The Huntress sailed for the
Mediterranean in May, 1805, with naval stores for
the squadron. She was provided with certificates from
the President and the British and French ministers,
but had none from the Spanish minister. June 1 she
was seized by a Spanish cruiser and a few days later
was recaptured by a British cruiser, and sent to Liver-

[1] Rep. Sen. Com. iv, p. 6.

pool.[1] The squadron was very far from being fully
manned, and the crews contained much poor material,
largely made up of foreigners, owing to the fact that
the government would not pay as high wages as merchantmen received; desertions were therefore common. There were other instances of faulty administration, which would not have occurred in a well-
organized department. The weather of 1804 was more
than usually severe and boisterous, adding greatly to
the difficulty of naval operations. All these things
increased to a large degree Preble's cares and per-
plexities, and his ability to rise above them distinguished him from commanders of ordinary capacity.[2]

In his negotiations with Tripoli, Preble was willing
to pay a fair price for the release of the unfortunate
captives, but absolutely refused to consider any payment for peace or tribute. He also refused to give an
amount for ransom which " would stimulate the avarice
of the other Barbary powers," and set a standard
likely to embarrass the United States and other
nations under similar circumstances in the future.
Colonel Lear authorized the offer of a much larger
sum, and the French consul, through whom negotiations were conducted, strongly urged it, but the commodore was firm in his determination not to yield.[3]
It would be a satisfaction to be able to record that
he refused to pay any ransom whatever.

Upon his arrival in the United States, Preble at
once set out for Washington. He reached the capital
March 4, 1805, the day of Jefferson's second inauguration, and was received by the President with great
distinction. He urged upon the government the need

[1] Claims, pp. 363, 364 ; Nat. Intell. Dec. 13, 1805, April 7, 1806.
[2] Preble, ch. vii.   [3] Ibid. ch. vi ; see above, pp. 164, 180, 182, 201.

of bomb-vessels and gunboats for use against Tripoli, of a larger and better class than could be obtained in the Mediterranean. Accordingly the equipment of nine gunboats was at once begun; these were seventy-one feet long, sloop-rigged, and carried two long thirty-two pounders, one at each end. Two bomb-vessels also were built, but as it became apparent that they could not be finished in time for the summer campaign, Preble was directed to procure two other vessels suitable for conversion into bombs. Thereupon he purchased in Boston two vessels of about one hundred tons each; they were fitted for the purpose, armed with a thirteen-inch mortar and two long nine-pounders each, and named Spitfire and Vengeance.[1]

Preble was received with enthusiasm wherever he went, and was honored during the remainder of his life; but this was for a brief period only. His health, which had long been declining, broke down completely, and he died August 25, 1807, at the age of forty-six.

Commodore Barron's squadron was organized in the spring of 1804. The John Adams, Captain Chauncey, sailed from Hampton Roads June 26, and after stopping at Gibraltar, Algiers, and Malta, arrived off Tripoli August 7, during the second assault on the town. The commodore's flagship, President, Captain Cox, and the Congress, Essex, and Constellation, Captains Rodgers, James Barron, and Campbell, sailed from the same port July 4 and arrived at Gibraltar August 12.[2] On board the flagship was William

[1] Nav. Chron. p. 244; Preble to Sec. of Navy: Preble Papers (April 9, June 24); Captains' Letters, i, no. 40, iii, no. 4 (April 25, Sept. 8).

[2] For the movements of Barron's squadron, see Nav. Chron. pp. 262-268; Cooper, ii, ch. vi; Eaton, pp. 268-274; Navy Dept. MSS.; Preble Papers; National Intelligencer.

Eaton, late consul at Tunis, who had been appointed navy agent for the Barbary States. Among the officers of the Constellation was Oliver H. Perry.

At Gibraltar Barron found letters from James Simpson, United States consul at Tangier, which intimated that the emperor of Morocco, not having seen an American man-of-war for several months, was beginning to regain his courage. He had asked for a passport for a ship with provisions for Tripoli, and was fitting out his cruisers. Barron wrote to Simpson that the blockade of Tripoli would not be raised for the emperor's vessel, and August 15 sent the Congress and Essex to Tangier. Their appearance doubtless had a salutary effect, and in two weeks, having examined the coast as far as Sallee, they returned to Gibraltar.[1] Captain Rodgers of the Congress, the senior officer, believing that the emperor would not go to extremities, proceeded up the Mediterranean, leaving Captain James Barron in the Essex at Gibraltar, with instructions to keep a watch on Morocco. The demonstrations of the emperor were probably made with the design of delaying American war vessels on their way to Tripoli, or of drawing others away from Tripoli.

Meanwhile Commodore Barron sailed from Gibraltar with the President and the Constellation August 16, arrived at Malta September 5, and off Tripoli on the 10th, where he found the Constitution, Argus, and Vixen, as already related. Three vessels were soon taken[2] for violation of the blockade, two of which were sent to Malta with the Constitution on the 14th, and the third with the Argus the next day. A

[1] Rodgers to Sec. of Navy, Nat. Intell. Oct. 29, 1804.
[2] See above, p. 211.

few days later the Congress arrived off Tripoli from Gibraltar by way of Algiers, where Consul Lear had joined her. On the 23d the President, with Lear on board, sailed for Syracuse, where she arrived four days later. The Vixen also left the blockade about this time, and soon afterwards her rig was altered from schooner to brig; Captain Smith had previously obtained Commodore Preble's permission to make this change.

There were now on blockade the Congress and Constellation, with Captain Rodgers the senior officer present. A small xebec was captured and held for examination. Four small coasting vessels laden with wheat were discovered one day creeping along shore from the westward. Two of them were driven ashore, and Captain Rodgers sent in boats after them, but they were supported by troops on the beach and escaped. Rodgers made a night reconnoissance in a boat along shore close to the batteries, took soundings and went inside the rocks, where he found the enemy's gunboats hauled up. October 25, the Nautilus having arrived, Rodgers sailed for Malta in the Congress, which needed repairs. A little later the Argus joined the blockaders, but soon returned to Syracuse on account of smallpox on board.

The Essex arrived at Malta from Gibraltar October 29, and her place in the Straits was taken by the Siren. Early in November most of the vessels not on blockade duty were at Syracuse, where Commodore Barron was sick on shore. On the 6th Rodgers took command of the Constitution and Decatur of the Congress. About the middle of November the President, Captain Cox, joined the blockade, and the Argus sailed for Egypt with Eaton. On the 30th the Scourge,

Lieutenant Izard, sailed for the United States with dispatches.

November 27 the Constitution, Captain Rodgers, sailed for Lisbon in order to recruit her crew, as it was believed that seamen could be procured there; she was also in need of new sails and other supplies. She arrived December 28, having touched at Gibraltar and Tangier, and remained until February 5, 1805. Having nearly filled her complement, she returned to Tangier, and there found the Siren. Leaving instructions with Captain Stewart to keep a watch on Morocco, Captain Rodgers returned to Malta February 25. He next proceeded off Tripoli, where he found the Constellation and Vixen. The blockade had been kept up by different vessels all winter and was continued during the spring. Rodgers soon returned to Malta. Commodore Barron was now there, and his condition was becoming serious. March 19 Captain Rodgers submitted to him a suggestion that a blockading force of two or three vessels should be constantly kept before Tripoli, others being held in readiness to relieve them at any time. In that way all the vessels would be ready for service as soon as conditions favored an attack on the town. He also recommended that other ports, such as Tunis, Bengazi, and Derne, should be closely watched, in order to intercept the enemy's cruisers attempting to enter them.

During the winter or early spring, the squadron was reinforced by the purchase of two small vessels. One of these was bought at Malta, converted into a sloop, armed with ten guns, and named Hornet. The other was a brig mounting eight guns called the Franklin; and from the fact that she had once been owned by the bey of Tunis, she was undoubtedly the same brig Franklin of Philadelphia which had been captured by the Tripolitans in 1802 and subsequently sold to the commercial agent of the bey.[1]

The views of President Jefferson on Barbary affairs at this time are expressed in a letter to Judge Tyler, dated March 29, 1805, in which he says: " The war with Tripoli stands on two grounds of fact. 1st. It is made known to us by our agents with the three other Barbary States, that they only wait to see the event of this, to shape their conduct accordingly. If the war is ended by additional tribute, they mean to offer us the same alternative. 2nd. If peace was made, we should still, and shall ever, be obliged to keep a frigate in the Mediterranean to overawe rupture, or we must abandon that market. . . . If in the course of the summer they cannot produce peace, we shall recall our force, except one frigate and two small vessels, which will keep up a perpetual blockade. Such a blockade will cost us no more than a state of peace, and will save us from increased tributes and the disgrace attached to them. There is reason to believe the example we have set begins already to work on the dispositions of the powers of Europe to emancipate themselves from that degrading yoke. Should we produce such a revolution there, we shall be amply rewarded for what we have done." [2]

The Constitution sailed again for Tripoli early in April, and was joined by the President. The Constellation and Vixen were then sent back to Malta for supplies. April 24, Rodgers captured a Tunisian xebec of eight guns, bound into Tripoli with two Neapolitan

[1] Letter Book (1799–1807), p. 177: Sec. of Navy to Campbell (Sept. 4, 1806); Eaton, p. 392; see above, p. 112.

[2] Jefferson, iv, p. 574.

ships she had taken. All three vessels were sent to
Malta under convoy of the President, which then
returned and rejoined the Constitution off Tripoli.

Commodore Barron's health at last became so far
impaired as to make it impossible for him longer to
manage the affairs of the squadron. Accordingly, on
May 22, he turned the command over to Captain
Rodgers. His letter conveying this intelligence he
sent to Rodgers by the Essex. This ship sailed for
Tripoli at once, having on board Colonel Lear, who had
spent the winter with Commodore Barron at Malta, so
as to be on hand when the time should come for peace
negotiations. The Essex arrived off Tripoli May 26,
and delivered Commodore Barron's letter on board
the Constitution. Captain Rodgers at once assumed
command of the squadron. On the 29th, by his order,
Captain James Barron of the Essex and Captain
George Cox of the President exchanged ships, Barron's
rank entitling him to the larger of the two frigates.

Commodore Rodgers's squadron was much the largest
and most powerful that had ever been organized under
the American flag, although it was never assembled
at any one place and the new mortar-vessels and gunboats had not yet arrived from the United States.
The force at this time in the Mediterranean consisted
of the frigates Constitution, 44, flagship of Commodore
Rodgers, of which Lieutenant David Porter became
acting captain very soon afterwards, President, 44,
Captain James Barron, Constellation, 36, Captain
Campbell, Congress, 36, Captain Decatur, and Essex,
32, Captain Cox; the brigs Siren, 16, Captain Stewart,
Argus, 16, Captain Hull, Vixen, 12, Captain Smith,
and Franklin, 8; the schooners Nautilus, 12, Captain
Dent, and Enterprise, 12, Captain Robinson, and the

sloop Hornet, 10, Lieutenant Samuel Evans. Dent and Robinson had been promoted to the grade of master commandant in September, 1804. There were also the two gunboats captured at Tripoli, August 3, 1804. The frigate John Adams, 28, which had taken Commodore Preble home, was now on her way back to the Mediterranean, under the command of Captain John Shaw.[1] The bomb-vessels Vengeance and Spitfire, under Lieutenants William Lewis and Daniel McNeill, Jr., sailed from Boston June 19 and 23.[2] The nine gunboats which had been equipped especially for this service by the advice of Commodore Preble, sailed from different ports about the middle of May; three of them sailed from New York in company with the John Adams. No. 2 carried one thirty-two pounder, No. 3, two twenty-four pounders, and all the others two thirty-two pounders each; these were all long guns and were stowed below during the passage across the Atlantic.[3] Eight of them had reached Gibraltar safely by the middle of June and arrived at Syracuse early in July, within forty-eight hours of each other.

Gunboat No. 7, Lieutenant Peter S. Ogilvie, sailed from New York May 14. Six days out she sprung her mast, returned to port, sailed again, and was never heard of afterwards.[4] No. 8 had a stormy passage, but her commander, Lieutenant Nathaniel Harraden, reported to Commodore Preble that she behaved well and he considered her "perfectly safe to cross the Atlantic."[5] No. 3, Lieutenant Joseph Maxwell, was

[1] Amer. Nav. Off. i, p. 141 ; Nat. Intell. Aug. 28, 1805.

[2] Preble Papers : Preble to Sec. of Navy (June 24, 1805).

[3] Emmons, p. 22 ; St. Pap. v, p. 435.

[4] Officers' Letters, i, no. 126 : Ogilvie to Sec. of Navy (May 30, 1805) ; also Nat. Intell. June 7, 1805.

[5] Nat. Intell. July 26, 1805.

JOHN RODGERS

seized by Spanish gunboats off Gibraltar and detained
for a short time.[1] No. 6 was held up off Cadiz by a
British squadron, and three of her crew were impressed,
against the protest of her commander, Lieutenant
James Lawrence.[2] July 12, Commodore Rodgers
published a general order setting forth this insult
to the American flag and directing his commanding
officers, under similar circumstances in the future,
after having resisted to the utmost of their power,
to strike the flag, go aboard the enemy's vessel, deliver
their swords, and insist upon remaining as prisoners
of war, unless put back on their own vessels by actual
force.[3] The remaining gunboats from the United
States, No. 2, No. 4, No. 5, No. 9, and No. 10, were
commanded by Lieutenants Ralph Izard, John Henley, Alexander Harrison, Samuel Elbert, and Seth
Cartee; their voyage across the ocean was uneventful.

The Enterprise spent several months in the Adri-
atic, where Captain Robinson purchased four gunboats
and two trabaccoloes, or small coasting vessels, which
assisted in towing the gunboats, and were apparently
to be themselves converted into gunboats, or possibly
into mortar-boats. The Enterprise sailed from Ancona
on the 24th of June with these six small vessels in
company, and after a stormy passage of over two
weeks arrived at Syracuse. One of the gunboats was
lost on the way, and was still missing July 12, when

[1] Captains' Letters, ii: Rodgers to Sec. of Navy (Aug. 21, 1805);
Nat. Intell. Aug. 12, Dec. 13, 1805; St. Pap. v, p. 66.

[2] Officers' Letters, i, nos. 156, 157: Lawrence to Rodgers (July 11,
1805), to Sec. of Navy (Aug. 30, 1805); Captains' Letters, ii: Rodgers
to Sec. of Navy (Aug. 21, 1805); Gleaves, Life of Lawrence (New
York, 1904), p. 59.

[3] Nav. Chron. p. 271.

Robinson made his report, but appears to have turned up later.[1]

It is thus evident that Commodore Rodgers might have brought against Tripoli by the end of July, 1805, if peace had not been concluded before that time, a force consisting of six frigates, four brigs, two schooners, one sloop, two bomb-vessels, and sixteen gunboats.

[1] Commanders' Letters, i, no. 28 : Robinson to Rodgers; Eaton, p. 392.

CHAPTER XIV

THE CAPTURE OF DERNE

SINCE his return home in the spring of 1803, ex-Consul Eaton had spent much time in Washington, and had succeeded in exciting a moderate amount of interest in his project to coöperate with Hamet Karamanli, the exiled pasha of Tripoli. He had been appointed navy agent May 26, 1804, and placed under the orders of Commodore Barron. To the latter the secretary of the navy wrote, June 6, 1804: "With respect to the ex-pasha of Tripoli, we have no objection to your availing yourself of his coöperation with you against Tripoli, if you shall, upon a full view of the subject, after your arrival upon the station, consider his coöperation expedient. The subject is committed entirely to your discretion. In such an event you will, it is believed, find Mr. Eaton extremely useful to you." [1]

It has been mentioned [2] that Hamet made his residence at Derne in the fall of 1802. About a year later, placing himself at the head of an army of Arabs, he took up arms against his brother, the pasha of Tripoli, whose forces he met in the field. He gained some advantages; but later, either on account of reverses or for lack of supplies, he was obliged to fall back, and early in 1804 withdrew to Egypt, leaving Derne in the hands of his enemies. Information of

[1] St. Pap. v, pp. 163, 164; Eaton, p. 368.
[2] See above, p. 123.

this had reached Washington some time before the fourth squadron sailed, and it was decided to withhold, at least temporarily, certain military supplies and money that it had been intended to send out to him.[1] But Commodore Barron was given the discretion indicated in the instructions quoted above.

September 15, 1804, having given Captain Hull of the Argus orders for a cruise, the commodore gave him also the following verbal orders in the presence of Eaton, and attested by Hull and Eaton: "The written orders I here hand you, to proceed to the port of Alexandria or Smyrna for convoying to Malta any vessels you may find there, are intended to disguise the real object of your expedition, which is to proceed with Mr. Eaton to Alexandria in search of Hamet Pasha, the rival brother and legitimate sovereign of the reigning Pasha of Tripoli; and to convey him and his suite to Derne or such other place on the coast as may be determined the most proper for coöperating with the naval force under my command, against the common enemy; or, if more agreeable to him, to bring him to me before Tripoli. Should Hamet Pasha not be found at Alexandria, you have the discretion to proceed to any other place for him, where the safety of your ship can be, in your opinion, relied upon. The Pasha may be assured of the support of my squadron at Bengazi or Derne, where you are at liberty to put in, if required, and if it can be done without too great risk. And you may assure him also, that I will take the most effectual measures, with the forces under my command, for coöperating with him against the usurper, his brother, and for reëstablishing him in the regency of Tripoli. Arrangements to this effect are

[1] Eaton, p. 265.

confided to the discretion with which Mr. Eaton is vested by the Government." [1]

The Argus sailed from Malta November 17, and arrived at Alexandria on the 27th.[2] From this point Eaton proceeded to Rosetta, at the mouth of the Nile. Letters from Sir Alexander Ball procured him a cordial reception and great assistance from English officials in Egypt, especially Major Misset, the British minister in Cairo, who was then at Rosetta. December 4, Eaton began the ascent of the Nile with a party including Lieutenant Presley N. O'Bannon of the marine corps, Midshipmen George Mann and Eli E. Danielson, the latter Eaton's stepson, Captain Vincent, secretary to Major Misset, Dr. Francisco Mendrici, whom Eaton met at Rosetta and had previously known in Tunis, and others, besides servants; eighteen in all. They embarked in two armed boats and arrived at Cairo on the 8th. A war was then in progress between the Mamelukes and the Ottoman government, and traveling was somewhat dangerous on account of bands of wild Arabs, who terrorized the country. The Americans represented themselves as officers traveling on leave of absence from the squadron during the winter's suspension of operations.

At Cairo Eaton found the secretary of state and two ex-governors of Hamet Pasha, " destitute of everything but resentment, for even hope had abandoned them." From them he learned that Hamet with a few Tripolitans and Arabs, after many vicissitudes, had

[1] St. Pap. v, p. 165; For. Rel. ii, p. 703; Eaton, p. 367.

[2] For the expedition to Derne, see Eaton, pp. 270–393, 422–424; Felton, ch. x, xi; St. Pap. v, pp. 163–175; For. Rel. ii, pp. 702–706; Nav. Chron. pp. 272–278; also Comdrs.' Letters, i, no. 26, Hull to Barron (Dec. 1804); letter of Mid. Peck in Nat. Intell. Oct. 9, 1805.

joined the rebellious Mamelukes, who at that time
were besieged at Minieh, one hundred and fifty miles
or more up the Nile from Cairo. The prospect of getting into communication with him seemed doubtful.

Eaton obtained an audience with the viceroy and
frankly explained the object of his visit. With the
aid of Dr. Mendrici, who had influence at court, he
succeeded in inducing the viceroy to grant a letter of
amnesty for Hamet and a passport through the Turkish lines. The chief difficulty then seemed to be to
get him away from the Mamelukes, who, it was feared,
would not allow him to leave them. Couriers were sent
by the viceroy in search of the exiled pasha, with
copies of these letters. Eaton sent on the same errand
a Tyrolese colonel of engineers named Johann Leitensdorfer, whom he met at Cairo, and other messengers
as well. Hamet was requested to come to Rosetta, and
Eaton himself proceeded to that place to meet him,
but after waiting a few days, went to Alexandria,
where he found a letter from Hamet appointing a
rendezvous on the edge of the desert a hundred and
ninety miles inland. Although it was believed that
the journey would be full of danger, on account of
the disturbed condition of the country, Eaton determined to make the attempt. He left Alexandria January 22, 1805, with Lieutenant Blake and Midshipman Mann of the Argus and an escort of twenty-three
men. On the evening of the next day, having traveled
seventy miles or more, they were arrested at Daman-
hur by a body of Turkish troops. The commander of
this post Eaton succeeded in conciliating by tact and
flattery, with the aid of a gratuity, and he was prevailed upon to send in search of Hamet an Arab chief,
who engaged to produce him within ten days. This

was done. Hamet finally appeared, and the party returned to the coast.

Eaton's plan had been to embark with Hamet on the Argus and proceed to a point near Derne where they would meet his troops. But new difficulties now arose through the intrigues of the French consul at Alexandria, who represented the American officers to be British spies, and persuaded the Turkish admiral and the governor of Alexandria not to permit the party to embark. It was therefore decided to march to Derne overland. Although the viceroy sent orders to the governor to allow the embarkation, it was still thought best to go by land, chiefly because it was feared that Hamet's army would evaporate in his absence. He therefore formed his camp some distance to the west of Alexandria. Arrangements were made with Captain Hull to meet the expedition at the Bay of Bomba with supplies and reinforcements. The Argus then sailed for Malta with Hamet's secretary as passenger bearing a letter to the commodore, and likewise with a letter from Eaton, dated February 14, requesting two additional small vessels and a bomb-ketch, two brass field-pieces, one hundred stands of arms, one hundred marines, and ten thousand dollars.[1]

February 23, Eaton entered into a convention with Hamet in which it was provided that " the government of the United States shall use their utmost exertions so far as comports with their own honor and interest, their subsisting treaties and the acknowledged law of nations, to reëstablish the said Hamet Pasha in the possession of his sovereignty of Tripoli." The expense incurred by the United States was to be repaid by Hamet out of the tribute derived from certain other

[1] St. Pap. v, pp. 169, 407.

nations. It was also provided that Eaton "shall be recognized as general and commander-in-chief of the land forces" operating against the usurping pasha.[1] Eaton undoubtedly exceeded his authority in committing his government to this compact.

March 2 the provisions of the party were seized and a guard sent to arrest Hamet, who was with difficulty restrained from fleeing to the desert. The trouble was found to be due to " the influence of the supervisor of the revenue, who had not yet been bought," and was soon arranged by the British consul. A few days later they marched to the Arab's Tower, forty miles west of Alexandria. Here the international army was assembled and organized with General William Eaton, commander-in-chief, Colonel Leitensdorfer, adjutant, an English volunteer named Farquhar, and a medical officer, possibly Mendrici, but this is not clearly stated in Eaton's journal ; nine Americans, including Lieutenant O'Bannon, Midshipman Pascal P. Peck, and a non-commissioned officer and six private marines; twenty-five cannoniers of various nationalities, with three officers ; thirty-eight Greeks, with two officers ; Hamet and his suite of ninety men ; a party of Arabian cavalry under Sheik el Tahib and another chief ; a number of footmen and camel-drivers ; altogether about four hundred men, and a caravan of one hundred and seven camels and a few asses. Eaton believed that he could easily have raised an army of twenty or thirty thousand Arabs and Moors, if he had had the means of arming and subsisting them.

On March 8 the march was begun across the Lybian Desert to Derne, a distance of between five and six hundred miles. For the greater part of the way the

[1] Appendix II.

route lay within sight of the sea. Water was generally
obtained from natural basins worn in the rocks by
the streams during the wet season, and filled with
rain-water; but there was often great scarcity of
water and suffering for want of it. An advance of
fifteen miles was made the first day, and then on the
following morning the owners and drivers of the
camels became mutinous and demanded advance pay.
In this they were encouraged by Sheik el Tahib, one
of the Arab chiefs, who made trouble during the
whole march. This difficulty caused a delay of a day
and a half. Hamet was irresolute and seemed to have
no influence with the Arabs. At last Eaton, finding
argument fruitless, assembled the Christians "and
feinted a countermarch, threatening to abandon the expedition." This had the effect of checking the mutiny
and the march was resumed. On the 13th a courier
from Derne appeared and announced to Hamet that
the province was preparing to support him. This
news caused rejoicing and a discharge of firearms,
which alarmed the Arabs in the rear, who thought
an attack was being made. They thereupon attempted
to disarm and massacre the Christians escorting the
caravan, but were restrained by one of their more
prudent chiefs.

March 16 and 17, there was a cold rain-storm, and
the Arabs again became mutinous. On the 18th, having advanced about one hundred and fifty miles,
Eaton learned that the caravan had been freighted by
Hamet for this distance only. The owners finally promised to proceed two days farther, upon being paid.
This took nearly all the money Eaton had, and when
they had received it, all deserted, part the first night
and part the second, setting out on their return to

Egypt. Sheik el Tahib and other chiefs now refused to proceed until news should be brought from Bomba that the United States vessels were there, and proposed to send a runner to ascertain the fact. Eaton ordered their rations stopped. These complications consumed three days. The Arabs finally yielded, about half the caravan was induced to return, and the march was resumed.

March 22, they arrived at a great plain, bordering upon the sea, inhabited by thousands of wild Arabs who had never before seen Christians or tasted bread. They had vast herds of camels, horses, and cattle, and countless sheep and goats. Hamet was here reinforced by eighty mounted warriors, and a caravan of ninety camels was freighted; and later another force of Arabs, including one hundred and fifty warriors, with their families, joined the expedition. On the 26th a courier announced that a large force, sent by Yusuf Pasha, was marching from Tripoli to Derne. This caused another panic, Hamet hesitated and wavered, the camel-drivers fled with the caravan, and Sheik el Tahib deserted with part of his tribe and a large number of other Arabs. Hamet begged Eaton to offer inducements for the sheik to return. This Eaton refused to do and was glad to be rid of him, but he soon came back of his own accord. On the 28th Hamet's slender stock of resolution seemed to have oozed away completely, and he decided to abandon the enterprise and return to Egypt. Eaton kept on with the baggage, and in two hours Hamet followed him. That evening all the Arabs that had joined a few days before deserted, having been discouraged by Sheik el Tahib. An officer was sent back after them and returned with them the following afternoon.

The next complication was a quarrel between Sheik el Tahib and another sheik, which ended in the latter's deserting with many others whom it was important to retain on account of their influence with Arabs near Derne. Hamet went back to induce them, if possible, to return. " From Alexandria to this place we have experienced continual altercations, contentions and delays among the Arabs. They have no sense of patriotism, truth nor honor ; and no attachment where they have no prospect of gain, except to their religion, to which they are enthusiasts. Poverty makes them thieves and practice renders them adroit in stealing. The instant the eye of vigilance is turned from an object on which they have fixed a desire, it is no more to be found. Arms, ammunition and provisions most engage their furtive speculations, but sundry of our people have been robbed of their clothes and other articles. With all their depravity of morals they possess a savage independence of soul, an incorrigible obstinacy to discipline, a sacred adherence to the laws of hospitality and a scrupulous pertinacity to their religious faith and ceremonies." [1] After an absence of four days, Hamet returned with the sheiks who had deserted. Meanwhile there had been more trouble with Sheik el Tahib, who demanded an increased ration. He became insolent, and Eaton threatened him with death if he attempted to incite a mutiny. He rode off with two other chiefs, but a few hours later returned very penitent and took an oath to remain faithful thereafter.

On the evening of April 2, Eaton held a meeting of Hamet and all the sheiks in his tent, and endeavored to impress upon them the importance of union and

[1] Eaton, p. 312.

perseverance, and they all "gave pledges of faith and honor." The force now consisted of between six and seven hundred fighting men, who with camel-drivers and camp-followers, including women and children, made a total of about twelve hundred. The next morning the march was resumed, but after advancing only ten miles the Arabs positively refused to go farther until a caravan had been sent to an oasis five days' journey inland for a supply of dates. Eaton finally agreed to this on condition that they should proceed the next day, being met at Bomba by the detachment sent after the dates. During the few days following there was much suffering for lack of water, but a good supply was found on the 8th.

On this day, also, occurred the most serious commotion yet experienced. Although there was only a six days' supply of rice and no other food, Hamet insisted upon encamping and sending a courier to Bomba to look for the American ships. Eaton stopped the Arabs' rations. They prevailed upon Hamet to return to Egypt and made a move to seize provisions. Eaton assembled the Christians and formed a line to resist this attempt. After facing each other for an hour the Arabs dispersed. "Supposing the tumult tranquilized, I ordered the troops to pass the manual exercise, according to our daily practice. In an instant the Arabs took an alarm, remounted and exclaimed: 'The Christians are preparing to fire on us.' The Pasha mounted and put himself at their head, apparently impressed with the same apprehension. A body of about two hundred advanced in full charge upon our people, who stood their ground motionless. The enemy withdrew at a small distance, singled out the officers and with deliberate aim cried ' *fire!* ' Some of the Pasha's officers exclaimed 'for God's sake do not fire. The Christians are our friends.' . . . I advanced towards the Pasha and cautioned him against giving countenance to a desperate act. At once a column of muskets were aimed at my breast. The Pasha was distracted. A universal clamor drowned my voice. I waved my hand as a signal for attention. At this critical moment some of the Pasha's officers and sundry Arab chiefs rode between us with drawn sabres and repelled the mutineers." [1] Hamet repented of his rashness, ordered the Arabs to disperse, called Eaton his friend and protector, and promised to take up the march if rations were issued. This was done, and the next morning they moved forward.

By April 10 there was "nothing but rice and water for subsistence and that at half rations" for three days. No news from Bomba. Hamet was beginning to entertain the idea that he was being used by the Americans merely "for the purpose of obtaining a peace with his brother," a suspicion that proved to be not wholly unreasonable. A mutiny was organized among the cannoniers, of which Eaton was secretly informed; they were to insist on a full ration. The situation seemed critical, and Eaton took O'Bannon into his confidence. Early in the evening, however, before any outbreak took place, a courier arrived from Bomba with news that the ships had been sighted. Confidence was now restored, and nothing more was heard of the mutiny. The last of the rice was issued on the 12th. The next day Hamet had one of his camels killed, and exchanged another for sheep with the Arabs; this gave the troops one full ration. For the next two days they subsisted on roots and herbs.

[1] Eaton, pp. 323, 324.

On the afternoon of the 15th they reached Bomba, but found there no trace of a human being and not a drop of water; moreover, not a vessel was in sight. The Arabs now became mutinous and abusive. Eaton took the Christians upon a mountain, where they built fires and kept them burning all night.

The next morning at eight o'clock, just as the Arabs were preparing to leave in disgust, a sail was sighted, which proved to be the Argus; she had seen the smoke of the fires. Eaton went aboard at noon. He found a letter from the commodore dated March 22, 1805,[1] informing him that stores and provisions were sent and seven thousand dollars in specie, but that no marines could be spared. Captain Hull also brought the commodore's reply to Hamet's letter.[2] The camp was moved around the bay to a cistern of water, and in the afternoon provisions were sent ashore. Either here or later, at Derne, Midshipman Mann came ashore and rejoined Eaton. April 17, the Hornet arrived with abundance of provisions. They remained in camp recuperating until the 23d, when they resumed the march with a sufficient supply of provisions to carry them to Derne, a distance of about sixty miles. The next day another courier arrived, with the news that an army from Tripoli was rapidly approaching Derne and would probably reach the place first. The Arabs were again seized with alarm and became mutinous. Sheik el Tahib, at the head of the cavalry, began a retreat. Hamet, as usual, was irresolute and despondent. After much persuasion and a promise of money, the sheiks were induced to advance, and on the afternoon of the 25th they encamped on a height overlooking Derne.

[1] St. Pap. v, p. 175; Eaton, p. 368.   [2] St. Pap. v, p. 408.

The town was reconnoitred, and information was also obtained from a number of sheiks who came out in the evening to meet Hamet and assured him that two of the three departments into which the city was divided were loyal to him. The third department, situated along the water front and containing a third of the inhabitants, was devoted to the interest of his brother Yusuf. This department was, however, the strongest in position and in its defenses, which consisted of a water battery of eight nine-pounders on the northeast, breastworks, and walls of old houses on the southeast, and a ten-inch howitzer on the terrace of the bey's palace; the walls of the houses were also pierced with loopholes for musketry. It was likewise learned that the bey had eight hundred fighting men, and that the Tripolitan army was near at hand. On the 26th Eaton sent in a flag of truce with a letter to the bey offering terms. His reply was: " My head or yours." Smoke signals were made, and in the afternoon the Nautilus appeared. The next morning the Argus and Hornet hove in sight. The Nautilus and Hornet came close in, and sent a boat ashore with two field-pieces. One of these was landed, but owing to the great difficulty and delay of hauling it up the steep and rocky precipice that bordered the bay, the other was left behind, as Eaton was very anxious to attack without any loss of time.

Eaton at once set about making his dispositions, and the attack was made that day, April 27, 1805. The enemy began by firing on the ships. The Hornet, Lieutenant Evans, anchored within a hundred yards of the water battery and opened fire. The Argus, Captain Hull, and Nautilus, Captain Dent, anchored about half a mile from shore, to the eastward of the

Hornet, and opened on the town and battery. The breastworks and a ravine at the southeast part of the town were held by a considerable force of the enemy, and opposite this point, on an elevation, were posted the squad of marines, twenty-four cannoniers with the field-piece, and thirty-six Greeks, all under the immediate command of Lieutenant O'Bannon; also a few Arabs on foot. Hamet occupied an old castle south-southwest of the town, with the Arabian cavalry drawn up in his rear. By two o'clock the action had become general, and forty-five minutes later the battery was silenced by the fire from the ships, and most of the enemy in that quarter being driven out reinforced the party opposed to the Christian land forces. At this point the enemy's musketry fire was very hot. In the excitement the rammer of the field-piece was shot away and its fire in consequence slackened. Eaton saw that his little force of undisciplined troops was falling into confusion, and as the only hope of restoring confidence, he ordered a charge. The enemy fled from their defenses, firing from behind trees and houses as they retreated. At this moment Eaton was shot through the left wrist by a musket ball. O'Bannon and Mann, with the marines, Greeks, and as many of the cannoniers as could be spared from the field-piece, pushed on towards the battery under a heavy fire from the houses. The way was cleared for them along the beach by the ships' guns. The battery was soon captured and the American flag was planted upon its walls. The guns, which were found ready loaded and primed, were turned on the town, and with the help of the ships' fire the enemy were soon dislodged from their houses. The bey fled from his palace and sought refuge in a mosque, and Hamet took possession of the deserted residence. The Arabian cavalry flanked the flying enemy, and a little after four o'clock the whole town was in the hands of the assailants. The ships' boats were sent ashore with ammunition for the battery, and took off the wounded. One marine was killed and two wounded, one of them mortally; eleven others were wounded, including Eaton and several Greeks. Practically all the fighting on this occasion was done by the Christians under Eaton's command, assisted by the ships' batteries.[1]

May 1, the Hornet sailed with dispatches for Commodore Barron. The bey of Derne left the mosque where he had taken refuge and sought asylum in the harem of an aged sheik, who, although a partisan of Hamet, could not be induced to break the laws of hospitality by giving him up. The town was now fortified against the Tripolitan army, which was approaching. The enemy advanced slowly, and on the 8th occupied the ground held by Eaton's forces before the capture. They spent several days in attempts to corrupt the inhabitants of the town, who were vacillating between the two parties, fearing that if they adhered to Hamet they would be slaughtered in case of his defeat. The late bey intrigued actively from his sanctuary, attempting to incite a counter-revolution in the town. At the head of fifty Christians Eaton proposed to enter the house of the old sheik and seize the bey. This course, however, was offensive to the Arabs, and Hamet begged that action be deferred until the next day. That night, May 12, the bey escaped to the Tripolitan camp.

Eaton believed that the enemy before Derne would

disperse, but they displayed more resolution than he gave them credit for. On the 13th, apparently encouraged by the bey's tales of disaffection towards Hamet, they made an attack on the town which fell only a little short of being successful. In the morning they appeared on the heights back of the town to the number of about twelve hundred, including Tripolitans, Arabs, and fugitives from Derne. After reconnoitring, they attacked an outpost about a mile from the town, consisting of one hundred of Hamet's cavalry, who held their ground firmly until overcome by numbers, when they were forced to give way. They retreated into the town, followed by the Tripolitans, who pursued as far as the bey's palace, now occupied by Hamet. Although exposed to the fire of the Argus and Nautilus, as well as of the battery and small arms from the houses, they made a vigorous attack on the palace, determined, if possible, to seize the person of the pasha. Their success seemed imminent, and Eaton began to fear that the day was lost. His little force of Christians was too weak for a sortie from the battery, and he turned the guns upon the town. A fortunate shot from a nine-pounder killed two of the enemy's mounted men. Immediately the undisciplined rabble beat a disorderly retreat, pursued by Hamet's cavalry and harassed by the fire from the ships. On this day Hamet's people surprised Eaton by an exhibition of courage and firmness of which their previous behavior had given him no reason to believe them capable. From deserters it was learned that the enemy had lost twenty-eight killed and fifty wounded, eleven of them mortally. Hamet lost twelve or fourteen killed and wounded.

The Tripolitans fortified their camp, about three

miles distant, and made preparations for another attack, but their leaders could not induce the Arabs to join in it. Eaton had the same difficulty. He wished to attack the enemy's camp, but Hamet and his people could not be prevailed upon to make the attempt. Eaton was beginning to fear a dearth of provisions, as the enemy cut off all supplies from the country. The Nautilus sailed May 18 with dispatches, leaving the Argus alone before Derne. Several times the enemy seemed about to attack, but they could never persuade the Arabs to expose themselves again to the fire of the Christians; artillery they could not face. Eaton believed that if he had had money he could have bought a wholesale defection of these allies of the Tripolitans. "We want nothing but cash to break up our enemy's camp without firing another shot." On the 28th the enemy sent a detachment of fifty or sixty, supported by cavalry, on a foraging expedition; they descended a ravine and attacked a party of Arabs, but were driven back. June 1, the Hornet returned with dispatches from the commodore, dated May 19,[1] announcing that peace negotiations were about to be entered upon, and that Derne must probably soon be evacuated. June 10, the enemy, who had been largely reinforced by Arabs, made another attack and were firmly resisted by Hamet's cavalry. The engagement which ensued lasted four hours. The Argus was occasionally able to use her long twelve-pounders when the enemy in their movements emerged from the hills and ridges, and one of Eaton's field-pieces also gave some assistance. The Tripolitans were finally repulsed with a loss, according to deserters, of forty or fifty killed, and seventy wounded.

[1] St. Pap. v, p. 191; Eaton, p. 371.

Hamet lost between fifty and sixty killed and wounded. O'Bannon wished to lead out the Christians and take an active part in the fight, but Eaton was unwilling to leave the defenses unmanned, and, moreover, doubted if offensive operations would be justifiable in view of the peace negotiations supposed to be in progress.

June 11, the Constellation, Captain Campbell, arrived with orders from Commodore Rodgers, dated June 5,[1] to evacuate Derne immediately, and announcing that peace had been concluded. It now became necessary to embark on the Constellation all the Christians, together with Hamet and his suite. This must be done secretly, moreover, as it was feared that the populace and the Arabs, enraged at being deserted, would attempt to revenge themselves by a massacre of those about to depart. Eaton was filled with disappointment and mortification at this ignominious ending of the expedition which he had hoped would result in the capture of Tripoli. But he had now no choice but to yield to necessity. To divert the attention of the people, preparations for an attack on the enemy were made June 12. In the evening patrols of marines were placed as usual to prevent communication between the town and the battery. The Constellation's boats came ashore and first took off the cannoniers and Greeks, with the field-pieces and the ten-inch howitzer captured April 27. Then Hamet and his suite were embarked, and next the American officers and marines. Lastly Eaton himself put off in a small boat, and had barely got clear " when the shore, our camp and the battery were crowded with the distracted soldiery and populace, some calling on the

1 Eaton, p. 375.

Pasha, some on me, some uttering shrieks, some exe-crations. Finding we were out of reach, they fell upon our tents and horses, which were left standing, carried them off and prepared themselves for flight." [1]

The next morning the Arabs and many of the inhabitants of Derne fled to the mountains. The enemy had already retired, under the impression that the Constellation had brought reinforcements to Eaton. A Tripolitan officer, a messenger from Yusuf Pasha, who had come from Tripoli in the Constellation, went on shore under a flag of truce, bearing letters of amnesty from the pasha " to the people of Derne on condition of their returning to allegiance; " but the people remaining in the town had no faith in Yusuf's promises, and in despair prepared to defend themselves to the last. This abandonment of Hamet's followers to the tender mercies of his brother was the most painful part of this whole transaction, but it is believed that no harm came to them and that Yusuf's promises in their case were fulfilled.

The Constellation sailed directly for Syracuse. From this point Eaton sailed for the United States in the brig Franklin August 6, and arrived at Hampton Roads November 10, 1805.[2]

[1] Eaton, p. 362.   [2] Nat. Intell. Nov. 20, 1805.

CHAPTER XV

PEACE WITH TRIPOLI

BEFORE Commodore Barron sailed for the Mediterranean he received instructions from the secretary of the navy, dated June 6, 1804, from which the following is an extract: " Colonel Tobias Lear, our consul-general at Algiers, is invested by the President with full power and authority to negotiate a treaty of peace with the Pasha of Tripoli, and also to adjust such terms of conciliation as may be found necessary with any of the other Barbary powers. He is, therefore, to be conveyed by you to any of these regencies, as he may request of you, and you will cordially coöperate with him in all such measures as may be deemed the best calculated to effectuate a termination of the war with Tripoli, and to ensure a continuance of the friendship and respect of the other Barbary powers." [1] He also conveyed to Colonel Lear instructions from the secretary of state, of the same date, containing the following: " Commodore Barron has orders to provide, at a suitable time, for your joining him, in order to the negotiating a peace with Tripoli. . . . The power of negotiation is confided to you in the first instance, but in case of accident it is to devolve on the acting commodore of the squadron." [2] From this it would appear that Lear was expected to take a more active

[1] St. Pap. v, p. 164.
[2] Ibid. pp. 433, 434.

part in the negotiations than he had during Preble's command.[1]

In December, Colonel Lear, who was at Malta, received a letter from the Spanish consul at Tripoli advising him to come to that place under a flag of truce, as the pasha seemed to be ready to negotiate.[2] Believing that he could make better terms on the approach of the season for active operations, Lear took no notice of this letter until the end of March, when he acknowledged it, but declined to make any proposal. In April, the pasha proposed, through the Spanish consul, "that the United States should pay him two hundred thousand dollars for peace and ransom, and deliver up to him gratis all his subjects in their power and make full restitution of the property taken from them." Lear in his report says : " These propositions were so completely inadmissible that after communicating them to Commodore Barron, I thought no more of them, fully expecting further advances." During the next few weeks "there were intimations made in various ways of the disposition of the Pasha to treat ; but none in a direct or official manner."

In the mean time Captain Bainbridge and Mr. Nissen, the Danish consul at Tripoli, had written letters [3] to Commodore Barron, in March, stating that peace could probably be bought for one hundred and twenty thousand dollars; that the Tripolitan minister of foreign affairs, Sidi Mohammed Dghies, who had opposed the war in the first place, had always been

---

[1] This chapter is based chiefly on St. Pap. v, pp. 159–203, 392–450; For. Rel. ii, pp. 695–725 ; iii, pp. 26–29. There is a condensed account of the negotiations in Nav. Chron. pp. 268–271.

[2] See Lear's report of July 5, 1805, to Sec. of State, St. Pap. v, pp. 441–450; For. Rel. ii, p. 716.

[3] St. Pap. v, pp. 410–415.

friendly to American interests, and had treated the captives with kindness, was strongly in favor of peace, partly because his private interests suffered by the war; that Dghies expected to go into the country soon, on account of his health; and as his influence with the pasha would be very valuable, it would be advisable to send some one empowered to treat as soon as possible. Bainbridge also expressed the opinion that it would be impossible to effect the release of the captives without paying a ransom, unless with the help of land forces.

May 18, Commodore Barron wrote to Colonel Lear and received a reply the next day. As they were both in Malta at this time, and had been for many months, they had doubtless discussed the question of peace many times, and these letters served to record their opinions, in which they agreed, that the time for entering upon negotiations had arrived, and plans were made accordingly. The subsequent events are described by Lear in his report to the secretary of state as follows: "On the 24th I embarked on board the United States frigate Essex, Captain James Barron, to proceed to Tripoli. On the 26th in the morning we saw the town of Tripoli . . . and the United States frigates Constitution and President. At ten o'clock, A. M., Captain Barron and myself went on board the former, when Captain Rodgers received the letter of Commodore Barron relinquishing to him the command of the squadron. He returned with us to the Essex, when we stood in for the town, and . . . hoisted the white flag, which was immediately answered by the same from the Pasha's castle. In half an hour a boat came off with the Spanish consul," whom " I informed . . . that the propositions which had been made through him were totally out of the question and must be relinquished before I would consent to move one step in the business." The Spanish consul went ashore, and on account of bad weather was not able to come aboard again until the 29th. " We now removed from the Essex to the Constitution. The Pasha relinquished all pretensions to a payment for peace or any future demand of any nature whatever, but demanded the sum of one hundred and thirty thousand dollars for the ransom of our countrymen, and the delivery of his subjects gratis. To this I objected as strongly as to the first proposition ; and after some time spent in discussing the subject, I told the Spanish consul that to prevent unnecessary delay and altercation, I would give him in writing my ultimatum, which must be at once decided upon, viz: That there should be an exchange of prisoners, man for man, so far as they would go ; that the Pasha should send all the Americans in his power on board the squadron now off Tripoli; that his subjects should be brought over from Syracuse and delivered to him with all convenient speed, and as he had three hundred Americans, more or less, and we one hundred Tripolitans, more or less, I would engage to give him for the balance in his favor sixty thousand dollars ; that a treaty of peace should be made upon honorable and mutually beneficial terms."

This ultimatum having been reported to the pasha, he replied on the 31st that he " had at length agreed to the sum of sixty thousand dollars for the balance of the prisoners, but that he could not think of delivering up the Americans until his subjects were ready to be delivered to him." Lear insisted, saying that he " would allow the Pasha twenty-four hours from this time to agree to my propositions in toto, or reject them." The next day, June 1, Captain Bainbridge came aboard the Constitution, his parole having been guaranteed by Nissen and Dghies. "He assured me that the Americans would not be delivered up until a treaty of peace should be made with the Pasha, as peace was more his object than the sum he might get for the captives." Lear agreed to negotiate the peace first "with any proper character," but "would have nothing more to do with the Spanish consul; " and "the Americans should be sent aboard without waiting the arrival of the Tripolines from Syracuse." Bainbridge then went on shore, and the next morning, June 2, Nissen came aboard with a commission to negotiate.

The treaty was then drawn up, and according to Nissen it contained "some articles more favorable to us than were to be found in any treaty which the Pasha had with any other nation." The pasha accepted the treaty on condition that the Americans should withdraw their forces from Derne, and should endeavor to persuade his brother Hamet also to withdraw, agreeing on his part, in the latter case, to restore to his brother his wife and children, if time were allowed him to do this. These details having been arranged, the preliminary articles were signed on board the Constitution June 3. "We went on board the Vixen to stand in near the harbor. When we were close to the town we fired a gun and hauled down the white flag. A salute of twenty-one guns was fired from the batteries and answered by the Constitution. I went into the harbor in the Constitution's barge, with the flag of the United States displayed, and was received at the landing place by the American officers, who had been in captivity, with a sensibility more easily to be conceived than described. An immense concourse of people crowded the shore and filled the streets, all signifying their pleasure on the conclusion of the peace. . . . On the 4th of June, at eleven A. M., the flag-staff was raised on the American house and the flag of the United States displayed, which was immediately saluted with twenty-one guns from the castle and forts and was returned by the Constitution." The American prisoners, after a captivity of over nineteen months, were then released and sent aboard the ships. Lear had an audience with the pasha, and says that "his court was much more superb than that of Algiers." On the 10th, Lear sent the pasha two copies of the treaty to be signed, and was invited to attend the divan. The treaty was there read, article by article, discussed, and finally signed and sealed. A week later the Constitution, which had gone to Syracuse, returned with the money and eighty-nine Tripolitan prisoners. Dr. John Ridgely, one of the late captives and formerly surgeon of the Philadelphia, was left at Tripoli as chargé d'affaires. June 21, the American vessels then at Tripoli sailed for Malta and Syracuse.

The treaty was liberal and enlightened, providing for the exchange of prisoners in case of future war and for their surrender, without ransom, at the conclusion of peace, and containing other articles advantageous to both parties. It involved no payment for peace, nor tribute, although it was tacitly understood, in accordance with ancient custom in Barbary, that when a consul was appointed, a present not exceeding six thousand dollars should be sent with him. It was ratified by the Senate April 12, 1806.[1]

[1] See Appendix II.

It is apparent from the published letters of Consul-General Lear, Commodores Barron and Rodgers, and Captain Bainbridge that they were all in favor of concluding peace at this time, even though it involved the payment of ransom. The long, tedious, and distressing captivity of the officers and crew of the Philadelphia appealed to the sympathies of all, and stimulated efforts to procure their early release. Colonel Lear, in spite of his military title, was a man of peace, and was very desirous of ending the war at the first opportunity. Success in diplomacy was doubtless his ambition. Yet he was firm in standing by his ultimatum, yielding only in allowing delay in the restoration of Hamet's family. Barron was suffering from physical disability, and at the time was mentally disqualified for the exercise of sound judgment on any question. Even Rodgers, contrary to what might have been expected, was not only acquiescent in a matter in which his authority was subordinate to that of Lear, but his letters [1] to Barron and to the secretary of the navy offer no suggestion of a final appeal to arms with the view of reducing the pasha's demands. There is no expression of protest or regret, but rather of approval. He says the pasha " acceded to peace on terms which left us no interest in a refusal of his wishes." The only hint we have of a warlike sentiment on his part is found in the following extract from Lear's report to the secretary of state : " I must here pay a tribute of justice to Commodore Rodgers, whose conduct during the negotiation on board was mixed with that manly firmness and evident wish to continue the war, if it could be done with propriety, while he displayed the magnanimity of an American

[1] St. Pap. v, pp. 429-432, 436.

in declaring that we fought not for conquest, but to maintain our just rights and national dignity, as fully convinced the negotiators that we did not ask, but grant peace. . . . Commodore Rodgers observed that if the Pasha would consent to deliver up our country-men without making peace, he would engage to give him two hundred thousand dollars, instead of sixty thousand, and raise the difference between the two sums from the officers of the navy, who, he was per-fectly assured, would contribute to it with the highest satisfaction." Bainbridge may not unnaturally have been somewhat biased in his view of the case by his painful situation as a captive. Preble also, when news of the peace reached him, appears to have approved of the terms, for not long after, September 29, 1805, he wrote to the secretary of the navy that Eaton's " ex-traordinary movements and the great increase of our naval forces undoubtedly occasioned the Pasha to sue for peace, and it is a pleasing circumstance and must be gratifying to every American that it has been estab-lished on more honorable terms than any other nation has ever been able to command." [1]

The preponderance of opinion, however, both con-temporary and later, has been that the conclusion of peace at this time was hasty and ill judged; that the payment of ransom was unjustifiable in view of the force then in the Mediterranean; that this force should have been used in an attack on Tripoli; that Eaton, having captured Derne, should have been rein-forced and supported in his design to attack Tripoli by land; and that the cause of Hamet Karamanli should have been upheld.

[1] Preble Papers. The treaty is defended in Nat. Intell. Oct. 9, 25, Nov. 6, 1805.

The secretary of state, Madison, in his instructions to Colonel Lear of June 6, 1804, expresses the hope that, in view of the strong force about to be sent out, peace may be effected "without any price or pecuniary compensation whatever." He authorizes the purchase of peace and the payment of ransom only in case of adverse events, accident to the squadron, or hostilities on the part of other Barbary powers. In his letter of April 20, 1805, he states his opinion that "the possibility of any considerable sacrifices being necessary should be considered as diminished by the spirited attack made on the enemy by Commodore Preble." [1]

It may reasonably be believed that if Preble had been in command, he would have made a vigorous attack on Tripoli with the fine squadron, which, a little later, could have been brought before the place, a squadron so much more powerful than that with which he had done such good work the year before. Yet it must be remembered that Preble offered a still larger sum for ransom, even after he had heard that Barron's squadron was on the way.[2] Preble's favorable opinion of the peace, quoted above, underwent a radical change within a few months, for he wrote to Eaton February 8, 1806, that he was sure "the Senate feel that just sense of indignation which they ought at the sacrifice of national honor which has been made by an ignominious negotiation." [3] When writing this, however, he evidently had in mind the treatment of Hamet, the exiled pasha, rather than the matter of ransom.

It is to be regretted that the negotiations were not deferred a few weeks, until the arrival of the bomb-

[1] St. Pap. v, pp. 433–435.   [2] See above, p. 201.
[3] Preble Papers.

vessels and gunboats from America, when the entire
squadron might have been made ready for united action against the enemy. The mere assembling of such
a formidable force before Tripoli might have fright-
ened the pasha into yielding any terms demanded,
especially if Eaton's movement on land had been reinforced and pushed. As it was, after Preble withdrew his force, there never appeared before Tripoli,
at any one time, more than a few blockading vessels,
and the real strength of the squadron was never
demonstrated to the pasha. The national honor was
vastly more important than hastening the release of
the captives in Tripoli, and the nation, having out-
grown the weakness and poverty of the earlier years,
should have been above haggling with a pirate.

Eaton's expedition, as a factor in the campaign
against Tripoli, particularly with regard to its effect
in disposing the pasha to peace, has been variously
estimated. When the plan was first proposed, it excited little interest among naval officers, who apparently were skeptical as to its practicability. Indeed,
with a leader of less than Eaton's indomitable energy
and perseverance, the enterprise must have proved a
failure. That Commodore Barron, when he first took
command, warmly approved of the project is shown by
his verbal orders of September 15, 1804, to Captain
Hull,[1] but later his attitude seems to have been modified by ill health and other influences, and he began
to express caution and a fear of having exceeded his
instructions. Lear was outspoken in his opposition to
the scheme, and doubtless had great influence with the
commodore. The following winter Captain Dent of
the Nautilus stated to a committee of the Senate:

[1] See above, p. 228.

" That I consider Commodore Barron's health, during the last winter and spring and until after the negotiation, such as to disqualify him from transacting any business, his mind being so much impaired as scarcely to recollect anything that transpired from one day to another. . . . It was generally believed by the officers in the Mediterranean that Mr. Lear had a great ascendency over the commodore in all his measures relative to the squadron, and from frequent observations of Mr. Lear's intimacy with the commodore, during his debilitated state, I am of the same opinion." [1]

Preble wrote to Eaton, October 28, 1805: "The arduous and dangerous services you have performed have justly immortalized your name and astonished not only your country, but the world. If pecuniary resources and naval strength had been at your command, what would you not have done ! . . . I have often regretted that you did not leave the United States with me. An earlier acquaintance might have given greater reputation to our arms, while I was on the station, but could not have increased your glory beyond its present zenith, for you have acquired immortal honor and established the fame of your country in the East." [2]

There was an idea that Eaton's expedition, if so far successful as to threaten the overthrow of the Tripolitan government and the restoration of Hamet, might have serious results for the American captives. The pasha informed Dr. Cowdery [3] that, if driven to extremity, he would put the prisoners to death, and Nissen expressed his belief that such would be their fate.[4] The secretary of the navy wrote to Preble,

[1] St. Pap. v, p. 406. [2] Preble Papers.
[3] Cowdery, pp. 26, 27. [4] St. Pap. v, p. 167.

September 18, 1805: "I have seen many of the officers that were prisoners. All say positively that if Lear had persisted in refusing paying a ransom for them, peace would not have been made and they would all have been certainly massacred." [1] There seems, however, to have been no apprehension in the squadron that this threat would be executed. Rodgers wrote to the secretary of the navy, June 8, 1805: "I never thought myself that the lives of the American prisoners were in any danger;" [2] although in the same letter he speaks of this danger as a possibility. To the Senate committee just mentioned, Lieutenant Wallace Wormeley, who had been a midshipman on the Philadelphia and a captive in Tripoli, said: "I do not believe that there was any danger to be apprehended for our lives." [3] There was also an idea that, if hard pressed, the pasha might have fled into the interior, taking the captives with him. There can be little doubt that the capture of Derne and the defeat of the Tripolitan army before that place had a disquieting effect on the pasha, and must in a great degree have stimulated his desire for an early peace.

The government has been accused of breach of faith with Hamet in abandoning his cause when there was a prospect of success. The degree of responsibility of the administration may be learned from the official utterances of its members. August 22, 1802, the secretary of state wrote letters to Consuls Eaton and Cathcart containing the earliest expression of the administration's views. Both letters refer to this matter in nearly the same words, and the following is an extract from the former: "Although it does not

[1] Preble Papers. [2] St. Pap. v, p. 437.
[3] Ibid. p. 405.

accord with the general sentiments or views of the United States to intermeddle in the domestic contests of other countries, it cannot be unfair, in the prosecution of a just war or the accomplishment of a reasonable peace, to turn to their advantage the enmity and pretensions of others against a common foe. How far success in the plan ought to be relied on, cannot be decided at this distance and with so imperfect a knowledge of many circumstances. The event, it is hoped, will correspond with your zeal and with your calculations. Should the rival brother be disappointed in his object, it will be due to the honor of the United States to treat his misfortune with the utmost tenderness, and to restore him as nearly as may be to the situation from which he was drawn, unless some other proper arrangement should be more acceptable to him. This wish of the President will be conveyed to Commodore Morris and Mr. Cathcart with a suggestion that, in the event of peace with the ruling Pasha, an attempt should be made to insert some provision favorable to his brother." Six days later the secretary of the navy wrote to Commodore Morris : " In adjusting the terms of peace with the Dey [pasha] of Tripoli, whatever regard may be had to the situation of his brother, it is not to be considered by you of sufficient magnitude to prevent or even to retard a final settlement with the Dey. Mr. Eaton in this affair cannot be considered an authorized agent of the government." The secretary of the navy in his instructions to Commodore Barron, June 6, 1804, already quoted,[1] says : " With respect to the ex-pasha of Tripoli, we have no objection to your availing yourself of his coöperation. . . . The subject is committed entirely to your

[1] See above, p. 227, also pp. 117, 124.

discretion." In his instructions to Consul-General
Lear, of the same date, the secretary of state says:
" Of the coöperation of the elder brother of the pasha
of Tripoli we are still willing to avail ourselves, if the
commodore should judge that it may be useful, and to
engage which, as well as to render it more effectual,
he has discretionary authority to grant him pecuniary
or other subsidies not exceeding twenty thousand
dollars; but the less reliance is placed upon his aid,
as the force under the orders of the commodore is
deemed sufficient for any exercise of coercion which the
obstinacy of the pasha may demand." [1] The above
expressions could hardly be construed as a promise
to restore Hamet to the throne of his ancestors, but
explicit orders might have been given that he should
be fully enlightened as to the exact position of the
administration in regard to his affairs.

It is to be considered next whether Barron and
Eaton exceeded their instructions and led Hamet to
expect more than was authorized by the administration. Eaton wrote to the secretary of the navy, December 5, 1805: " Commodore Barron's instructions
to Captain Hull of September 15th, 1804, and my
convention with Hamet Pasha of February 23rd, 1805,
comprise all the obligations entered into with Hamet." [2]
These two documents have already been quoted; [3] in
the first Barron says: "The Pasha may be assured
of the support of my squadron at Bengazi or Derne.
. . . And you may assure him also that I will take
the most effectual measures, with the forces under
my command, for coöperating with him against the

---

[1] For the letters referred to in this paragraph, see Morris, pp. 45–
51; St. Pap. v, pp. 162, 164, 434.

[2] St. Pap. v, p. 199.   [3] See above, pp. 228, 231.

usurper, his brother, and for reëstablishing him in the regency of Tripoli." Eaton, in the second article of his convention, commits the United States to "use their utmost exertions" under certain conditions "to reëstablish the said Hamet Pasha." It is not improbable also that, on various occasions during their long march through the desert, Eaton may have revived the drooping spirits of the exile by confident assurances of support on the part of the United States. In his letter of March 22, 1805, to Eaton, Barron, apparently fearful of having gone too far in his instructions to Hull, says: "You must be sensible that in giving their sanction to a coöperation with the exiled pasha, Government did not contemplate the measure as leading, necessarily and absolutely, to a reinstatement of that prince in his rights on the regency of Tripoli. They appear to have viewed the coöperation in question as a means which, if there existed energy and enterprise in the exile and attachment to his person on the part of his former subjects, might be employed to the common furtherance and advantage of his claims and our cause, but without meaning to fetter themselves by any specific and definite attainment as an end, which the tenor of my instructions and the limited sum appropriated for that special purpose clearly demonstrate. . . . Under my present impressions I feel it my duty to state explicitly that I must withhold my sanction to any convention or agreement committing the United States, or tending to impress upon Hamet Pasha a conviction that we have bound ourselves to place him upon the throne. . . . I wish you to understand that no guaranty or engagement to the exiled prince, whose cause, I must repeat, we are only favoring as an instrument to our

advantage and not as an end in itself, must be held to
stand in the way of our acquiescence to any honorable and advantageous terms of accommodation which
the reigning pasha may be induced to propose; such
terms being once offered, and accepted by the representative of Government appointed to treat of peace,
our support to the ex-pasha must necessarily cease." [1]
This letter reached Eaton April 16, too late to relieve
Barron of the responsibility assumed in his order of
September 15.

A summary of the case from the point of view of
the administration is given by the President in his
message to Congress of January 13, 1806: "We
considered that concerted operations by those who have
a common enemy were entirely justifiable and might
produce effects favorable to both, without binding
either to guarantee the objects of the other. . . . Our
expectation was that an intercourse should be kept up
between the ex-pasha and the commodore; that while
the former moved on by land, our squadron should
proceed with equal pace, so as to arrive at their destination together and to attack the common enemy by
land and sea at the same time. The instructions of June
6th to Commodore Barron show that a coöperation
only was intended and by no means an union of our
object with the fortune of the ex-pasha; and the
commodore's letters . . . prove that he had the most
correct idea of our intentions. His verbal instructions, indeed, to Mr. Eaton and Captain Hull, if the
expressions are accurately committed to writing by
those gentlemen, do not limit the extent of his co-
operation as rigorously as he probably intended. . . .
If Mr. Eaton's subsequent convention should appear

[1] St. Pap. v, p. 176; Eaton, p. 368.

to bring forward other objects, . . . the second article, as he expressly states," guards "it against any
ill effect. . . . In the event it was found that, after
placing the ex-pasha in possession of Derne, one of
the most important cities and provinces of the country,
where he had resided himself as governor, he was
totally unable to command any resources or to bear
any part in coöperation with us. This hope was then
at an end, and we certainly had never contemplated
nor were we prepared to land an army of our own, or
to raise, pay or subsist an army of Arabs, to march
from Derne to Tripoli, and to carry on a land war at
such a distance from our resources. . . . While, therefore, an impression from the capture of Derne might
still operate at Tripoli, and an attack on that place
from our squadron was daily expected, Colonel Lear
thought it the best moment to listen to overtures of
peace then made by the pasha. He did so, and while
urging provisions for the United States, he paid attention also to the interests of Hamet, but was able
to effect nothing more than to engage the restitution
of his family. . . . In operations at such a distance
it becomes necessary to leave much to the discretion
of the agents employed. . . . In all these cases the
purity and patriotism of the motives should shield the
agent from blame and even secure a sanction where
the error is not too injurious. Should it be thought
by any that the verbal instructions, said to have been
given by Commodore Barron to Mr. Eaton, amount to
a stipulation that the United States should place
Hamet on the throne of Tripoli, a stipulation so entirely unauthorized, so far beyond our views and so
erroneous, could not be sanctioned by our Government.
. . . Something equivalent to the replacing him in his

former situation might be worthy its consideration. A nation, by establishing a character of liberality and magnanimity, gains in the friendship and respect of others more than the worth of mere money." [1]

As usual in such cases, the discussion of this question at the time took a political turn, and the administration and its agents were warmly attacked by the opposition. The following extract from a letter written March 21, 1806, by Timothy Pickering, then in the Senate, serves to show this feeling : " Lear's conduct is inexcusable, and can be resolved into nothing but the basest treachery on the basest principles. The President in his message on the subject labored to justify him, but in vain." [2]

The situation of the unfortunate Hamet was by no means befitting a royal exile. In a letter to Eaton, dated June 29, 1805, he acknowledges that everything had been done for him which he had any reason to expect, but suggests " some small assistance to enable me to subsist myself and suite." Accordingly, by order of Commodore Rodgers, he was allowed two hundred dollars a month for the support of himself and his twelve or fifteen dependents in Syracuse. A few weeks later he appealed to the President and to the people of the United States for relief. He was allowed for a time to suffer in neglect. In April, 1806, Congress appropriated twenty-four hundred dollars for his benefit, but it was not delivered to him until more than a year later. The allowance authorized by Commodore Rodgers was then stopped. In the mean time, February 18, 1807, he had addressed a memorial to Congress in which he says : " I will not, like the world,

---

[1] St. Pap. v, p. 159 ; For. Rel. ii, p. 695.
[2] Pickering, xxxviii, p. 105 ; see also xlvi, pp. 412–415, lv, p. 210.

reproach the representatives of the American nation with ingratitude. I rather implore their commiseration towards me; at least so far as to restore to me my family and to grant me a competence." In May, 1807, Dr. George Davis, who had been for some years chargé d'affaires of the United States at Tunis, went to Tripoli as consul, and one of his first acts was to demand of the pasha the fulfillment of the third article of the treaty of June 4, 1805, which provided for the restoration to Hamet of his wife and children. It was now learned that Colonel Lear had agreed to a secret article of that treaty,[1] allowing the pasha four years to comply with this stipulation. This fact had never been communicated to the state department nor to Congress, although Eaton had stated his suspicion of some such secret agreement in a letter to the chairman of the Senate committee on Hamet's application. The President, in his message of November 11, 1807, expresses surprise at this affair, and says: " How it has happened that the declaration of June 5th has never before come to our knowledge cannot with certainty be said. But whether there has been a miscarriage of it or a failure of the ordinary attention and correctness of that officer in making his communications, I have thought it due to the Senate, as well as to myself, to explain to them the circumstances which have withheld from their knowledge, as they did from my own, a modification which, had it been placed in the public treaty, would have been relieved from the objections which candor and good faith cannot but feel in its present form." Dr. Davis, however, prevailed upon the pasha to restore his brother's family without further delay, and this was done in October, 1807.

[1] See Appendix II.

December 18, 1807, a committee of the House of Representatives recommended further pecuniary aid for Hamet. In 1808 provision was made by the pasha for his brother's residence in Morocco, with a pension; and in the following year, through the influence of Consul Davis, Hamet was appointed by the pasha to the government of Derne. Two years later he was again expelled by his brother and fled with his family to Egypt, where he died.[1]

Upon his return to America, Eaton was received with marked distinction. The legislature of Massachusetts made him a grant of ten thousand acres of land in Maine. But he could never get over his chagrin and disappointment at the inglorious termination of his expedition, which he had hoped and believed would end with the capture of Tripoli, the restoration of Hamet, a brilliant victory for the United States forces afloat and ashore, and an honorable peace. The remainder of his life was embittered. Towards those who, he believed, had in any degree thwarted his plans, Lear especially, he was unsparing of his reprobation. He therefore not unnaturally made enemies, and a resolution to present him a medal was defeated in Congress by a small majority. He was embarrassed by long delay in settling his claims against the government, especially the twenty-two thousand dollars expended in 1803 for the furtherance of his plans regarding Hamet,[2] which had not yet been allowed. Finally, in February, 1807, a bill passed in Congress authorizing the state department to settle the accounts accord-

---

[1] St. Pap. v, pp. 196–203, 403, 489–493; vi, pp. 51–57; x, pp. 496–502; Rep. Sen. Com. viii, p. 17; Eaton, pp. 420–425; Greenhow, p. 33; Pickering, xxix, p. 12; Nat. Intell. June 25, 1806.

[2] See above, p. 122.

ing to equity. Many years later his heirs applied to
Congress for relief. The total expense of the Derne
expedition was a little less than forty thousand dollars;
Eaton would accept for his own services during this
campaign only enough to cover his personal expenses.
His relations with Hamet continued cordial, and for
years they kept up a friendly correspondence. Eaton
died in 1811, at the age of forty-seven.[1]

[1] Claims, pp. 299–307, 323–332; Mil. Aff. vi, p. 1; Eaton, pp. 243–256, 267, 405, 406; Felton, pp. 339, 354.

CHAPTER XVI

FURTHER TROUBLE WITH THE BARBARY STATES

AFTER the peace, the squadron rendezvoused at Syracuse, and on June 29, 1805, the inquiry into the loss of the Philadelphia was held.[1] One of the first things to engage the attention of Commodore Rodgers was a threatened difficulty with Tunis. It has been mentioned[2] that on April 24 Rodgers captured a Tunisian xebec with two prizes attempting to run the blockade of Tripoli. The bey of Tunis, who either would not or could not understand the law of blockades, was much incensed, and demanded of Dr. Davis, the United States chargé d'affaires, that the vessels should be given up to him. Davis assured him that this would not be done. May 28, he made the same demand of the commodore. Early in June, Rodgers sent the crew of the xebec to Tunis by the Essex, retaining the vessels, and in a letter to Davis announced his intention of taking the squadron to Tunis as soon as possible. On her return the Essex brought information that the bey still insisted on the surrender of the captured vessels. July 1, Rodgers wrote to him "that a compliance with your demands to deliver up the xebec and her two prizes is totally inadmissible." The bey felt himself affronted, assumed a menacing attitude towards Davis, and threatened war against the United States.[3]

---

[1] See above, p. 148.　　　　　　　　[2] See above, p. 222.
[3] For this difficulty with Tunis, see Nav. Chron. pp. 279-287; Captains' Letters, i, no. 59, Rodgers to Davis (June 11 and 29, 1805).

Rodgers at once sent the Congress and Vixen to Tunis, and on July 23 followed with the Constitution, Constellation, Essex, John Adams, Siren, Nautilus, Enterprise, Hornet, and several gunboats. All these vessels anchored in Tunis Bay August 1, and the next day the commodore wrote to the bey asking whether his intentions were peaceful or otherwise, and declaring his purpose to begin hostilities if he did not receive a reply within thirty-six hours. Rodgers waited, however, until the 5th, when he sent Captain Decatur ashore to demand a reply. The bey refused to receive Decatur, who at once returned to the squadron. The bey's discretion then got the better of his valor, and he sent off a messenger in such haste that he arrived on board the flagship before Decatur. He bore a conciliatory letter from the bey, inviting the commodore and Consul-General Lear to a friendly conference with him. At the same time he complained of the whole squadron's being anchored before the city, which, he said, constituted an act of hostility.

Lear went on shore and remained several days. August 11, Rodgers demanded " a guarantee for the maintenance of peace, to be witnessed by the English and French consuls ; " and to the bey's complaint of all the squadron's being present, replied that he was mistaken, that a frigate, a brig, two bomb-vessels, and eight gunboats had not yet arrived. The bey appeared to be waiting only for the departure of the squadron in order that he might send out his cruisers. August 15, Rodgers wrote to Lear that the bey " must do one of three things, by simple request, or else must do all three by force. He must give the guarantee already required, or he must give sufficient security for peace and send a minister to the United States, or he must make such alterations in the treaty as you may require and as may satisfy you that there is confidence to be placed in what he does. I have only to repeat that if he does not do all that is necessary and proper, at the risk of my conduct being disapproved by my country, he shall feel the vengeance of the squadron now in this bay." But the bey had already yielded, and Lear returned to the flagship with his letter of the 14th, in which he declared his intention of sending an ambassador to the United States to claim the captured vessels, and promised to keep the peace until the result of this mission should be known. This solution of the difficulty was accepted by the commodore, but he kept the squadron before Tunis until September. The envoy, whose name was Mellimelni, was then ready, and embarked on the Congress, Captain Decatur. These proceedings astonished the European consuls at Tunis, who said that "no other nation has ever negotiated with the present bey on such honorable terms."

In a letter to the secretary of the navy, dated August 21, 1805, Rodgers says : " Peace on honorable terms is always preferable to war, and if Government thinks proper to overlook the late unfriendly conduct of the Bey of Tunis, I think I can almost with certainty say that he never will again attempt to behave in a similar manner, as I feel satisfied this lesson has not only changed his opinion of our maritime strength, but has caused him to discover more distinctly his own weakness in every sense. However, should the Government determine to chastise him for what has passed, permit me to solicit the honor of bearing the standard of their vengeance, and as a guarantee for the fulfillment of their wishes, I will pledge all that is sacred and dear to me in this world, provided such intention is made known to me by the first of March next, that before the ensuing first of September following that my country shall not only obtain an honorable peace, but make him pay the expenses of the war, and this too with no more force than what remains this winter in the Mediterranean." [1]

After the affair with Tunis had been settled, Commodore Rodgers sailed for Algiers, where Consul-General Lear was landed. About this time Mustapha, who had been dey of Algiers since 1798, was murdered by the soldiery, and a new dey named Achmet was chosen.[2]

The squadron was gradually reduced as the vessels composing it returned to the United States. The President, with Commodore Barron, Captain Bainbridge, and most of the officers recently released from captivity in Tripoli, had already sailed from Malta homeward bound, July 13.[3] In the Straits of Gibraltar she was fired upon by Spanish gunboats, to which she replied only by hoisting the Spanish flag under her own. Late in August the Constellation sailed for America under Captain Stewart, Captain Campbell having been transferred to the Essex. About the same time the John Adams was ordered home by way of Syracuse and Malta, where she took on board the invalids of the squadron. The brig Franklin, Captain Robinson, with Eaton on board, was also sent home by way of Tunis and Gibraltar. No other vessels sailed until the following year. One of the late captives, Lieutenant Porter, remained with the squadron, and was given command of the Enterprise, having served for a time as acting captain of the Constitution.

---

[1] Captains' Letters, ii.   [2] Greenhow, p. 37.
[3] Nat. Intell. Sept. 18, 1805.

In April, 1806, he was promoted to the grade of master-commandant.[1]

December 7, 1805, the American brig Friendship was sent into Algiers, having been seized by one of the dey's cruisers. The reason given for this was that the brig had no passport, and it was not considered an act of hostility, especially as she was promptly released. Consul Lear believed that she would have been condemned as a prize, had it not been for the impression produced by the American conduct of affairs at Tripoli and Tunis.[2]

The Congress upon her arrival in the United States landed the Tunisian ambassador in Washington, and he forthwith presented the bey's claim to the three vessels captured before Tripoli. They were of small value, and the administration, as a matter of policy, thought best to restore them. The ambassador then demanded a supply of naval stores as a condition of peace for three years, and threatened war as an alternative. This met with a prompt and decisive refusal. In the Senate, however, there appears to have been a more conciliatory sentiment, judging by a report made by the committee on foreign relations. Whether or not in deference to this feeling, the administration, in the summer of 1806, determined to send the brig Franklin to the bey as a present, and the ambassador was to return home in her; but he declined to do so, and the brig was not sent. He remained in the United States nearly a year altogether, and then sailed in the

[1] For movements of vessels in this chapter, see Porter, pp. 67–69; C. Morris, pp. 37–40; Perry, pp. 69–73; Emmons, pp. 10, 22, 90–93; Life and Adventures of James R. Durand (Rochester, N. Y., 1820), pp. 34–71; MSS. in Navy Dept.

[2] Captains' Letters, iii, no. 51, Lear to Rodgers; Nat. Intell. May 19, 1806.

ship Two Brothers, chartered by the government, without retracting his demands or his threat of war.[1] War, however, did not follow. The bey had become involved in a difficulty with Algiers, and the impression produced by the American squadron anchored before his city had not wholly faded. It may have been strengthened by his ambassador's accounts of the size and resources of the United States.

In the spring of 1806 the Hornet, 18, Captain Dent, a new sloop-of-war, arrived in the Mediterranean. Her namesake, the ten-gun sloop, seems to have left for the United States about the same time. In the summer Commodore Rodgers sailed home in the Essex, leaving the Constitution and the squadron under the command of Captain Campbell. The Argus, Siren, Nautilus, Vixen, Spitfire, Vengeance, and the American gunboats also returned to the United States in the summer of 1806; the boats procured in the Mediterranean were disposed of there. After this there remained in the Mediterranean only the Constitution, Hornet, and Enterprise. On the 15th of August, while beating to the eastward through the Straits of Gibraltar, the Enterprise was attacked by seven Spanish gunboats. Captain Porter hoisted his colors and hailed the gunboats, but received no reply. They kept up a running fight for some time, but were finally driven off by the fire of the Enterprise.[2]

In the summer of 1807, an incipient mutiny took place on the Constitution on account of the period of enlistment of most of her crew having long elapsed.[3]

---

[1] St. Pap. v, p. 452 ; For. Rel. ii, p. 799 ; Rep. Sen. Com. viii, p. 20 ; Letter Book (1799–1807), pp. 170–174, 177–180 ; see Nat. Intell. March 20 and May 27, 1807.

[2] Comdrs'. Letters, ii, no. 51, Porter to Sec. of Navy (Aug. 19, 1806).

[3] Hollis's Constitution, p. 120 ; Durand, p. 59 et seq.

It was quickly quelled, and she soon sailed for home, arriving at Boston in October. The Enterprise had already sailed, and the Hornet soon followed, being the last to leave. Meanwhile the Wasp, 18, Captain Smith, another new sloop-of-war, having been to Europe, touched at Gibraltar in August, but almost immediately returned to America. As relations between the United States and England became more strained, the navy was kept at home as much as possible. It seems to have been not uncommon for vessels visiting Europe to look into the Mediterranean, and the Argus and Enterprise did so in 1809. Except for such brief and infrequent cruises, American interests in the Mediterranean were left unguarded for several years. If the navy had been enlarged at this time, as it should have been, in view of the likelihood of a collision with England, further complications with Barbary might have been prevented.

No sooner had the Hornet departed than difficulty with Algiers began. Two years' supplies of naval stores, stipulated by treaty, were due, and the dey refused to accept their equivalent in cash, although it was repeatedly offered by Consul Lear. The dey preferred warlike measures, and sent out a frigate on a cruise for Americans. October 26, 1807, the schooner Mary Ann of New York, Captain Ichabod Sheffield, and the brig Violet of Boston were captured in the Straits of Gibraltar, and the ship Eagle of New York was taken about the same time. The Mary Ann sailed for Algiers in charge of a prize crew of eight men and a boy. Three days later the crew of the schooner recaptured her, after a struggle in which four of the Algerines were thrown overboard; they then set four others adrift in a boat, keeping the boy. The Mary

Ann was brought safely into Naples, arriving there
November 4. Notice of the hostilities was at once sent
to American consuls and shipmasters in the Mediterranean. At about the same time the other two prizes
arrived at Algiers. The captives were well treated, and
in about six weeks Lear succeeded in settling the
affair. The dey, apparently satisfied with the commotion he had stirred up, consented to receive the arrears
in cash, released the vessels and crews, and promised
that American commerce should be no further molested. At this time it was believed that the Mary
Ann had been taken into some other port by her prize
crew. Yet when it was learned that she had escaped,
it made no difference, at first, with the dey's decision.
He still assured the consul that there would be no
further trouble.[1]

Three months later, however, the dey suddenly
demanded of Lear the payment of eighteen thousand
dollars for his nine subjects, the prize crew of the
Mary Ann. Lear declined to pay without authority
from his government. The dey threatened him with
imprisonment. On the same day the Danish consul
was arrested and put to work with the slaves, loaded
with chains, because his government was behindhand
with its tribute; he was released, however, on the
intercession of the other consuls. Lear expected the
same treatment, but firmly persisted in his refusal to
pay. But a week later, March 31, 1808, two frigates,
which had been fitting out, were ordered to sea. Lear
was formally notified that they had orders to cruise
against Americans, and he had " other indubitable
evidence " that such was the fact. In order, therefore,

[1] St. Pap. vi, pp. 69-72; For. Rel. iii, pp. 32, 33.

to prevent a piratical raid on his countrymen, he consented, under protest, to pay the money.[1]

In 1810 the ship Liberty of Philadelphia was seized by a French privateer, acting under the Berlin and Milan decrees, and taken into Tunis. She was there sold at auction by the French consul to the first minister of the bey. She was subsequently sent to Malta under the Tunisian flag. United States Consul Pulis thereupon claimed her for her American owners, and applied to the Maltese court for judgment. When the bey of Tunis heard of this he threatened to arrest all the Americans in Tunis and sequester their property. Another American ship, the Rolla, had also been captured by the French and bought by the bey's agents, and he made the same threat in case she should be given up to her American owners. He declared that he had always released American vessels taken within his jurisdiction, but the case of "those taken on the high seas was an affair between the American and French governments," and he claimed the right to purchase such prizes and dispose of them as he pleased. The United States consul at Tunis, C. D. Coxe, having remonstrated in vain, proceeded to Malta and consulted with Consul Pulis, who finally withdrew his claim and surrendered the Liberty to the bey's representative.[2] The claim was no doubt ultimately settled with the many other cases of French spoliation.

In 1812 the dey of Algiers was a ferocious old man named Hadji Ali. His two immediate predecessors, Achmet and Ali, had been assassinated by the soldiery, the first in November, 1808, the second in 1809.[3] Early

[1] St. Pap. vii, pp. 70–75 ; For. Rel. iii, pp. 34, 35.
[2] St. Pap. vii, pp. 488–490 ; For. Rel. iii, p. 394; Claims, p. 484.
[3] Greenhow, p. 37.

in 1812 a British envoy was sent to Algiers with a letter which says: "The Prince Regent in the name of his father George III ... expresses the strongest friendship for the Dey; ... assures the Dey that he will protect his capital with his fleets so long as the present friendship shall subsist between the two nations; declares that the British fleets are masters of every sea and are the terror of all maritime states and that whoever attempts to oppose them will be subdued; ... begs the Dey not to permit those who are enemies of Great Britain to lessen the harmony now subsisting between the two nations and that he will not hearken to their evil sayings."[1] This letter was shown to Consul Lear, and is supposed to have encouraged the dey in the aggressive attitude that he soon afterwards assumed towards the United States.

July 17, the ship Alleghany arrived from the United States loaded with naval stores for Algiers. On the 20th, when they were partly unloaded, the dey expressed dissatisfaction with the articles sent, ordered them reshipped, and demanded of Colonel Lear the instant payment of twenty-seven thousand dollars in liquidation of all arrearages of tribute to that time. Since the treaty was signed, September 5, 1795, about three hundred and fifty thousand dollars in annuities had been paid, and the amount that would actually be due September 5, 1812, was less than sixteen thousand dollars. But the dey claimed that, reckoning according to the Mohammedan calendar, three hundred and fifty-four days to the year, the time elapsed was seventeen and a half instead of seventeen years. He also commanded Lear, with all other Americans in Algiers, to embark on the Alleghany and leave his dominions

[1] Shaler, p. 118.

within three days. If the money was not paid and the Americans not ready to depart by that time, he threatened to seize the ship, enslave Lear and his countrymen, over twenty in all, including the crew of the Alleghany, and declare war against the United States. In vain Lear protested and endeavored to arrange the matter. The dey was obdurate; he extended the time limit to the 25th, allowing two more days, but would grant no other concession. With difficulty the Jew broker Bacri was persuaded to advance the money, charging a commission of twenty-five per cent. On the morning of July 25, the money was paid, and Lear embarked with his wife and son and three other American citizens. The affairs of the United States were left in the hands of Mr. John Norderling, the Swedish consul.[1]

The Alleghany sailed at once for Gibraltar. On the passage she fell in with a British brig-of-war, but was not detained, the fact of war having been declared by the United States against England about six weeks before being still unknown in the Mediterranean. In his report Lear says: "Should our differences with Great Britain be so accommodated as to admit of sending a naval force into this sea, I am sure there is only one course which the government will pursue, and what has now taken place may be a happy and fortunate event for the United States, by relieving them from a disgraceful tribute and an imperious and piratical depredation on their commerce. If our small naval force can operate freely in this sea, *Algiers will be humbled to the dust.* . . . I shall proceed in the Alleghany to Gibraltar, where I shall dispose of her

[1] For the events of 1812 at Algiers, see Lear's report of July 29 to the Sec. of State, St. Pap. ix, pp. 127-144.

cargo, which has been refused by the Dey of Algiers,
to meet, as far as it will go, the bill before mentioned
[due to Bacri], and for the remainder shall draw
upon the honorable the Secretary of State."

The Alleghany arrived at Gibraltar August 4. On
the 8th, news of the declaration of war against England having come, the ship was seized. The captain
was allowed to go on parole, but the crew were put on
a prison ship and later sent to England. Lear, with
his family, remained at Gibraltar until December,
then went to Cadiz on a British transport, and there
procured a passage to the United States.[1]

Before the Alleghany's arrival in Algiers, the dey
had sent to sea a squadron of five frigates and several
smaller vessels, heavily manned and carrying many
guns, but not formidable, on account of the small
calibre of the guns, the inefficiency of the crews, and
the poor condition of the ships. Lear says: " I am
sure that our brave officers and seamen would rejoice
to meet them with only half their force." [2]

On the 25th of August, 1812, the brig Edwin of
Salem, Captain George C. Smith, with a crew of ten
men, including the mate, while proceeding from Malta
to Gibraltar, was captured and sent into Algiers.
This was the dey's only American prize, although
a vessel under the Spanish flag was also taken, on the
ground that she was an American under false colors,
and an American citizen on board of her, named Pollard, was detained. The crew of the Edwin were
" subjected to the well known horrors of Algerine
slavery," but the captain and mate and Pollard were

[1] Niles's Register, iv, p. 128, April 24, 1813; Claims, pp. 435, 476,
500, 615, 699.
[2] St. Pap. ix, pp. 141–143.

not made to work nor kept in confinement.[1] The war
between the United States and Great Britain kept
American merchantmen out of the Mediterranean for
three years, which accounts for the small returns
derived by the dey from his enterprise. He chose
the wrong time for his hostile demonstration.

In 1813, Mordecai M. Noah was appointed United
States consul to Tunis, and was instructed to attempt
the release of the American captives in Algiers, being
allowed to offer for them a ransom of three thousand
dollars apiece. At Cadiz, on his way to Tunis, Noah
engaged the services of Richard R. Keene, an American in business at that place, who proceeded to
Algiers in February, 1814. He represented himself
as a Spanish subject and " as the bearer of despatches
from the Spanish Regency to their consul." Upon
his arrival he consulted with the Spanish consul, and
it was agreed to inform the dey that he had come in
the interest of the American merchants of Cadiz
and under the auspices of the Spanish government,
to offer a ransom for the American captives; at the
same time insinuating that the United States government was indifferent to the fate of the captives, as
any hindrances to commerce were an aid to the em-
bargo policy of the administration. Keene was shown
great attention and courtesy by the British consul,
Mr. McDonell, who, with the Spanish consul, did all
in his power to influence the dey in favor of the
project, but without success. His reply was : " My
policy and my views are to increase, not to diminish
the number of my American slaves; and not for
a million dollars would I release them." The Swedish
consul, Norderling, also tried, but could make no

---

[1] St. Pap. ix, pp. 435-438; For. Rel. iii, p. 748.

impression on the dey. About this time an American who had been impressed on an English frigate deserted at Algiers, and to prevent arrest turned Mohammedan. He was claimed by the British consul, but was protected by the dey, then fled into the interior, and could not be found. The consul threatened to impress two Algerines; but as a favor to Keene, he finally consented to accept in exchange two of the Edwin's crew; to save the dey's pride they were claimed as British subjects. They were thereupon turned over to Keene, who paid for them a ransom of two thousand dollars each. The dey picked out the two poorest workmen in the crew for liberation. Four other Americans impressed on a British frigate which came into Algiers were also turned over to Keene by the consul, for a consideration of six thousand dollars, without the dey's knowledge. With these six Americans Keene returned to Gibraltar, leaving ten others in captivity at Algiers: Captain Smith, Mr. Pollard, and the mate and seven of the crew of the Edwin.[1]

[1] Noah, pp. 69-76, 109, 141-152, 159-161, 369, 370, 386, 412-414, app. ii-v.

CHAPTER XVII

WAR WITH ALGIERS — FINAL PEACE

As soon as the war with Great Britain was over, it was possible for the government to turn its attention to Algiers, and on February 23, 1815, President Madison sent a message to Congress recommending a declaration of war. Congress thereupon passed an act, which was approved March 2, declaring war against Algiers.[1]

Two squadrons were organized, one at Boston under Commodore William Bainbridge, the other at New York under Commodore Stephen Decatur. The latter was ready first and sailed May 20, 1815. It comprised the frigates Guerrière, 44, flagship, Captain William Lewis, Constellation, 36, Captain Charles Gordon, and Macedonian, 38, Captain Jacob Jones; the sloops-of-war Epervier, 18, Captain John Downes, and Ontario, 16, Captain Jesse D. Elliott; the brigs Firefly, Spark, and Flambeau, each 14, Lieutenants George W. Rodgers, Thomas Gamble, and John B. Nicholson; and the schooners Torch and Spitfire, 12, Lieutenants Wolcott Chauncey and Alexander J. Dallas. Mr. William Shaler, who had been appointed consul-general for the Barbary States, to reside at Algiers, and joint commissioner with Commodores Bainbridge and Decatur to treat for peace, was a passenger on the Guerrière. A few days after sailing, the squadron

[1] St. Pap. ix, p. 436; For. Rel. iii, p. 748; Rep. Sen. Com. iv, p. 8; Niles's Register, viii, p. 24, March 11, 1815.

encountered a heavy gale, in which the Firefly sprung her masts and was obliged to put back to New York for repairs.[1]

Before entering the Mediterranean, Decatur communicated with the United States consuls at Cadiz and Tangier, in order to learn, if possible, whether or not there was an Algerine squadron in the Atlantic. He was informed that a squadron under the command of Reis Hammida had been outside, but had passed up the Mediterranean. Decatur arrived at Gibraltar June 15, where his squadron attracted much attention. Dispatch vessels were at once sent by partisans of Algiers to warn the dey and Hammida. Decatur was informed that Hammida was probably off Cape de Gat, and remaining only long enough to communicate with the American consul, he proceeded in search of the Algerine, hoping to take him by surprise.

On the morning of the 17th, the squadron being much scattered in search of strange sails, the Constellation sighted a large frigate under topsails twenty miles or more southeast of Cape de Gat and signaled an enemy. Decatur, thinking that the Algerine would believe his squadron to be English, wished to avoid any appearance of being in chase, so as to carry out the deception until he was within striking distance of the enemy. But the Constellation, through the mistake of a quartermaster, hoisted the American ensign; and although the other vessels, following the Guerrière's example, immediately showed British colors, the Al-

---

[1] This chapter is based on Decatur, ch. xiii, xiv, app. viii; Bainbridge, ch. ix; Perry, ch. xii; Life of Farragut, by his son (New York, 1879), ch. vi; Cooper (New York, 1853), iii, ch. i; Shaler, ch. v, app. D, E, G. See also Naval Monument (Boston, 1830), pp. 296–314; Naval Temple (Boston, 1816), pp. 214–224; Analectic Magazine (Jan. and Feb. 1816); Mrs. Decatur, pp. 25, 26, 51–56; Nav. Aff. i, p. 396.

gerine at once took alarm, and, rapidly spreading all
sail, headed for Algiers. The Constellation was nearest
the stranger and about a mile from her. Half a mile
astern of the Constellation was the Epervier, with the
Guerrière on her starboard quarter and the Ontario
on her port beam. The other vessels were scattered
far behind. The Constellation opened fire on the
enemy, who returned it and then wore ship and headed
for the Spanish coast, evidently in despair of escaping
in the long chase to Algiers and hoping to make a
neutral port. The Ontario crossed her bow, and the
Guerrière, passing between the Constellation and Epervier, approached so close to the Algerine as to receive
a musketry fire from her tops which wounded several
of the crew. Without returning this fire, Decatur
brought his ship close up alongside the enemy and gave
her a broadside, which caused great havoc on her deck.
Hammida had already been wounded by a shot from
the Constellation and was seated in an exposed position
on the quarter-deck directing the working of his ship
with great fortitude. He was now cut in two by a
forty-two pound shot from one of the Guerrière's carronades. A second broadside drove all the Algerines
below, except a few musketeers, who with cool courage
kept up the fight. Wishing to prevent unnecessary
loss of life, Decatur ceased firing and drew ahead out
of range, although the Algerine had not struck her
colors. The Epervier now came up on the starboard
quarter of the enemy, who seemed to be attempting to
escape. The little brig manœuvred skillfully about the
big frigate and gave her nine broadsides, receiving
only musketry fire in return. At last the Algerine
brought her head to the wind and surrendered.

She was the frigate Mashuda of forty-six guns and

the flagship of Reis Hammida. Four hundred and
six prisoners were taken in her, many of whom were
wounded. About thirty had been killed, most of
them by the Guerrière's two broadsides; very few of
her crew were on deck during the Epervier's fire. The
Guerrière lost one killed and three wounded by the
enemy's fire, three killed and seven wounded by the
bursting of a gun. The Mashuda was sent into Carthagena under convoy of the Macedonian. Hammida
was a remarkable man and one of the greatest of the
race of Barbary corsairs. He was a member of a tribe
of Kabyles, warlike mountaineers of southern Barbary.
He had come to Algiers when a boy to seek his fortune
and, going to sea, had risen from the lowest to the
highest rank.

Decatur continued his cruise in the hope of falling
in with the remainder of the Algerine squadron, and
on June 19, off Cape Palos, a brig was discovered and
chased. After three hours she got into shoal water
near the shore, where the frigates could not follow. The
Epervier, Spark, Torch, and Spitfire kept up the chase.
The brig ran aground, and part of her crew escaped
in boats, one of which was sunk by the fire of the
squadron, and the others reached the shore in safety.
The remainder of the brig's crew, eighty in number,
surrendered, and when she was boarded twenty-three
dead were found on her deck. She proved to be the
Algerine brig Estedio, of twenty-two guns, and was
floated and sent into Carthagena with most of the prisoners from both prizes. No other Algerine cruisers
were found, and Decatur decided to proceed at once
to Algiers, so as to intercept any of the enemy who
should attempt to get back there. He called a council
of his captains, and to them expressed his hope that

what had already been accomplished would bring the
dey to terms, and his determination, should the dey
be unwilling to treat, to attack the batteries and
destroy the shipping in the harbor. The squadron
arrived off Algiers on the 28th of June.

The old dey, Hadji Ali, as well as his immediate
successor, had been murdered by the soldiery a few
months before, and the present dey was a Lesbian
by birth named Omar, a man of courage and determination and of more character than most Algerine
rulers.

On the morning after his arrival, Decatur hoisted
a white flag at the foremast head of the flagship and
Swedish colors at the main, meaning that he wished
to negotiate through the Swedish consul, Mr. Norderling. Thereupon Norderling came off to the Guerrière,
with the captain of the port, who was astonished and
distressed to learn of the capture of two vessels and
the death of Reis Hammida. He would not believe the
news until it was confirmed by an Algerine officer
on board the Guerrière. A letter from the President
to the dey, dated April 12, 1815, was delivered; it
announced that war had been declared against Algiers
by Congress, and expressed a hope that the dey
would choose peace rather than war. " But peace, to
be durable, must be founded on stipulations equally
beneficial to both parties, the one claiming nothing
which it is not willing to grant to the other; and on
this basis alone will its attainment or preservation by
this government be desirable." [1] Shaler and Decatur
sent with this a letter signed by themselves as commissioners, dated June 29, in which they say that
" they are instructed to treat upon no other principle

[1] Shaler, app. D.

than that of perfect equality and on the terms of the most favored nations. No stipulation for paying any tribute to Algiers under any form whatever will be agreed to." [1] The captain of the port suggested that the commissioners should go on shore to negotiate, and that an amnesty should be declared, any Algerine cruisers that might return being unmolested; but the commissioners insisted that negotiations should be conducted on board the Guerrière, and Decatur declared his intention to seize any Algerine vessel that should appear before the conclusion of peace.

The Swedish consul and the captain of the port then went ashore, and the next day, June 30, came aboard the flagship again with the authority of the dey to negotiate. The draft of a treaty was presented to them, from which the American commissioners declared that they would not depart in any essential particular. It provided for the total abolition forever of tribute in any form; for the release of the Americans in the dey's power and also of the Algerines recently captured by Decatur; for the payment by the dey of ten thousand dollars as compensation for the Edwin and other American property seized by him, and for the restoration of certain American property still in his hands; for the emancipation of any Christian slave in Algiers who should escape to a United States man-of-war; for the treatment of captives in case of future war, not as slaves, but as prisoners of war exempt from labor. In other respects, also, the treaty was liberal and enlightened. The captain of the port feared that it could not be ratified. The Algerines were not prepared to surrender their system of exacting tribute, and the dey would not dare to defy public

[1] Shaler, app. D; Decatur, p. 383; For. Rel. iv, p. 7.

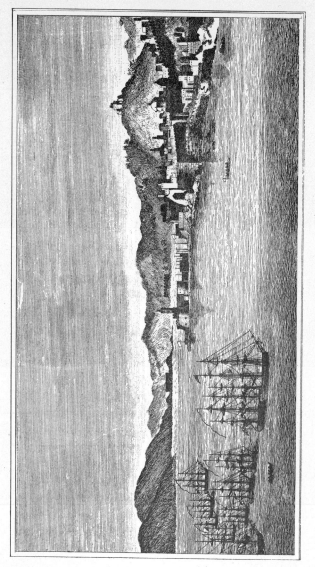

DECATUR'S SQUADRON OFF ALGIERS

opinion. On this point the commissioners intimated that, in accordance with the custom of all other nations, a present might be expected upon the arrival of a consul. It was further objected that the payment of indemnity for property seized by the dey's predecessor and already distributed would be unprecedented in Algiers. The commissioners, however, stood firmly by these conditions. The Algerine then begged for the restoration of the vessels lately captured by Decatur. This also was refused, but after some deliberation, the commissioners agreed to return the vessels. This provision, however, was not to be incorporated in the treaty. The dey's commissioners then requested a truce until peace should be finally concluded. This was refused. They begged for three hours. The reply was: "Not a minute. If your squadron appears in sight before the treaty is actually signed by the dey, and the prisoners sent off, ours will capture them." It was agreed, however, that hostilities should cease when a boat should be seen coming from the shore with a white flag hoisted; it being understood that this signal should mean that the treaty had been signed and that the American captives were in the boat.

This being settled, the Swedish consul and the captain of the port went ashore; and although the distance to the landing was five miles, they returned with a white flag, the captives, and the treaty signed and sealed within three hours. Meanwhile, an Algerine cruiser had hove in sight, making for the port. Decatur signaled a general chase, and bore down on her in the Guerrière. He was determined to capture her if possible, but the boat of the dey's commissioners with the flag of truce was sighted just in time to save her.

The boat came alongside the flagship, the ten liberated captives stepped aboard, and the treaty was delivered into Decatur's hands.

In a letter to the secretary of the navy, Benjamin W. Crowninshield, dated July 5, 1815, Decatur says of the treaty: "It has been dictated at the mouths of our cannon, has been conceded to the losses which Algiers has sustained and to the dread of still greater evils apprehended. And I beg leave to express to you my opinion that the presence of a respectable naval force in this sea will be the only certain guarantee for its observance. Having concluded the treaty, I have, in conformity with your instructions to dispose of such vessels we might capture as would be unsafe to send home in such manner as should seem to me most expedient, restored them in their present state to the Dey of Algiers. This was earnestly requested by the Dey, as it would satisfy his people with the conditions of the peace, and it was determined by Mr. Shaler and myself that, considering the state of those vessels, the great expense which would be incurred by fitting them for a voyage to the United States, and the little probability of selling them in this part of the world, it would be expedient to grant the request." [1]

Consul-General Shaler went ashore the same day, June 30, and was received with the honors due to his office. The ten thousand dollars stipulated in the treaty and all the American property that could be recovered was delivered to him. The dey's minister said to the British consul: "You told us that the Americans would be swept from the seas in six months by your navy, and now they make war upon us with

[1] Captains' Letters, xlvii, no. 22; Analectic, February, 1816.

some of your own vessels which they have taken."[1]
This treaty[2] was much the most advantageous that
had ever been made by any Christian nation with
Algiers, and it contributed more than had anything
else up to that time to the breakdown of the system of
piracy and white slavery in the Barbary States.[3] It
undoubtedly hastened the action taken by Great
Britain the following year.

The peace was concluded in less than six weeks
after the departure of the squadron from New York.
The Epervier, under the command of Lieutenant John
T. Shubrick, was at once sent back to the United
States with the treaty. Captain Downes of the Epervier was transferred to the command of the Guerrière,
relieving Captain Lewis, who, with Lieutenant B. J.
Neale, took passage in the Epervier; Lewis was bearer
of the treaty. These two officers had recently married
sisters, and they were granted leave by the commodore
to return home. Two other officers and the liberated
captives also sailed as passengers with Lieutenant
Shubrick. The Epervier passed Gibraltar on her
homeward passage July 12, and was never heard of
again. She was supposed to have foundered in a violent gale which raged off the American coast about
the time she should have arrived.

The presence of the squadron was now needed at
Tunis and Tripoli. Early in the year 1815 the American privateer Abællino[4] of Boston had captured a
number of British vessels in the Mediterranean, one
of which had been sold in Tunis at the request of
Consul Noah and against the protest of the British

---

[1] Decatur, p. 269.   [2] Appendix II.
[3] St. Pap. xi, p. 5; For. Rel. iv, pp. 4–7.
[4] For an account of her cruise, see Nat. Intell. Aug. 17, 1815.

consul. Later, two prizes had been taken into Tunis and two into Tripoli. The bey of Tunis and the pasha of Tripoli had each allowed British men-of-war to retake these prizes of the Abællino in violation of their treaties with the United States and against the protests of the American consuls. Consul Noah demanded of the first minister of the bey the value of the prizes seized at Tunis, but this proposition was treated with ridicule. Consul Richard B. Jones at Tripoli, where the Abællino had not only been robbed of her prizes, but was blockaded by a British brig-of-war, after vain remonstrance hauled down his flag. As these facts were unknown in America when Decatur sailed, he had no instructions in the matter, but decided to act on his own responsibility. He accordingly took his departure from Algiers July 8 with all his squadron except the Epervier and the Spark and Torch, the two latter having been sent to Carthagena for the Algerine prizes. After touching at Sardinia for fresh provisions and water, he sailed for Tunis, and anchored in the bay on the 26th. Having consulted with Mr. Noah, Decatur demanded the instant payment of forty-six thousand dollars, at which sum the two prizes of the Abællino were valued. The bey of Tunis at this time was Mahmud, the old bey, Hamuda, having died in 1814, after a reign of thirty-two years. Mahmud did not consider that he was treated with due respect because the commodore refused to come on shore until the dispute was settled. At first he assumed indifference, then proposed to defer payment for a year, but soon yielded, and the money was turned over to the consul.[1]

The squadron left Tunis August 2, and arrived at

[1] Noah, pp. 264–268, 285–288, 318, 337, 338, 377, 378, 382–385.

Tripoli on the 5th. Here Decatur demanded thirty thousand dollars as indemnity for the loss of the two prizes given up to the British. Yusuf, who was still pasha and reigned many years longer, was inclined to reject the terms and declare war against the United States; but on learning what had just taken place at Algiers and Tunis and reflecting on his previous acquaintance with Decatur, he decided to yield. Negotiations took place on board the Guerrière. On the representation of Consul Jones that the vessels seized were worth no more than twenty-five thousand dollars, Decatur agreed to reduce his demand to that sum, on condition, however, that the pasha would liberate ten of his Christian captives. Two of these were young Danes who were to be released in remembrance of the kindness of their countryman, Consul Nissen, to the Philadelphia's crew. The other eight captives were a Sicilian family, consisting of husband, wife, and children, and were liberated by Decatur in consideration of the aid given to Commodore Preble by the king of the Two Sicilies. The money was paid to the American consul, acting as agent for the owners of the Abællino.

The squadron sailed from Tripoli August 9, and after touching at Syracuse arrived off Messina on the 20th. The wind was not favorable for entering the harbor, and the pilot refused to take in the Guerrière, whereupon Decatur, being assured that his chart was correct and not wishing to throw on Captain Downes the responsibility of going against the pilot's advice, took the ship in himself. The liberated Sicilians were here put ashore, and Decatur received the thanks of the king. The commodore next proceeded to Naples, where the young Danes he had freed were turned over

to the consul-general of their country. After a short
stay the squadron sailed for Carthagena, and thence
all proceeded immediately to Malaga, except the Guerrière, which followed a few days later. As the flagship was beating down alone from Carthagena, she fell
in with the Algerine squadron, of seven vessels. Half
expecting and perhaps hoping that they might be
tempted to attack him, with such odds in their favor,
in spite of the peace, and confident of his ability to
handle them all, Decatur cleared ship for action, but
the Algerines prudently let him pass unmolested. He
arrived at Malaga October 2.

Having been informed that Commodore Bainbridge
was at Gibraltar, Decatur sent all the vessels then at
Malaga to that place, and followed in the Guerrière
a few days later. He arrived off Gibraltar October 6,
just as Bainbridge was leaving that place with his
squadron, homeward bound. Having communicated
with his superior, Decatur went into port for necessary supplies. He sailed for home the next day, and
arrived at New York November 12. He was received
with honor by the administration and with enthusiasm by the people. It was the first time that the
Barbary States had been dealt with in a manner that
met with the unqualified approval of every one. Congress appropriated one hundred thousand dollars to
indemnify Decatur and the officers and men of his
squadron for the prizes that had been restored to
Algiers.

Commodore Bainbridge sailed from Boston July 3,
1815, and arrived at Carthagena August 5. His squadron, part of which sailed with him and part joined
him in the Mediterranean, consisted of the Independence, 74, flagship, Captain William M. Crane, the

SQUADRON OF COMMODORE BAINBRIDGE

first ship of the line to show the American flag in the Mediterranean; the frigates United States, 44, Captain John Shaw, and Congress, 36, Captain Charles Morris; the sloop-of-war Erie, 18, Captain Charles G. Ridgely; the brigs Chippewa, Saranac, Boxer, and Enterprise, each 14, commanded by Lieutenants George C. Read, John H. Elton, John Porter, and Lawrence Kearney; and the schooner Lynx, 6, Lieutenant George W. Storer. The Enterprise was the old schooner of that name altered into a brig. The Firefly, which had started with Decatur and put back for repairs, joined Bainbridge at Carthagena, and he found there on his arrival the Spark and Torch, also of Decatur's squadron. The Congress had come out by way of Holland, and arrived at Carthagena August 9. David G. Farragut, then fourteen years old, was a midshipman and captain's aide on board the Independence.

Although Bainbridge had learned on his arrival that peace had already been concluded with Algiers, he soon sailed for that place with the Independence, Congress, Erie, Chippewa, and Spark, as his orders were to show his squadron at the various Barbary ports. From Algiers he proceeded to Tripoli and thence to Tunis. The appearance of a second powerful squadron so soon after the first had a very salutary effect on the Barbary powers. The Independence produced a decided impression, as it had been represented to them that the United States were bound by treaty with England not to build vessels of this class. Bainbridge then sailed for Malaga, where he arrived September 13, and later proceeded to Gibraltar. Here he was joined by the United States, which arrived from home September 25, and by all of Decatur's squadron except the Guerrière. After making some changes among the officers, a small squadron made up of the United States, Captain Shaw, senior officer, Constellation, Captain Gordon, Erie, Captain Crane, and Ontario, Captain Downes, was left in the Mediterranean for the protection of American interests. The John Adams, 28, Captain Edward Trenchard, Alert, 20, Lieutenant Walter Stewart, and the schooner Hornet, 5, Lieutenant Alexander Claxton, arrived a little later with stores; this was the third Hornet to serve in the Mediterranean. Commodore Bainbridge sailed for the United States October 6, as has been mentioned, with all the other vessels of both squadrons, except Decatur's flagship, the Guerrière, which shortly followed. Bainbridge arrived at Newport November 15, 1815.

Commodore Shaw sailed from Gibraltar October 30, and on the 5th of November arrived at Port Mahon, on the island of Minorca, which he made his winter quarters. Here the United States remained until spring, except for a visit to Gibraltar and Malaga in December and January. The other vessels cruised a little, but spent most of the winter at Mahon.[1]

The frigate Java, 44, Captain Oliver H. Perry, sailed from Newport for the Mediterranean January 22, 1816, with the ratified treaty with Algiers and dispatches for Consul-General Shaler. She arrived off Gibraltar February 13, and joined Commodore Shaw at Port Mahon March 7. On the 31st the United States sailed for Algiers, followed on April 5 by the rest of the squadron. They found there a powerful

[1] The movements of vessels in this chapter have been traced, as far as possible, in the authorities already named, in the log of the United States and other manuscripts in the navy department, and in the National Intelligencer.

British squadron under Admiral Lord Exmouth, who was negotiating a treaty with the dey. The English historian Brenton says : " It was not to be endured that England should tolerate what America had resented and punished ; " [1] and Perry wrote home : " The Algerines are extremely restive under the treaty made with Decatur, considering it disgraceful to the Faithful to humble themselves before Christian dogs. These feelings are encouraged and their passions are fomented by the consuls of other powers, who consider the peace we have made a reflection upon them." [2] Exmouth had been instructed to make the best terms possible for the Mediterranean powers under England's protection, and he agreed to the payment of a heavy ransom for twelve hundred Neapolitans and Sicilians. This won him no respect at Algiers, and, together with other circumstances, caused such dissatisfaction among his countrymen that he was soon sent back with a still more powerful fleet to compel submission.

Apparently, the dey of Algiers had not taken his treaty with the United States very seriously, after the danger, which threatened his navy at the time he signed it, had passed. Consul-General Shaler was informed more than once that the Algerines expected to force the United States again into the position of a tributary nation. When the ratified treaty was presented to the dey by Commodore Shaw and the consul, he declared the document null and void on the ground that one of his vessels captured by Decatur had not been restored to him as had been promised. The frigate had been returned, but the brig, having been

[1] Naval History of Great Britain (London, 1837), ii, p. 559.
[2] Perry, ii, p. 115.

captured in neutral waters on the Spanish coast, had been seized by the Spanish government. Negotiations were at that time being carried on for her release. As the dey refused absolutely to yield, Shaler hauled down his flag and retired aboard the flagship.

Plans were then laid for a night attack by twelve hundred men in the boats of the squadron, under the command of Captain Gordon. One party was to land and spike the guns of the batteries while another was to destroy the Algerine navy by boarding and firing the ships. Preparations were actively pushed, scaling ladders for carrying the batteries were made, and arms got ready for service. There was some discussion as to whether the attack would be justifiable, as the treaty bound both parties to give three months' notice of projected hostilities; but Shaler was evidently of the opinion that, as the dey had rejected the treaty, it was no longer binding on the United States. However, the preparations were discovered by a French frigate and reported to the dey, which made a surprise impossible. The attempt, therefore, was abandoned, as it would certainly have been attended with a great loss of life, and as there were still doubts as to the obligation of giving the three months' notice. These warlike preparations, however, won the respect of the dey; and when Perry was sent ashore under a flag of truce to attempt further negotiations, he was well received. The dey declared that the treaty was at an end, but that he would allow the commodore time to communicate with his government and receive instructions, in which case the consul might continue his residence at Algiers; or hostilities might be begun at once. It was decided to wait, and Shaler returned to the consulate and hoisted his flag. The dey wrote a letter to the President proposing to renew the treaty of 1795.[1] Perry found that the British, French, and Spanish consuls were unfriendly, and endeavored so far as they could to influence the dey.

The John Adams was sent to America with dispatches and the dey's letter. The United States sailed April 19 for Barcelona, thence to Marseilles. She returned to Port Mahon June 9. The Constellation, Java, Erie, and Ontario visited Tripoli and Tunis, to see that everything was quiet at those places, and also touched at Sicilian ports. These vessels then separated, and the Java returned down the Mediterranean, arriving at Gibraltar early in July. The other vessels came in later. On the first of that month there had arrived from the United States, after a passage of twenty-two days, the ship of the line Washington, 74, Captain John O. Creighton, bearing the broad pennant of Commodore Isaac Chauncey, who had come out to take command of the squadron. The sloop-of-war Peacock, 18, Captain G. W. Rodgers, also arrived about this time, having come by way of France. Most of the squadron sailed for Naples about the middle of July. The Washington arrived there on the 22d, and United States Minister William Pinkney was landed. The different vessels gradually assembled at Naples. The United States arrived August 20, and Commodore Shaw reported to his superior.[2] About the end of August Commodore Chauncey sailed with the squadron for Messina, and at this place Captain Gordon of the Constellation died from the effects of an old wound. From Messina the

[1] See Appendix VII.
[2] Captains' Letters, 1, nos. 4, 70, Chauncey to Sec. of Navy (July 3, and Aug. 24, 1816).

ships proceeded to Tripoli late in September, thence
to Tunis and to Algiers, where they arrived in October. The United States left the squadron here, and
sailed direct to Port Mahon.

In August a combined British and Dutch fleet under
Lord Exmouth had appeared off Algiers, and in a
terrific bombardment, with heavy losses on both sides,
had nearly destroyed the Algerine navy and severely
damaged the fortifications. Consul Shaler viewed the
battle from his house, which was partially destroyed
by shells. The dey was compelled to submit, and
signed a treaty with England which provided for the
total abolition of Christian slavery. Upon the arrival
of the American squadron, so soon after this disaster,
the Algerines, in their helpless condition, were apprehensive of being attacked. The dey's fears were
quieted when Shaler assured him that the visit was
a peaceful one. Shaler embarked on the flagship in
order that he and the commodore might be together
upon the receipt of their instructions and the President's reply to the dey's letter. The squadron then
sailed for Gibraltar, and there found the brig Spark,
Lieutenant Gamble, with the President's letter,[1] and
orders appointing Chauncey and Shaler commissioners
to treat for peace.

The Washington and Spark thereupon sailed for
Algiers and arrived December 8. The weather was so
very boisterous that the commodore did not venture to
anchor in the bay. Midshipman Farragut, who was on
the Washington, says : " We lay off Algiers during
the whole month of December, and were I to say in
one continual gale, it would scarcely be an exagger-
ation." It was therefore decided that Shaler should

[1] See Appendix VII.

land and represent the United States alone in the negotiations. Conditions had changed since Commodore Shaw's visit in the spring. In the first place the brig captured by Decatur had been given up by Spain and restored to Algiers, so that the dey no longer had a pretext for rejecting the treaty. Then the bombardment in August had left him almost defenseless, although he had shown extraordinary energy in rebuilding his navy and fortifications. A letter signed December 9, 1816, by Shaler and Chauncey was presented to the dey and contained their ultimatum. It stated that their instructions were not to admit his pretended right to reject the treaty, and called attention to the fact that both of his vessels had been restored, and that the delay was not chargeable to the neglect or indifference of the United States. They proposed a modification of the eighteenth article[1] of the treaty, by which the United States disclaimed " any advantage in the port of Algiers over the most favored nations," because this article was supposed to be incompatible with an old treaty between England and Algiers. The subject of presents was made clear by the following : " The Regency of Algiers having misunderstood the liberal principles upon which the treaty of June, 1815, was concluded, and, contrary to a distinct understanding between them and the American commissioners, having introduced into the translation of that treaty an obligation on the part of the United States to pay to the Regency a present on the presentation of their consuls, the same is formally denied ; and the undersigned declare in the most distinct and formal manner, that no obligation binding the United States to pay anything to the Regency or to

[1] Appendix II.

its officers, on any occasion whatsoever, will be agreed to." The letter further states that "the undersigned believe it to be their duty to assure his Highness that the above conditions will not be departed from; thus leaving to the Regency of Algiers the choice between peace and war. The United States, while anxious to maintain the former, are prepared to meet the latter." The negotiations were begun December 17. The dey was driven into a corner. He used every art to evade the issue and vainly sought some avenue of escape. When finally forced to yield, he begged Shaler for a certificate that he had accepted the treaty under compulsion. Shaler agreed to this and gave the dey a note certifying "that in conference with him on the 19th instant the proposition of his Highness to delay the negotiation for eight months and a day was repeatedly rejected, the undersigned always replying that he could not depart from the tenor of the note which he had the honor to address to his Highness, conjointly with his colleague under date of the 9th current, and that if those propositions were rejected, he should consider himself in duty bound to embark immediately, leaving the Regency of Algiers in the predicament of declaring war." This certificate may have prolonged the dey's life a few months, but his ill luck pursued him, and he finally fell a victim to assassination in September, 1817. The treaty was signed December 23, 1816.[1]

Having settled this business, the Washington sailed for Port Mahon, where the squadron went into winter quarters. According to Farragut it was not until this time that the command was formally turned over by

[1] For these negotiations see Shaler, pp. 149–153, app. G; see also Appendix II.

Commodore Shaw to Commodore Chauncey. Early in January, 1817, the Java, Captain Perry, was sent home with the treaty, and arrived in Newport March 3. The Ontario also returned to the United States during the winter.

Trouble with the Barbary States, so far as concerned the United States, was now at an end, except occasional trivial difficulties with consuls. But it was considered prudent to keep a naval force in the Mediterranean for several years. The need of this is alluded to in nearly all the annual messages of the presidents down to 1830. In 1818 Commodore Chauncey was relieved by Commodore Charles Stewart, who came out in the Franklin, 74.

It was hardly to be expected in the early days, with the country exhausted and impoverished by the struggle for independence, that a correct course governing our relations with Barbary should have been laid out and pursued. It was easier and more natural to follow in the footsteps of Europe. A few wise and far-seeing men knew what ought to be done, and urged it; but as always happens in such cases, the politicians and the people were slow to follow, giving the matter little thought, with an exaggerated idea of the power of the corsairs, and preferring measures which seemed easiest and cheapest at the moment. Time was required to form a healthy, self-respecting public opinion. Meanwhile the wrong course was entered upon and led to a succession of later false steps and complications.

The first treaty with Algiers was on a level with the worst European practice, and its only excuse was the urgency of redeeming the unfortunate captives. It was followed by an awakening sense of national dignity, and each of the later negotiations and treaties marked an advance upon old world precedents. Their favorable terms, however, were to a great extent nullified, during the earlier years, by the necessity, imposed by the bad example set in the case of Algiers, of maintaining peace by a system of concessions and gratuities which practically constituted a sort of tribute. But the insolent demands of the Barbary rulers were resisted to a great extent and war was preferred to servile compliance.

The barbarians themselves hastened the settlement of the difficulty by their overreaching arrogance, which culminated in the declaration of war by Tripoli and later by Algiers. In each case an opportunity was presented of improving existing conditions by vigorous offensive action; opportunities turned to good advantage by the Navy.

APPENDIX

APPENDIX

I

SOURCES OF INFORMATION

THIS list includes most of the authorities consulted. The abbreviations used in the footnotes are here indicated. Other works, cited only once or twice, are also referred to in footnotes.

The Barbary Corsairs. By Stanley Lane-Poole. New York, 1902. [Poole.]

White Slavery in the Barbary States. By Charles Sumner. Boston, 1853. [Sumner.]
These books cover the history of Barbary and the system of Christian slavery. They give copious references.

The Captives. By James Leander Cathcart, Eleven Years a Prisoner in Algiers. Compiled by his Daughter, J. B. Newkirk. La Porte, Ind. [1897 ?]. [Cathcart, I.]
This is an account of conditions at the time of the first American captures.

Tripoli. First War with the United States. Letter Book. By James Leander Cathcart, First Consul to Tripoli. Compiled by his Daughter. La Porte, Ind., 1901.
[Cathcart, II.]

Journal of the Captivity and Sufferings of John Foss, Several Years a Prisoner in Algiers. [First Edition.] Newburyport [1797 ?]. [Foss.]

A Short Account of Algiers and its Several Wars. [By Mathew Carey. Second Edition.] Philadelphia, 1794.
[Carey.]

Historical and Geographical Account of Algiers. By James Wilson Stephens. Second Edition. Brooklyn, 1800.

[Stephens.]

These three books relate the experiences of the captives of 1793.

History and Present Condition of Tripoli. By Robert Greenhow. Richmond, 1835. [Greenhow.]

A history of all the Barbary States and of their relations with the United States to about 1830. Greenhow was librarian to the State Department.

Travels in England, France, Spain, and the Barbary States. By Mordecai M. Noah, Late Consul at Tunis. New York, 1819. [Noah.]

Sketches of Algiers, Political, Historical, and Civil. By William Shaler, Consul-general. Boston, 1826. [Shaler.]

American Captives in Tripoli, or Dr. Cowdery's Journal. Boston, 1806. [Cowdery.]

Horrors of Slavery; or, The American Tars in Tripoli. By William Ray. Troy, 1808. [Ray.]

Cowdery was an officer and Ray a private marine on the frigate Philadelphia, lost at Tripoli.

History of the War between the United States and Tripoli. [By Stephen C. Blyth.] Salem, 1806. [Blyth.]

Includes a general history of Barbary. This book, although contemporary, is unreliable.

The Works of John Adams. By Charles Francis Adams. Boston, 1853. [Adams.]

Writings of Thomas Jefferson. Edited by H. A. Washington. Washington, 1853. [Jefferson.]

Writings of Thomas Jefferson. Collected and Edited by Paul Leicester Ford. New York, 1892.

[Ford's Jefferson.]

Life and Letters of Joel Barlow. By Charles Burr Todd. New York, 1886. [Barlow.]

Notes upon the Treaties of the United States. By J. C. B. Davis. Washington, 1873. [Davis.]

Contains a summary of negotiations with the Barbary powers, which are also treated in Lyman's Diplomacy of the United States (Boston, 1828) and Schuyler's American Diplomacy (New York, 1886), each of which has a chapter devoted to the subject.

Secret Journals of Congress. [1774–1789.] Boston, 1820.
[Secr. Jour.]

The Diplomatic Correspondence of the American Revolution. Edited by Jared Sparks. Boston, 1830.
[Dipl. Corr. Rev.]

The Diplomatic Correspondence of the United States of America. From Sept. 10, 1783, to March 4, 1789. Washington, 1837. [Dipl. Corr. U. S.]
There is much important official correspondence in these publications.

State Papers and Publick Documents of the United States. [Edited by T. B. Wait.] Third Edition. Boston, 1819.
[St. Pap.]

American State Papers. Edited by Lowrie and Clarke. Class I. Foreign Relations. Class V. Military Affairs. Class VI. Naval Affairs. Class IX. Claims. Class X. Miscellaneous. Washington, 1832.
[For. Rel., Nav. Aff., etc.]
These papers, both series published by authority of Congress, are indispensable. The papers in Wait's series are generally duplicated in Class I of Lowrie and Clarke. Vol x of Wait's series comprises confidential documents.

Compilation of Reports of Committee on Foreign Relations, U. S. Senate, 1789–1901. Washington, 1901.
[Rep. Sen. Com.]

The National Intelligencer, a newspaper published in Washington, contains many letters, papers, and reports, some of them not elsewhere published; also news items of value.
[Nat. Intell.]

Narrative and Critical History of America. Edited by

Justin Winsor. Vol. vii, chap. vi. Wars of the United States. By James R. Soley. Boston, 1888.

[Narr. and Crit. Hist.]

Contains an extensive bibliography with critical discussion of authorities.

United States Naval Chronicle. By Charles W. Goldsborough. Vol. i. Washington, 1824. [Nav. Chron.]

One volume only was published. The author, who was forty-four years in the navy department and therefore had easy access to original material, has presented much valuable and reliable information.

Statistical History of the Navy of the United States. By Lieutenant George F. Emmons, U. S. N. Washington, 1853. [Emmons.]

Useful for statistics and movements of vessels.

History of the Navy of the United States of America. By J. Fenimore Cooper. London, 1839. [Cooper.]

Lives of Distinguished American Naval Officers. By J. Fenimore Cooper. Auburn, N. Y., 1846.

[Amer. Nav. Off.]

Cooper was in the navy for a time and doubtless had a personal acquaintance with several of the officers who served in the Mediterranean. His statements are occasionally inaccurate. The Lives include Dale, Preble, Bainbridge, Somers, Shaw, and Perry. Cooper also published in Putnam's Magazine, vol. i, nos. 5 and 6 (May and June, 1853), an article on the frigate Constitution.

Life of the Late General William Eaton. [By Charles Prentiss.] Brookfield, 1813. [Eaton.]

Life of William Eaton. By Cornelius C. Felton. New York, 1840. [Felton.]

Prentiss's book is composed chiefly of Eaton's letters and papers. Felton's is one of Sparks's Library of American Biography, and is based partly upon Prentiss and partly upon other original material.

Life of Edward Preble. By Lorenzo Sabine. Boston, 1847.
[Preble.]

Commodore Preble and Tripoli. American Historical
Record, vol. i, no. 2 (Feb. 1872).   [Am. Hist. Rec.]

Operations of the Mediterranean Squadron under Commodore Edward Preble, in 1803–04. By Prof. James R.
Soley, U. S. N. Record of U. S. Naval Institute, vol. v,
no. 2 (whole number 7), 1879.   [Nav. Inst.]

Sabine's Life, also in Sparks's Library, is based on
Preble's letters and papers. The Historical Record article
contains a memorandum diary of the commodore, from
June, 1803, to April, 1805. Soley's article contains several
of Preble's letters and his journal of the operations before
Tripoli in 1804. The latter was also published in the
Magazine of American History, vol. iii, no. 3 (March,
1879). The Port Folio, for May and December, 1810,
contains a good biographical sketch of Preble.

Life and Services of Commodore William Bainbridge,
U. S. N. By Thomas Harris, M.D., Surgeon U. S. N.
Philadelphia, 1837.   [Bainbridge.]

Life of Stephen Decatur. By Alexander Slidell Mackenzie,
U. S. N. Boston, 1846.   [Decatur.]

This book is in Sparks's Library. The author was a
naval officer and served with Perry in the Mediterranean
in 1816. He had Decatur's papers at his disposal, and
obtained first-hand information from officers who served
in the Tripolitan and Algerine wars.

Documents Relative to the Claim of Mrs. Decatur. George-
town, D. C., 1827.   [Mrs. Decatur.]

Memoir of Commodore David Porter. By Admiral David
D. Porter. Albany, 1875.   [Porter.]

Life of Commodore Oliver Hazard Perry. By Alexander
Slidell Mackenzie, U. S. N. New York, 1843.   [Perry.]

A Defence of the Conduct of Commodore Morris during his
Command in the Mediterranean. New York, 1804.
[Morris.]

This is the chief authority for the operations of Commodore R. V. Morris in 1802–03; it contains many official letters not elsewhere published.

Autobiography of Commodore Charles Morris. Boston, 1880. [C. Morris.]

This is reprinted from Naval Institute, vol. vi, no. 2 (whole number 12), 1880. Morris was a midshipman under Preble.

MANUSCRIPT SOURCES.

Massachusetts Historical Society. Pickering Papers.

[Pickering.]

Timothy Pickering was secretary of state from 1795 to 1800, during the most important of the earlier negotiations with the Barbary States.

Navy Department. The correspondence consists of letters received and letters sent. The former are classed as Miscellaneous Letters, Officers' Letters, Masters' Commandant Letters [Comdrs'. Letters], and Captains' Letters. Among the letters sent are Instructions to Officers of Ships of War and a volume entitled Letter Book, 15 May, 1799, to 18 July, 1807, which relates chiefly to Barbary affairs. There are also a few Log Books, a volume called Ships' Service, which gives details relating to the movements of vessels, a Letter Book of Captain Alexander Murray, etc.

Library of Congress. Preble Papers. The Papers relating to Barbary are contained in four volumes marked Letters, besides one volume of Autograph Letters, 1799 to 1807, one of Navy Department Letters, 1799 to 1807, an Order Book, 1803 to 1805, three Letter Books for the years 1803 and 1804, and a Log Book, containing the log of the Constitution from May 21, 1803, to October 27, 1804, and that of the John Adams from October 30, 1804, to February 23, 1805. At the end of this volume is inserted a manuscript Journal of Preble, extending from March 19, 1803, to August 21, 1804; this differs from either of his two published journals. As in most of the volumes neither the letters nor the pages are numbered, the letters, which are arranged chronologically, are generally referred to by date only.

II

TREATIES

On account of their great length, the treaties are here condensed. The full text is given in volume viii of Peters's Public Statutes at Large, Boston, 1848.

1. France. Treaty of Amity and Commerce, February 6, 1778.

Art. VIII. The Most Christian King will employ his good offices and interposition with the King or Emperor of Morocco or Fez, the regencies of Algier, Tunis, and Tripoli, or with any of them; and also with every other Prince, State, or Power of the coast of Barbary, in Africa, and the subjects of the said King, Emperor, States, and Powers, and each of them, in order to provide as fully and efficaciously as possible for the benefit, conveniency, and safety of the said United States, and each of them, their subjects, people, and inhabitants, and their vessels and effects, against all violence, insult, attacks, or depredations, on the part of the said Princes and States of Barbary or their subjects.

2. Morocco. Treaty of Peace and Friendship, June 28, 1786. Ratified by Congress July 18, 1787.

Art. I. Treaty agreed upon.

Art. II. Neither party shall take commissions from an enemy of the other.

Art. III. Citizens or property of either party, found on a

prize taken by the other party from an enemy of the latter, shall be released. Property of an enemy of either party, loaded on vessels of the other, shall pass free.

Art. iv. Vessels of both parties to be given passes.

Art. v. Either party, being at war, shall board a vessel of the other with two or three men only and shall make good any damage.

Art. vi. American citizens or goods seized by a Moor shall be released.

Art. vii. Vessels of either party shall be furnished with necessary supplies in ports of the other.

Art. viii. American vessels undergoing repairs in Morocco may land and reload their cargoes without paying duty.

Art. ix. American vessels may take refuge from the weather in Morocco, and if wrecked shall be protected by the Emperor.

Art. x. A vessel of either party engaged with any Christian vessel, within gunshot of a fort of the other party, shall be protected.

Art. xi. When a vessel of either party sails from a port of the other, enemies shall not follow within 24 hours.

Art. xii. United States ships of war in Morocco shall not be examined, even for fugitive slaves, nor shall payment be demanded for such.

Art. xiii. Ships of war of both parties shall be saluted.

Art. xiv. Commerce shall be on the footing of the most favored nation.

Art. xv. Regulations in the interest of merchants.

Art. xvi. In case of war between the parties, prisoners are not to be made slaves, but exchanged.

Art. xvii. Merchants may buy and sell all goods except those prohibited to other Christian nations.

Art. xviii. Goods to be examined before sent on board, and not after, unless in case of fraud.

Art. xix. Vessels not to be detained, and commanders may decline to ship any article.

Art. xx. Disputes between Americans to be settled by the consul.

Art. xxi. If an American kill or wound a Moor, or vice versa, the law of the country shall take place, the consul assisting at the trial.

Art. xxii. If an American die intestate, the consul shall take charge of his effects.

Art. xxiii. American consuls may live in any seaport and shall not be liable for debts of Americans.

Art. xxiv. In case of disputes between the parties, peace shall continue until they can be arranged if possible. If war follow, citizens of both parties shall be allowed nine months to retire with their property.

Art. xxv. Treaty shall be in force for fifty years.

Supplementary to Article x. American vessels in Morocco shall be protected and their enemies shall not be permitted to follow them.

TAHER BEN ABDELKACK TENNISH,
THOMAS BARCLAY.

3. Algiers. Treaty of Peace and Amity, September 5, 1795.
   Ratified by the President and Senate, March 2, 1796.
   Art. i. Declaration of friendship.

Art. ii. American vessels may trade on paying usual duties. Naval and military stores free.

Art. iii. Vessels of both nations shall pass unmolested.

Art. iv. Algerine cruisers to be given passports by American consul; and on meeting American merchantmen shall send two men only to examine passports.

Art. v. Commanders of Algerine cruisers shall not remove any person from American vessel or molest him.

Art. vi. Stranded vessels to be assisted.

Art. vii. Algerines not to sell vessels of war to enemies of United States.

Art. viii. When a prize condemned by Algiers becomes property of American citizen, certificate of consul shall serve as passport.

Art. IX. No Barbary State, at war with United States, may sell American prizes in Algiers.

Art. X. United States, at war with any nation, may sell prizes in Algiers, free of duty.

Art. XI. United States ships of war in Algiers shall receive usual hospitalities. Slaves escaping to such vessels shall be returned.

Art. XII. Redemption and sale of slaves to be arranged by agreement. Americans taken by Algerines on enemy's ships, and having passports, to be released.

Art. XIII. Property of Americans dying intestate to be delivered to consul.

Art. XIV. Americans not compelled to purchase goods. Consul not responsible for debts of Americans. The dey, wishing to freight American vessel not engaged, shall have preference on paying full freight.

Art. XV. Disputes between Americans and Algerines to be decided by the dey; between Americans, by the consul.

Art. XVI. An American, having killed an Algerine, shall be punished as a Turk; should he escape, consul shall not be answerable for him.

Art. XVII. Consul shall have security and religious freedom, and may board any vessel.

Art. XVIII. In case of war between the parties, consul and other Americans may depart unmolested.

Art. XIX. Citizens of either nation captured by the other, on vessels of an enemy, shall be released.

Art. XX. Vessels of war to be saluted with 21 guns.

Art. XXI. Private property of consul free of duty.

Art. XXII. In case of dispute, war not to be declared until after investigation and attempt at adjustment.

The dey will observe the treaty on consideration of the United States paying annually the value of 12,000 Algerine sequins [21,600 dollars] in maritime stores.

HASAN PASHA,

JOSEPH DONALDSON, Jr.

4. Tripoli. Treaty of Peace and Friendship, November 4, 1796, and January 3, 1797. Ratified June 10, 1797.

Art. I. Declaration of perpetual peace guaranteed by the dey of Algiers.

Art. II. Enemies' goods on vessels of either party shall pass free.

Art. III. Citizens and property of either party on a prize taken by the other party shall be released.

Art. IV. All vessels of both parties shall be given passports.

Art. V. Condemnation and bill of sale of prize available as passport for one year.

Art. VI. Parties shall furnish each other's vessels with supplies or repairs when needed.

Art. VII. Parties shall assist and protect each other's vessels and citizens in case of shipwreck.

Art. VIII. Parties shall defend each other's vessels against an enemy when in port or within gunshot of a fort; and enemy not allowed to pursue within 24 hours.

Art. IX. Relations of parties on footing of most favored nations.

Art. X. Pasha acknowledges receipt of money and presents demanded by him for the treaty. No pretense of any periodical tribute or farther payment is ever to be made by either party.

Art. XI. As the United States government is not founded on Christianity nor opposed to Mohammedanism, religious differences shall never disturb the harmony of the parties.

Art. XII. Disputes between the parties which the consul cannot settle shall be referred to the dey of Algiers.

<table>
<tr><td>Tripoli.</td><td>YUSUF PASHA,</td></tr>
<tr><td>Algiers.</td><td>HASAN PASHA,</td></tr>
<tr><td></td><td>JOEL BARLOW.</td></tr>
</table>

5. Tunis. Treaty of Peace and Friendship, August, 1797. Ratification advised by Senate March 6, 1798, on condition that Article XIV be suspended. Alterations in

Article XI, XII, and XIV agreed to March 26, 1799. Ratified January 10, 1800.

Art. I. Declaration of peace.

Art. II. Citizens and goods of either party, found in enemy's vessel, to be restored.

Art. III. Goods of enemy of one party, on board vessel of other party, to pass free.

Art. IV. Passports to be given to vessels of both parties.

Art. V. Commander of convoy to be believed on his word, in order to exempt it from search.

Art. VI. War vessels of neither party shall exact anything from merchantmen of the other. A slave taking refuge on any American vessel shall be restored; the same with prisoners escaping to Tunisian vessels.

Art. VII. Prizes purchased at Tunis by Americans shall be given passports good for one year.

Art. VIII. Parties to extend hospitality to each other's vessels in need of supplies or repairs.

Art. IX. Parties shall assist each other's vessels when wrecked.

Art. X. Parties shall defend each other's vessels, near forts, against enemies; and shall not permit an enemy to pursue within 48 hours of departure.

Art. XI. The war vessels of the parties shall be saluted in each other's ports, on request; and for each gun fired the vessel shall pay one barrel of powder. But salutes shall not be fired if not requested.

Art. XII. Merchants of the parties shall enjoy the same privileges as those of other nations. A Tunisian, freighting an American vessel, shall not remove his cargo until disputes are decided by other merchants. Merchant vessels may be detained only when ports are shut for those of all nations. Parties shall protect each other's citizens.

Tunis may freight any American merchant vessel, in case of need, upon paying a suitable freight.

Art. XIII. Enemies of Tunis among crews of American

merchant vessels shall be free, if less than one third of crew
in number ; if more, they shall be made slaves. Passengers
shall in no case be molested.

Art. XIV. A merchant of either party, trading in the country of the other with goods of his country, shall pay the
lowest duty paid in United States by merchants of other
nations. But American goods under a foreign flag and
foreign goods under the American flag shall pay six per
cent. in Tunis.

Art. XV. Americans may trade as they please in Tunis,
except in prohibited articles.

Art. XVI. Prescribes anchorage fees.

Art. XVII. Consuls may import free of duty articles for
their own use, and shall be protected.

Art. XVIII. Neither party responsible for debts of its
citizens in country of the other.

Art. XIX. Consuls to take charge of property of citizens
of either party dying intestate in country of the other.

Art. XX. Consul shall settle all disputes between his fellow countrymen.

Art. XXI. A citizen of either party, killing or injuring
one of the other party, shall be punished according to law
of the country ; consul shall be present at trial.

Art. XXII. In civil disputes consul shall be present.

Art. XXIII. Disputes between the parties shall not disturb
peace until an attempt at adjustment has failed; if war
follow, citizens of both parties shall be allowed one year to
arrange their affairs and withdraw.

HAMUDA PAƠĦA,

WILLIAM EATON,

JAMES LEANDER CATHCART.

6. Tripoli. Convention between the United States and Hamet
   Karamanli. Alexandria, Egypt, February 23, 1805.[1]
   Art. I. Declaration of peace.

[1] St. Pap. v, p. 171 ; For. Rel. ii, p. 706 ; Eaton, p. 297.

Art. II. The United States shall use their utmost exertions, so far as comports with their own honor and interest, their subsisting treaties, and the law of nations, to reëstablish Hamet Bashaw in the possession of Tripoli, against the pretensions of Joseph Bashaw.

Art. III. The United States shall furnish Hamet on loan, cash, ammunition, and provisions, and debark troops, if necessary, to aid his operations.

Art. IV. American prisoners in Tripoli to be released without ransom.

Art. V. The United States to be indemnified from tribute of certain nations.

Art. VI. For that purpose existing treaties between Tripoli and those nations are to be observed.

Art. VII. Peace to be offered to king of the Two Sicilies.

Art. VIII. William Eaton shall be commander-in-chief of land forces serving against the common enemy.

Art. IX. Amnesty granted to those in service of usurper who return to their allegiance.

Art. X. In case of war between the parties, captives shall be treated as prisoners of war and not as slaves, and shall be exchanged. Neither ransom nor tribute shall be required as a condition of peace.

Art. XI. United States consulate in Tripoli shall be asylum to all persons, except for crimes of treason and murder.

Art. XII. Hamet to be left in possession of Tripoli.

Art. XIII. Future articles to be on footing of most favored nations.

Art. XIV. This convention to be submitted to President of United States for ratification, and meanwhile is to go into effect.

In presence of
P. N. O'BANNON,
FRANCISCO MENDRICI,
PASCAL PAOLI PECK.

HAMET KARAMANLI,
WILLIAM EATON.

Additional Article, secret. Hamet will endeavor to deliver to United States commander-in-chief in Mediterranean Joseph Bashaw and Murad Reis, to be held as hostages.

7. Tripoli. Treaty of Peace and Amity, June 4, 1805. Ratified April 12, 1806.

Art. I. Peace on terms of most favored nation.

Art. II. Prisoners of the two parties to be exchanged, and for balance in favor of Tripoli, United States is to pay 60,000 dollars.

Art. III. United States forces in Derne to be withdrawn and no supplies given Tripolitan subjects in rebellion. Americans will endeavor to persuade Hamet to withdraw, but will not use force; and his family will be restored to him.

Art. IV. Goods of an enemy of one party, on vessel of the other, shall pass free.

Art. V. Citizens of either party, taken on a prize by the other party, shall be released.

Art. VI. All vessels shall have passports, and upon showing them may pass unmolested. Tripolitan war vessels shall board American merchantmen with two men only.

Art. VII. For prizes purchased by citizens of either party, certificate of condemnation and bill of sale shall serve as passport for two years.

Art. VIII. Vessels of both parties shall be furnished with necessary supplies and repairs in each other's ports, and may land and reload cargo without duty.

Art. IX. Parties shall protect each other's vessels and crews in case of shipwreck.

Art. X. Parties shall defend each other's vessels against enemies within gunshot of forts, and enemy not to be allowed to pursue vessel within 24 hours of departure.

Art. XI. Commerce on footing of most favored nations.

Art. XII. Consul not answerable for debts of his countrymen.

Art. XIII. War vessels to receive and return salute of 21 guns.

Art. XIV. Religious differences not to disturb harmony.

Art. XV. Disputes between the parties shall be settled if possible, one year being allowed. If war follow, consuls and citizens may depart unmolested.

Art. XVI. In case of war, prisoners shall be exchanged and not made slaves.

Art. XVII. American vessels, prizes of any nation, shall not be sold in Tripoli; but Americans may sell their prizes in Tripoli, duty free.

Art. XVIII. Disputes to be settled by consuls.

Art. XIX. If citizens of the parties kill or wound each other, the law of the country shall take place. Consul not answerable for escape of criminal.

Art. XX. Consul shall take charge of property of American dying intestate. YUSUF PASHA,
TOBIAS LEAR.

Additional Article or Declaration, secret, in modification of Article III.[1] The pasha believes that his brother Hamet, should his wife and children be immediately restored to him, would renew hostilities against him. Therefore the pasha is allowed four years within which to deliver up his brother's family. TOBIAS LEAR.
TRIPOLI, June 5, 1805.

8. Algiers. Treaty of Peace and Amity, June 30, 1815. Ratified Dec. 26, 1815.

Art. I. Peace on terms of most favored nations.

Art. II. No tribute, either as biennial presents or under any other form, shall ever be required by Algiers from the United States on any pretext.

Art. III. All prisoners now in possession of either party shall be immediately released without ransom.

[1] St. Pap. x, p. 500.

Art. IV. As compensation for American citizens and property detained by the dey, he shall deliver to consul American property left by late consul and also pay 10,000 dollars.

Art. V. Enemy's goods on vessels of either party to pass free.

Art. VI. Citizens of either party, on a prize taken by the other party, shall be released.

Art. VII. All vessels shall be given passports and upon showing them may pass unmolested. Algerine war vessels shall board American merchantmen with two men only, who shall be punished if they give offense.

Art. VIII. For prizes purchased by either party certificate and bill of sale shall serve as passport for six months.

Art. IX. Vessels of both parties shall be furnished with necessary supplies and repairs free of duty.

Art. X. Citizens and property of both parties, in case of shipwreck, shall be assisted and no duties exacted.

Art. XI. Neutrality of ports to be enforced. Enemy not allowed to pursue vessel within 24 hours.

Art. XII. Commerce on footing of most favored nations.

Art. XIII. Consul not answerable for debts of his countrymen.

Art. XIV. Same salutes exchanged as with most favored nations. Christian slaves escaping to United States war vessels shall be free without ransom.

Art. XV. Harmony not to be interrupted by religious differences. Consul may board any vessel.

Art. XVI. Disputes between the parties shall be settled if possible, three months being allowed ; if war follow, consuls and citizens may depart unmolested.

Art. XVII. In case of war, prisoners shall be exchanged and not enslaved.

Art. XVIII. American vessels, prizes of any nation, shall not be sold in Algiers. Americans may sell their prizes in Algiers, paying customary duties.

Art. XIX. Disputes of Americans with each other or

with other foreigners shall be settled by the consuls ; with Algerines, by the dey.

Art. xx. If a citizen of either party kill or wound one of the other party, the law of the country shall take place. Consul not answerable for escape of criminal.

Art. xxi. Consul's private property free of duty.

Art. xxii. Consul shall take charge of property of American dying intestate in Algiers.

OMAR PASHA,
WILLIAM SHALER.

9. Algiers. Treaty of Peace and Amity, December 23, 1816. Ratified February 11, 1822 (late date due to its being overlooked).

Practically identical with treaty of 1815, except that Articles iii and iv, having been executed, had become obsolete, and that the treaty was modified by

Article Additional and Explanatory. The United States agree to annul so much of Article xviii as gives to United States any advantage in Algiers over the most favored nations.

OMAR PASHA,
WILLIAM SHALER,
I. CHAUNCEY.

10. Tunis. Convention for Amendment of Treaty of 1799, February 24, 1824. Ratified January 13, 1825. Amended articles :

Art. vi. Tunisians shall board American vessels with two men only, who shall exact nothing. A slave escaping to a United States war vessel shall be free.

Art. xi. Salutes of 21 guns shall be given and returned, and no powder will be given.

Art. xii. Tunis, being in need of the service of an American vessel, not previously engaged, shall have the preference, on paying customary freight.

Art. xiv. Vessels of either party may trade in ports of the other, paying same duties paid by nations most favored by the latter.

S. D. Heap,
Sidi Mahmud.

III

SQUADRONS

The following list, it is believed, includes all the vessels of war of the United States which served in the Mediterranean before the year 1818 :

I. Dale.	President, 44, J. Barron.
1801–1802.	Philadelphia, 36, S. Barron.
	Essex, 32, Bainbridge.
	Enterprise, 12, Sterrett.
	Boston, 28, McNeill.
	George Washington, 24, Shaw.
II. Morris.	Chesapeake, 36, Chauncey, J. Barron.
1802–1803.	Constellation, 36, Murray.
	John Adams, 28, Rodgers.
	New York, 36, J. Barron, Chauncey.
	Adams, 28, Campbell.
	Enterprise, 12, Sterrett, Hull.
	Boston, 28, McNeill.
	George Washington, 24, Shaw.
III. Preble.	Constitution, 44, Dent, Robinson.
1803–1804.	Philadelphia, 36, Bainbridge.
	Siren, 16, Stewart.
	Argus, 16, Hull.
	Vixen, 12, Smith.
	Nautilus, 12, Somers.
	Enterprise, 12, Decatur.
	John Adams, 28, Chauncey.

Scourge, 16, Dent, Izard.

Intrepid, 4, Decatur, Somers.

Two bomb-vessels.

Nine gunboats.

IV. Barron. President, 44, Cox.
1804–1805. Constitution, 44, Decatur, Rodgers.

Constellation, 36, Campbell.

Congress, 36, Rodgers, Decatur.

Essex, 32, J. Barron.

John Adams, 28, Chauncey.

Siren, 16, Stewart.

Argus, 16, Hull.

Vixen, 12, Smith.

Nautilus, 12, Dent.

Enterprise, 12, Robinson.

Hornet, 10, Evans.

Two gunboats.

V. Rodgers. Constitution, 44, Porter, Blake.
1805–1806. President, 44, J. Barron.

Constellation, 36, Campbell.

Congress, 36, Decatur.

Essex, 32, Cox.

John Adams, 28, Shaw.

Siren, 16, Stewart.

Argus, 16, Hull.

Vixen, 12, Smith.

Nautilus, 12, Dent.

Enterprise, 12, Robinson, Porter.

Hornet, 10, Evans.

Franklin, 8, Robinson.

Vengeance, 3, Lewis.

Spitfire, 3, McNeill.

Sixteen gunboats.

VI. Campbell. Constitution, 44, Ludlow.
1806–1807. Hornet, 18, Dent.

Wasp, 18, Smith.

VII. Decatur.   Guerrière, 44, Lewis, Downes.
    1815.   Constellation, 36, Gordon.
               Macedonian, 38, Jones.
               Epervier, 18, Downes, Shubrick.
               Ontario, 16, Elliott.
               Firefly, 14, Rodgers.
               Spark, 14, Gamble.
               Flambeau, 14, Nicholson.
               Torch, 12, W. Chauncey.
               Spitfire, 12, Dallas.
VIII. Bainbridge. Independence, 74, Crane.
    1815.   United States, 44, Shaw.
               Congress, 36, Morris.
               Erie, 18, Ridgely.
               Chippewa, 14, Read.
               Saranac, 14, Elton.
               Boxer, 14, Porter.
               Enterprise, 14, Kearney.
               Lynx, 6, Storer.
IX. Shaw.   United States, 44, Gregory.
    1815–1816.   Constellation, 36, Gordon.
               Java, 44, Perry.
               Erie, 18, Crane.
               Ontario, 16, Downes.
               John Adams, 28, Trenchard.
               Alert, 20, Stewart.
               Hornet, 5, Claxton.
X. Chauncey.   Washington, 74, Creighton.
    1816–1818.   United States, 44, Shaw.
               Constellation, 36, Gordon.
               Java, 44, Perry.
               Erie, 18, Crane.
               Ontario, 16, Downes.
               Peacock, 18, Rodgers.
               Spark, 14, Gamble.

IV

OFFICERS IN COMMODORE PREBLE'S SQUADRON[1]

U. S. Frigate Constitution, Flagship.

Edward Preble, captain, commanding squadron.
Thomas Robinson, lieutenant, acting captain.
Charles Gordon, lieutenant.
Joseph Tarbell, lieutenant.
Samuel Elbert, lieutenant.
Nathaniel Harraden, sailing-master.
James Wells, surgeon.
Noadiah Morris, purser.
Peter Leonard, chaplain.
John Hall, captain of marines.
Robert Greenleaf, lieutenant of marines.
Hethcote J. Reed, master's mate.
David Deacon, master's mate.
Patrick Simms, surgeon's mate.
Louis Alexis, midshipman.
Charles G. Ridgely, midshipman.
Daniel S. Dexter, midshipman.
Alexander Laws, midshipman.
Henry P. Casey, midshipman.
John M. Haswell, midshipman.
Joseph Israel, midshipman.
William Lewis, midshipman.
Francis C. Hall, midshipman.
Leonard Hunnewell, midshipman.
Joseph Nicholson, midshipman.
John N. Cannon, boatswain.
William Sweeny, gunner.
Thomas Moore, carpenter.
Isaac Steel, sailmaker.
John Thompson, acting midshipman.

[1] Preble Papers (April 19, 1804).

U. S. Brig Siren.

Charles Stewart, lieutenant commandant.
James R. Caldwell, lieutenant.
Michael B. Carroll, lieutenant.
Joseph Maxwell, acting lieutenant.
William Burrows, acting sailing-master.
Samuel R. Marshall, surgeon.
Nathan Baker, purser.
John Howard, lieutenant of marines.
Thomas O. Anderson, midshipman.
John Dorsey, midshipman.
Frederick C. de Krafft, midshipman.
William R. Nicholson, midshipman.
Thomas Brown, midshipman.
John Unsworth, boatswain.
James Willman, gunner.
John Felt, carpenter.
Thomas Crippen, sailmaker.

U. S. Brig Argus.

Isaac Hull, lieutenant commandant.
Joshua Blake, lieutenant.
Sybrant Van Schaick, lieutenant.
Samuel B. Brooks, sailing-master.
Nathaniel Weems, surgeon.
Timothy Winn, purser.
John Johnson, lieutenant of marines.
John W. Dorsey, surgeon's mate.
William G. Stewart, midshipman.
John Pettigrew, midshipman.
Samuel G. Blodget, midshipman.
Pascal Paoli Peck, midshipman.
George Mann, midshipman.
George Nicholson, boatswain.

U. S. Schooner Vixen.

John Smith, lieutenant commandant.
John Trippe, lieutenant.
William M. Crane, lieutenant.
Richard Butler, sailing-master.
Michael Graham, surgeon.
Thomas Hunt, purser.
Lewis Warrington, midshipman.
William Ballard, midshipman.
John D. Henley, midshipman.
John Nevitt, midshipman.
John Clark, boatswain.

U. S. Schooner Nautilus.

Richard Somers, lieutenant commandant.
James Decatur, lieutenant.
George W. Reed, lieutenant.
Stephen Cassin, acting sailing-master.
Gershom R. Jacques, surgeon.
James Tootell, purser.
Octavius A. Page, master's mate.
William Miller, midshipman.
James Pinkerton, gunner.
William Johnson, boatswain.
Robert Fell, carpenter.

U. S. Schooner Enterprise.

Stephen Decatur, lieutenant commandant.
James Lawrence, acting lieutenant.
Joseph Bainbridge, acting lieutenant.
Jonathan Thorn, acting lieutenant.
Seth Cartee, sailing-master.
Lewis Heermann, surgeon.

Samuel Robertson, purser.
Thomas Macdonough, midshipman.
George Mitchell, midshipman.
Walter Boyd, midshipman.
William Hook, gunner.
John Newman, boatswain.
Patrick Keogh, sailmaker.
John Williams, carpenter.

U. S. Brig Scourge.

John H. Dent, lieutenant commandant.
Henry Wadsworth, acting lieutenant.
Ralph Izard, acting lieutenant.
Charles Morris, acting sailing-master.
Thomas Marshall, acting surgeon.
John Green, acting purser.
John Davis, midshipman.
John Rowe, midshipman.

U. S. Frigate Philadelphia (Oct. 31, 1803).

William Bainbridge, captain.
David Porter, lieutenant.
Jacob Jones, lieutenant.
Theodore Hunt, lieutenant.
Benjamin Smith, lieutenant.
William S. Osborne, lieutenant of marines.
John Ridgely, surgeon.
Keith Spence, purser.
William Knight, sailing-master.
Jonathan Cowdery, surgeon's mate.
Nicholas Harwood, surgeon's mate.
Bernard Henry, midshipman.
James Gibbon, midshipman.

[1] Nav. Chron. p. 252.

James Biddle, midshipman.
Richard B. Jones, midshipman.
Daniel T. Patterson, midshipman.
William Cutbush, midshipman.
Benjamin F. Reed, midshipman.
Wallace Wormeley, midshipman.
Robert M. Gamble, midshipman.
Simon Smith, midshipman.
James Renshaw, midshipman.
Joseph Douglass, sailmaker.
George Hodge, boatswain.
Richard Stephenson, gunner.
William Godby, carpenter.
William Anderson, captain's clerk.
Minor Fontaine, master's mate.

V

THE CREW OF THE INTREPID (Feb. 16, 1804)

List of the officers and men who took part in the destruction of the Philadelphia:

Stephen Decatur, commander.
James Lawrence, lieutenant.
Joseph Bainbridge, lieutenant.
Jonathan Thorn, lieutenant.
Lewis Heermann, surgeon.
Thomas Macdonough, midshipman.
John Rowe, midshipman.
Ralph Izard, midshipman.
Alexander Laws, midshipman.
Charles Morris, midshipman.
John Davis, midshipman.
Thomas O. Anderson, midshipman.

William Wiley, boatswain.
William Hook, gunner.
George Crawford, quartermaster.
George Brown, quartermaster.
John Newman, quartermaster.
Paul Frazier, quartermaster.
James Metcalf, boatswain's mate.
Nicholas Brown, boatswain's mate.
Edward Kellen, master's mate.
Samuel Endicott, quarter gunner.
James Wilson, quarter gunner.
John Ford, quarter gunner.
Richard Doyles, quarter gunner.
Joseph Boyd, ship's steward.
Edward Burk, seaman.
Peter Munell, seaman.
Richard Ormond, seaman.
Samuel Jackson, seaman.
James Pasgrove, seaman.
Joseph Goodwin, seaman.
John Boyles, seaman.
Augustus C. Fleur, seaman.
Charles Berryman, seaman.
Daniel Frazier, seaman.
William Graham, seaman.
Reuben James, seaman.
Robert Love, seaman.
John Williams, seaman.
Joseph Fairfield, seaman.
George Fudge, seaman.
James Robinson, seaman.
Matthew Yeates, seaman.
William Ducket, seaman.
Andrew Espey, seaman.
William Tumbo, seaman.
Thomas James, seaman.

Joseph Numond, seaman.
George Murray, seaman.
Robert McKnight, seaman.
William Dixon, seaman.
Henry Davenport, seaman.
Joseph Parker, seaman.
Dennis O'Brian, ordinary seaman.
Jacob Kurgen, ordinary seaman.
John Burtson, ordinary seaman.
William Rodgers, ordinary seaman.
Charles Robinson, ordinary seaman.
William Trippet, ordinary seaman.
John Joseph, ordinary seaman.
Michael Williams, ordinary seaman.

Marines:
Solomon Wren, sergeant.
Duncan Mansfield, corporal.
Noble James, private.
John Quin, private.
Isaac Camfield, private.
Reuben O'Brian, private.
William Pepper, private.
John Wolsfrandorf, private.

Salvadore Catalano, pilot.

VI

CASUALTIES IN COMMODORE PREBLE'S SQUADRON

" Names of the officers, seamen, and marines, killed and
wounded, on board the squadron of the United States,
under command of Commodore Edward Preble, in the

several attacks made on the city and harbor of Tripoli in
Barbary, in July, August, and September, 1804, with the
names of the vessels they belonged to." [1]

Killed.

July   7. Siren, William Williams, marine, boat attack.

Aug.   3. Nautilus, James Decatur, lieutenant, gunboat
        No. 2.

Aug.   7. Siren, James R. Caldwell, lieutenant, gunboat
        No. 9.

        Siren, John Dorsey, midshipman, gunboat No. 9.

        Siren, William Davis, boatswain's mate, gunboat
        No. 9.

        Siren, James Farrell, quarter gunner, gunboat
        No. 9.

        Siren, John Spear, quartermaster, gunboat No. 9.

        Siren, John Robinson, seaman, gunboat No. 9.

        Siren, John Holmes, seaman, gunboat No. 9.

        Siren, George Irving, seaman, gunboat No. 9.

        Siren, Jonathan Meredith, sergeant marines, gun-
        boat No. 9.

        Siren, Nathaniel Holmes, private marines, gunboat
        No. 9.

        Vixen, John Brown, seaman, gunboat No. 8.

        Vixen, John Jones, seaman, gunboat No. 8.

Aug. 28. John Adams, Thomas Macdonough, seaman, in
        ship's boat.

        John Adams, William Fountain, seaman, in ship's
        boat.

        John Adams, John Bartlett, seaman, in ship's boat.

Sept.   4. Nautilus, Richard Somers, captain, Intrepid.

        Nautilus, James Simms, seaman, Intrepid.

---

[1] Nav. Chron. p. 240. The list varies slightly from the returns
given in Preble's report of September 18, 1804. A few obvious errors
have been corrected.

Sept. 4. Nautilus, Thomas Tompline, seaman, Intrepid.

Nautilus, James Harris, seaman, Intrepid.

Nautilus, William Keith, seaman, Intrepid.

Constitution, Henry Wadsworth, lieutenant, Intrepid.

Constitution, Joseph Israel, lieutenant, Intrepid.

Constitution, William Harrison, seaman, Intrepid.

Constitution, Robert Clark, seaman, Intrepid.

Constitution, Hugh McCormick, seaman, Intrepid.

Constitution, Jacob Williams, seaman, Intrepid.

Constitution, Peter Penner, seaman, Intrepid.

Constitution, Isaac W. Downes, seaman, Intrepid.

Wounded.

July 7. Siren, William Cooper, marine, boat attack.

Siren, Thomas Riveness, marine, boat attack.

Siren, Samuel Henry, marine (mortally), boat attack.

Aug. 3. Enterprise, Stephen Decatur, captain, gunboat No. 4.

Enterprise, Thomas James, seaman, gunboat No. 4.

Enterprise, Daniel Frazier, seaman, gunboat No. 4.

Enterprise, Solomon Wren, sergeant marines, gunboat No. 4.

Vixen, John Trippe, lieutenant, gunboat No. 6.

Vixen, C. Allen, boatswain's mate, gunboat No. 6.

Vixen, M. Cannon, marine, gunboat No. 6.

Vixen, J. Ryan, marine, gunboat No. 6.

Constitution, Charles Young, marine, on board ship.

Nautilus, Samuel Rodney, marine, gunboat No. 1.

Nautilus, Neapolitan, seaman, gunboat No. 1.

Nautilus, ———, seaman, gunboat No. 2.

Nautilus, ———, seaman, gunboat No. 2.

Aug. 7. Siren, Francis Rodgers, seaman (mortally), gunboat No. 9.

      Siren, James Desney, seaman, gunboat No. 9.

      Siren, Anthony Currin, seaman, gunboat No. 9.

      Siren, Thomas Deven, seaman, gunboat No. 9.

      Siren, William Mitchell, seaman, gunboat No. 9.

      Siren, John Lamott, seaman, gunboat No. 9.

      Siren, Antonio Morrell, seaman, gunboat No. 9.

      Siren, Isaac Happs, seaman, gunboat No. 9.

      Total : 30 killed, 24 wounded.

VII

THE DEY'S LETTER TO PRESIDENT MADISON AND REPLY

The Dey of Algiers to the President of the United States :

With the aid and assistance of Divinity, and in the reign of
our sovereign, the asylum of the world, powerful and great
monarch, transactor of all good actions, the best of men, the
shadow of God, director of the good order, king of kings,
supreme ruler of the world, emperor of the earth, emulator
of Alexander the Great, possessor of great forces, sovereign
of the two worlds, and of the seas, king of Arabia and Per-
sia, emperor, son of an emperor and conqueror, Mahmoud
Khan, (may God end his life with prosperity, and his reign
be everlasting and glorious,) his humble and obedient servant, actual sovereign Governor and Chief of Algiers, submitted forever to the orders of his Imperial Majesty's noble
throne, Omar Pashaw (may his government be happy and
prosperous).

To his Majesty, the Emperor of America, its adjacent
and dependent provinces and coasts, and wherever his government may extend, our noble friend, the support of the
kings of the nation of Jesus, the pillar of all Christian sov-

ereigns, the most glorious amongst the princes, elected amongst many lords and nobles, the happy, the great, the amiable James Madison, Emperor of America, (may his reign be happy and glorious, and his life long and prosperous,) wishing him long possession of the seal of his blessed throne, and long life and health, Amen. Hoping that your health is in good state, I inform you that mine is excellent, thanks to the Supreme Being, constantly addressing my humble prayers to the Almighty for your felicity.

After many years have elapsed, you have at last sent a squadron, commanded by Admiral Decatur, your most humble servant, for the purpose of treating of peace with us. I received the letter of which he was the bearer, and understood its contents; the enmity which was between us having been extinguished, you desired to make peace as France and England have done. Immediately after the arrival of your squadron in our harbor, I sent my answer to your servant the Admiral, through the medium of the Swedish Consul, whose proposals I was disposed to agree to, on condition that our frigate and sloop of war, taken by you, should be returned to us, and brought back to Algiers; on these conditions we would sign peace according to your wishes and request. Our answer having thus been explained to your servant the Admiral by the Swedish Consul, he agreed to treat with us on the above mentioned conditions; but having afterwards insisted upon the liberation of all American citizens, as well as upon a certain sum of money, for several merchant vessels made prizes of by us, and of other objects belonging to the Americans, we did not hesitate a moment to comply with his wishes, and in consequence of which we have restored to the said Admiral, your servant, all that he demanded from us. In the mean time, the said Admiral having given his word to send back our two ships of war, and not having performed his promise, he has thus violated the faithful articles of peace which were signed between us, and by so doing a new treaty must be made.

I inform you, therefore, that a treaty of peace having been signed between America and us, during the reign of Hassan Pashaw, twenty years past, I propose to renew the said treaty on the same basis stipulated in it, and if you agree to it, our friendship will be solid and lasting.

I intended to be on higher terms of amity with our friends the Americans than ever before, being the first nation with whom I made peace ; but as they have not been able to put into execution our present treaty, it appears necessary for us to treat on the above mentioned conditions. We hope that with the assistance of God you will answer this our letter, immediately after you shall have a perfect knowledge of its contents. If you agree, according to our request, to the conditions specified in the said treaty, please to send us an early answer. If on the contrary, you are not satisfied with my propositions, you will act against the sacred duty of man, and against the laws of nations.

Requesting only that you will have the goodness to remove your Consul as soon as possible, assuring you that it will be very agreeable to us, these are our last words to you, and we pray God to keep you in his holy guard.

Written in the year of the Hegira, 1231, the 20th day of the moon, Dge Mazirl Covel, corresponding to 1816, April 24th. Signed in our well beloved city of Algiers.

(Signed)   OMAR, son of Mohammed,
Conqueror and great.

The President of the United States to the Dey of Algiers:

I have received your letter, bearing date the twenty-fourth of April last. You represent that the two vessels of war captured by the American squadron were not restored, according to the promise of its Commodore, Decatur, and inferring that his failure violated the treaty of peace, you propose as an alternative, a renewal of the former treaty, made many years ago, or a withdrawal of our Consul from Algiers. The

United States being desirous of living in peace and amity
with all nations, I regret that an erroneous view of what has
passed, should have suggested the contents of your letter.

Your predecessor made war without cause on the United
States, driving away their Consul, and putting into slavery
the captain and crew of one of their vessels, sailing under
the faith of an existing treaty. The moment we had brought
to an honorable conclusion our war with a nation the most
powerful in Europe on the sea, we detached a squadron
from our naval force into the Mediterranean, to take satisfaction for the wrongs which Algiers had done to us. Our
squadron met yours, defeated it, and made prize of your
largest ship, and of a small one. Our commander proceeded
immediately to Algiers, offered you peace, which you accepted, and thereby saved the rest of your ships, which it
was known had not returned into port, and would otherwise
have fallen into his hands. Our commander, generous as
brave, although he would not make the promise a part of
the treaty, informed you that he would restore the two captured ships to your officer. They were accordingly so restored. The frigate, at an early day, arrived at Algiers.
But the Spanish government, alleging that the capture of
the brig was so near the Spanish shore as to be unlawful,
detained it at Carthagena, after your officer had received it
into his possession. Notwithstanding this fulfilment of all
that could be required from the United States, no time was
lost in urging upon that government a release of the brig,
to which Spain could have no right, whether the capture
were or were not agreeable to the law of nations. The
Spanish government promised that the brig should be given
up, and although the delay was greater than was expected,
it appears that the brig, as well as the frigate, has actually
been placed in your possession.

It is not without great surprise, therefore, that we find
you, under such circumstances, magnifying an incident so
little important as it affects the interests of Algiers, and so

blameless on the part of the United States, into an occasion for the proposition and threat contained in your letter. I cannot but persuade myself, that a reconsideration of the subject will restore you to the amicable sentiments towards the United States which succeeded the war so unjustly commenced by the Dey who reigned before you. I hope the more that this may be the case, because the United States, whilst they wish for war with no nation, will buy peace with none. It is a principle incorporated into the settled policy of America, that as peace is better than war, war is better than tribute.

Our Consul, and our naval Commander, Chauncey, are authorized to communicate with you, for the purpose of terminating the subsisting differences by a mutual recognition and execution of the treaty lately concluded. And I pray God that he will inspire you with the same love of peace and justice which we feel, and that he will take you into his holy keeping.

Written at the city of Washington, this twenty-first day of August, 1816.

    (Signed)   JAMES MADISON.

By the President.
 (Signed) JAMES MONROE,
    Secretary of State.

INDEX

INDEX

ABÆLLINO, American privateer, 289–291.

Abdurrahman, Tripolitan ambassador, 32, 33.

Achmet, dey of Algiers, 270, 273–275.

Acton, Sir John, 131.

Adams, John, commissioner in Paris, 25, 27; appointed to treat with Barbary powers, 28; negotiations with Morocco and Algiers, 29, 30; minister to England, interviews with Abdurrahman, 32, 33; favors peace with Barbary, 35; correspondence with Jefferson, 36–38; president, advises building cruisers for Algiers, 60; letter to the bey of Tunis, 70.

Adams, U. S. frigate, in Morris's squadron, 106, 107; at Gibraltar, 114, 115, 118; sails for Malta, 123; off Tripoli, attack on gunboats, 128; on blockade, 129; at Tunis, 132; in the Straits, 133, 144; sails home with Commodore Morris, 134, 143.

Alert, U. S. sloop-of-war, 294.

Alexandria, 228–231.

Algiers, 1; early history, 3–5; government, 6; in 17th and 18th centuries, 7, 8; French conquest, 11; attacks American commerce, 14–17; slavery in, 19–22; negotiations with, 29–31, 51–55; truce with Portugal, 47, 48; first treaty with United States, 23, 53, 56, 313; vessels built for, 60–62; new difficulties with, 271, 273, 274, 276–280; United States declares war against, 281; vessels of, captured, 283, 284; negotiations with, 285–287; second treaty with, 288, 289, 320; repudiated by, 295, 296; bombarded by the British, 298; renewed negotiations with, 299; third treaty with, 300, 322.

Alleghany, ship, 276–278.

Amazon, British frigate, 159.

Anderson, Thomas O., midshipman, 168, 169.

Anna Maria, ship, 71.

Arabs, 229; mutinous, 233–238; Eaton's description of, 235; at Derne, 241–243.

Arago, 8.

Argus, U. S. brig, built, 136; in Preble's squadron, 139; at Gibraltar, 158, 159; cruising, 180; captures a prize off Tripoli, 181; at Tunis, 182; on blockade, 183; before Tripoli, 185, 187; supports gunboats, 193, 194, 206; struck by a shot, 201; attacks the batteries, 203, 205; supports Intrepid, 207; on blockade, 211; convoys a prize, 219; sent to Egypt, 220, 228; in Rodgers's squadron, 223; at Alexandria, 229; returns to Malta, 231; at Bomba, 238; at Derne, 239; bombards the town, 240; and the enemy, 242, 243; returns to United States, 272; and to Mediterranean, 273.

Bacri, broker in Algiers, 23, 51; aids negotiations, 52; lends money for ransom, 54; demands indemnity, 55; unfriendly to American interests, 73; lends money to Lear, 277.

Bagnio Baleck, prison in Algiers, 17, 19; described, 20.

Bainbridge, Joseph, midshipman, fights a duel, 120; lieutenant, takes part in burning the Philadelphia, 167, 169; commands a gunboat, 188, 189.

Bainbridge, William, captain, in command of the George Washington, 75; ordered by the dey to Constantinople and forced to go, 76–79; arrives, 80; well treated, 81–84; returns to Algiers, 84; audience with the dey, 85; returns home, 86; in command of the Essex, 94; at Barcelona, 99; offended with Eaton, 104; commands the Philadelphia, 139; captures the Mirboka, 140, 141; at Gibraltar, 142; off Tripoli, 145; wrecked, 146; his efforts to save his ship, 147–149; surrenders, 148; acquitted by court, 149, 150; his captivity, 151–157; receives a letter from his officers, 151, 152; his letters to Preble, 148, 152, 154, 159, 164, 165, 179, 182; writes to Smith, 160; receives letters and supplies, 162, 163; suggests destroying the Philadelphia, 164, 173; injured in bombardment, 204; sees dead bodies from Intrepid, 209; favors peace, 247, 252, 253; on parole, 250;